Understanding Hume

Understanding Hume

by
JOHN J. JENKINS

and edited by
Peter Lewis and Geoffrey Madell

EDINBURGH UNIVERSITY PRESS
BARNES & NOBLE BOOKS

© Edinburgh University Press, 1992

Edinburgh University Press
22 George Square, Edinburgh

First published in the United States
of America 1992 by
Barnes & Noble Books
4720 Boston Way
Lanham, MD 20706

Set in Linotronic Ehrhardt by
Koinonia Ltd, Bury and
printed in Great Britain by
Hartnoll Ltd, Bodmin

A CIP record for this book is
available from the British Library
ISBN 0 7486 0112 0

*Library of Congress Cataloging-in-
Publication Data*
Understanding Hume/edited by John
      Jenkins, P. Lewis, and G. Madell.
         p.   cm.
      Includes bibliographical
      references.
      ISBN 0-389-20986-4
      1. Hume, David, 1711-1776.
   I. Jenkins, John J. II. Lewis, P.
   III. Madell, Geoffrey.
   B1498.U53   1992
   192—dc20   92-1118
                                 CIP

Contents

Preface

John Jenkins was fatally injured in a road accident on 8 December 1987. At the time of his death he had completed rough drafts of about twelve chapters of this book on Hume. The editors revised the existing manuscript and added new material (the final section of Chapter 12, as well as Chapter 13) based on John's lecture notes.

During a career at Edinburgh University spanning nearly twenty five years, John Jenkins was involved in teaching Hume at all levels, from first year undergraduates to postgraduates. However, his book on Hume, like its companion volume, *Understanding Locke* (Edinburgh University Press, 1983), is principally aimed at students beginning philosophy. For this reason it avoids entering into the numerous scholarly controversies concerning the interpretation of Hume's philosophy. Reference to the more important of these disputes can be found in the notes to each chapter. There too, some indication is given of recent work on the philosophical problems discussed by Hume.

Edinburgh, April 1991   P. L. and G. M.

Abbreviations

T   *A Treatise of Human Nature*, edited by L. A. Selby-Bigge,
    revised by P. H. Nidditch. References to this work will be to
    page numbers, e. g. (*T.*, p. 64).

E   *Enquiries Concerning the Human Understanding and Concerning
    the Principles of Morals*, edited by L. A. Selby-Bigge, revised by
    P. H. Nidditch. References to these works will be by page
    number, e. g. (*E.*, p. 83). *An Enquiry Concerning Human Under-
    standing* will sometimes be referred to as the First *Enquiry*, but
    more commonly as the *Enquiry*. *An Enquiry Concerning the
    Principles of Morals* will sometimes be referred to as the Second
    Enquiry.

D   *Dialogues Concerning Natural Religion*, edited by Martin Bell.
    References to this work will give part number followed by page
    number, e. g. (*D.*, IV, p. 158).

1. *Introduction*

Man and Background

Seven years after the death of Locke, and when Berkeley was a young man of twenty-six, Hume came into the world. The date was 26 April, 1711, and the place was Edinburgh. Commentators are fond of saying that he came 'of a good family', or that his parents were 'well-connected'. What this means is that his mother and father were members of the landed gentry class. His father, Joseph Home, an Edinburgh lawyer, owned an estate called 'Ninewells', close to the Whiteadder river in Berwickshire. Joseph Home died young and the estate was inherited early in life by Hume's elder brother, John. Hume's boyhood, then, was divided between country life in the Scottish border country and city life at the family's home in Edinburgh.

Hume, only two years old when his father died, was brought up by his mother, for whom he had a great deal of affection and respect. In his mini-autobiography, written shortly before his death, Hume says of his mother that she was 'a woman of singular merit, who, though young and handsome, devoted herself entirely to the rearing and educating of her children'.[1] The implication seems to be that her youth and 'handsomeness' made her eligible to remarry: the fact that she did not do so is a mark of her devotion to her children.

About his education, Hume is rather reticent, but it is known that he entered Edinburgh University in 1723. It now appears extraordinary that at this point Hume was barely twelve years old. He probably left university at the age of fourteen. The only comment he was prepared to make upon his progress there was that 'I passed through the ordinary course of education with success'.[2] Granted that Hume was not famed for his modesty, the brevity of his remark probably indicates that he was not a conspicuous success. But it was probably his time at the university which gave him an appreciation of literature, something that was to become the ruling passion of his life. In view of some subsequent remarks on Hume's part, it is unlikely that his university education advanced that passion very much. He speaks of 'college education' as being restricted very largely to language teaching.[3]

What his time at Edinburgh University obviously did was to

provide him with the incentive for the pursuit of literary interests. That incentive had immediate effect, for he spent the next eight years or so in private study, partly for its own sake and partly as a prelude to becoming a lawyer. His interest in law studies was not an enthusiastic one. It was probably the result of pressure from his family, combined with the consideration on his part that, at least until his literary pursuits could sustain him, a career as a lawyer was the next best thing. He did not receive any formal training for the purpose. He underwent, instead, a form of apprenticeship. Nevertheless, his legal knowledge would have been sufficient, in the end, to have qualified him as an advocate: his limited interest in law subjects, however, never provided him with the requisite ambition for going that far. Indeed, it is at least possible that one of the contributory motives for taking up law studies was his knowledge that this would provide him with access to the famous Advocates' Library in Edinburgh. At that time, the University Library was not open to former students of the university and in any case its collection of books was limited as compared with that of the Advocates' Library. The latter, then, was an obvious source from which his love of literature could be fed. Few could then have guessed that Hume was eventually to become its Keeper.

It has already been said that, after leaving university, Hume spent eight years engaged in private study. But the specifically legal aspect of his study was abandoned in 1729. The remaining years, to about 1734, were devoted to philosophy, classical literature and perhaps general history. they were not years of uninterrupted study since he was plagued by a 'disease' which we would now probably call psychosomatic, the symptoms of which included scurvy spots on his fingers and 'watryness in the mouth'. He tried very hard to combat it by means of various remedies, none of which had any lasting effect. Eventually, he decided for himself that the source of the trouble was an overdose of 'learning' and that the remedy would have to be an intermission from his studies. He therefore resolved to commit himself to some purely practical activity, and with this end in view he applied for and obtained employment with a sugar merchant in Bristol. This was in 1734, and the sugar merchant was a Mr Michael Miller, with whom Hume did not get on. One of the sources of friction between them was Miller's literary and grammatical style in his business correspondence. Hume, being employed as a clerk, took it upon himself to correct his employer's written work, repeatedly, much to Miller's annoyance. Hume left, or was forced to leave, the company about four months after his arrival at Bristol. Shortly after, still bearing deep resentment towards the illiterate Miller but entirely cured of his 'complaint', he went to Paris. There he resumed the studious life: the 'disease of the learned' was never to recur.

It may be mentioned that, while in Bristol or very soon afterwards, Hume changed the spelling of his surname. What had been spelt 'Home' but pronounced 'Hume' was changed to its present form, so that the spelling and the pronunciation coincided. Englishmen were obviously averse to pronouncing 'Home' as 'Hume', and Hume must have thought that joining them was preferable to beating them.

The Paris of 1734 was an expensive place in which to live, especially on an income as meagre as Hume's then was. He therefore moved to Rheims which, being a less expensive city, but being equipped with a university and one with good library facilities, was the next best thing to Paris. During his twelve months in that city he began the work for which he is now most famous, and with which the present book will be principally concerned, the *Treatise of Human Nature*. He also taught himself French, made a number of friends, and generally acquainted himself with French manners and customs, for which he formed an abiding affection. However, at the end of a year, perhaps because his very active social life prevented him from devoting sufficient energy to the *Treatise*, and perhaps because, even at Rheims, his income was insufficient to support him, he moved to the small country town of La Fleche. Here he completed much of the writing of the *Treatise*, living as a paying guest in the seclusion of a country manor house. He returned to London in 1737, having spent three years in France. His first objective was to seek a publisher for what he had written. In this he succeeded, with the result that the first two books of the *Treatise* appeared in January 1739. The third book, produced by a different publisher, appeared in November 1740.

By 1745, after a long stay at Ninewells and after a further spell of writing, Hume felt confident enough to apply for the vacant Chair of Ethics and Pneumatical Philosophy at Edinburgh University. His decision to apply for the post was not entirely surprising, if only because he had been exploring the possibility of an academic position as early as 1739. That he did not obtain the Edinburgh Chair is a well-known fact. It is generally thought that this was due to his reputed atheism. This may well have been true, or partly; but, officially, the charge against Hume, made at an influential meeting shortly before the main City Council meeting itself, was based upon his views in the

Treatise. The precise character of this charge made by William Wishart, the Principal of the university at that time, has never been known. Were it to be known, fresh light might well be cast upon certain aspects of the *Treatise*.[4] One thing is certainly striking about the whole affair. It is that, when Hume described his *Treatise* as falling 'dead-born from the Press', he had, from one important point of view, misdescribed the situation. It looks as though the *Treatise* was well enough known to figure as an obstacle when it came to his candidature for the Chair. It was, perhaps, still an obstacle some six years later when Hume also failed to obtain the chair of Logic at Glasgow University.

However, his academic aspirations had not been entirely frustrated in 1745. Early in that same year he had received an invitation to become tutor to the Marquis of Annandale. He accepted the invitation and went to join the Marquis, staying partly in London and partly in the family's country house near St Albans. It was a part of Hume's contract of employment with Lord Annandale that if Hume was eventually offered the Edinburgh professorship he would be entitled to resign his post immediately. In the event, as we have already seen, Hume was never called upon to utilise this part of his contract. His time spent in the Annandale household was not a happy one, partly because the Marquis himself was partially insane when Hume joined him and became increasingly so during the ensuing months, and partly because of the friction that developed between Hume and other members of the Annandale family. Hume took his leave of the mad Marquis in April 1746, having spent twelve months in his service. However, the job had its compensations. It had strengthened Hume's financial position quite considerably and it had also provided him with good opportunity to continue his literary career.

Hume then spent some weeks in London and was all set for returning to Scotland when, on 18 May, he received an invitation from General St Clair, a distant relative, to join him as secretary on a military expedition. The expedition was originally intended for Canada but was eventually switched to the coast of France. Militarily speaking, the expedition was abortive, but, for Hume personally, the eight months spent with General St Clair were not wasted. They gave him valuable experience of war at first-hand, which provided him with many new friends and, with many a long hour in which to pass the time, he learned to play whist, for which, it turned out, he had some talent.

After a short spell of writing in the seclusion of Ninewells, Hume spent a further period of time as secretary/companion to General St Clair, this time on a diplomatic mission to Vienna and Turin. And by 1749 he was able to say that he was financially independent: 'In short I was now master of near a thousand pounds'.[5]

In the summer of 1749 Hume returned to Scotland where he spent two years with his brother John and sister Katherine at Ninewells, occupying himself almost entirely with literary pursuits. He was to remain in Scotland, with some brief exceptions, until his death in 1776. He might well have continued to reside at Ninewells had it not been for the fact that his brother married in 1751. Hume judged it prudent to move out. He thought, in any case, that the city was a more appropriate place than the country for a 'man of letters' as he now regarded himself. Accordingly, he and his sister moved into a house at 'Riddle's Land' on the south side of Edinburgh's Lawnmarket.

In 1752 Hume was elected Keeper to the Advocates' Library in Edinburgh, thus returning to a favourite haunt of his immediate post-university days. He remained in that office until his resignation in 1757. In *My Own Life* he described the office as one 'from which I received little or no emolument, but which gave me the command of a large library'.[6] The library contained 30,000 volumes. To Hume, then engaged in writing his *History of England*, this was a valuable asset. The privilege of using the library continued after his resignation.

It has already been said that there were some brief exceptions to Hume's stay in Scotland after 1749. There were three main excursions. In 1758-9 and in 1761 he visited London for business purposes concerning the publication of his *History of England*. Then again, in 1763 he spent a few weeks in London prior to his departure for Paris. He had been invited earlier in that year to accompany the Earl of Hertford to the British Embassy in Paris, where Lord Hertford was to become Ambassador. The offer had been unexpected. Hume did not know Lord Hertford, and he was initially reluctant to accept the post. Eventually, however, partly because of his love of Paris and partly because Hume was well aware of his high reputation and popularity in that city as contrasted with his ambivalent standing in his native Scotland, Hume was persuaded to accept the invitation. He spent two happy years in Paris, later becoming an official secretary to the Embassy. From the start his reception in France was, by all accounts, ecstatic, certainly a reception beyond what he had ever imagined. In a letter to friends at Edinburgh Hume states that the French seem eager to convince him 'that they consider me one of the greatest geniuses in the world'.[7] Indeed, in his first three weeks in Paris the adulation was so constant and so intense that Hume found it embarrassing and even painful. He relates that, during this period, he longed for the comfort and security of his own fireside and easy chair back in Edinburgh.[8] But, after this initially difficult period, and as his proficiency in the language increased, this 'distant admiration' gradually gave place to more intimate friendships, and Hume settled down. Indeed, he eventually became a figure of affectionate fun, rather in the way in which he had been in Edinburgh and London, and this made him feel quite at home.

Hume's resignation from the Embassy staff in Paris where, in the last few months he had become Chargé d'Affaires in Lord Hertford's absence, was brought about by the latter's departure for Ireland where he was appointed Lord Lieutenant. Hume was invited to accompany him to Ireland to perform an office comparable to his Paris appointment but, judging that he might be unpopular there, Hume declined. Hume's return to London from Paris in January, 1766, was remarkable for the fact that he was accompanied by Rousseau, whom he had met in Paris. Being something of a refugee from Switzerland, and feeling unsafe in France also, Rousseau was persuaded to take up residence in England. Hume assumed responsibility for the necessary arrangements. For some months a close friendship developed between the two men, but, largely due to Rousseau's paranoic disposition, the relationship ended in conflict, the visitor returning to France early in 1767.

In September of 1766 Hume returned briefly to Scotland and would have remained longer had there not been a pressing invitation from Lord Hertford's brother, General Conway, to join him as Under-Secretary of State in what was known as the Northern Department. Hume accepted the invitation and held the appointment for eleven months. He finally returned to Edinburgh in August 1769, feeling that nothing further could now be done to enhance his reputation as a man of affairs and as a man of letters. For good or ill his active life was at an end and he was content to sit back upon his laurels in the city of his birth. He did not anticipate crossing the Tweed again, a fact he was happy to convey to all and sundry.

Hume was, as he later described himself, 'opulent' when he returned to Edinburgh, and one of his first thoughts was to build himself a larger house. This was begun in 1770, under Hume's own supervision, and was situated on the south-west corner of St Andrew's Square in the recently begun New Town development of Edinburgh. He settled there with his sister Katherine in 1771 and led a very content existence until his death in 1776. His death was made remarkable not only by the tranquillity and composure with which he met it but also by the retention, to the end, of his belief that nothing would follow it.

Hume's writings

Although Hume wrote extensively on a variety of subjects, he is now best known for the very forthright brand of philosophy that was set out in his *Treatise of Human Nature*. It is largely with this work that the present volume will be concerned. The *Treatise*, as we have already stated, consists of three books. The first of these deals with the origin of ideas and with the character and limits of human intellectual powers; the second book deals with the 'emotional' side of human nature; and the third book attempts to show how human sentiment, rather than reason, explains the phenomenon we know as morality.

It was his disappointment with the reception given to the *Treatise* that led to the writing of the two *Enquiries* some ten years later. Hume reasoned that if he was to reach a larger and also a more sympathetic audience he would need to simplify both the style and the doctrines contained in the earlier work. The result was, first of all, the *Enquiry Concerning Human Understanding*, published in 1738, which covered most of the main doctrines from Book 1 of the *Treatise*. The second work, the *Enquiry Concerning the Principles of Morals*, was published in 1751. It contained, in much less detailed form, the main conclusions of Book III of the *Treatise*. Much of the material from Book II of the *Treatise*, containing as it did some very close psychological analysis of certain central human passions, was omitted from these later publications.

The other main philosophical work for which Hume became famous was something called the *Dialogues Concerning Natural Religion*. It is not known when it was completed. Some version of the *Dialogues*, in manuscript form, was circulating in Edinburgh during the 1750s, though Hume was advised not to publish it at that point because of its potentially damaging effect upon orthodox Christian belief. Hume reluctantly accepted this advice but made careful preparations for its posthumous publication. The first edition appeared three years after his death. Despite the fact that Hume was popularly known as an atheist in his own day, the *Dialogues* does not openly argue the case for atheism or indeed agnosticism. The work has been the subject of a great deal of controversial interpretation over the years and it would be foolish to make any hasty pronouncement here. But one thing can safely be said: in total it presents a strong and articulate case for what may be called rational theism, but it also presents, sometimes in disguised form, a very powerful critical response to that position.

Another work in the same area, though possibly written just prior to the *Dialogues*, was called the *Natural History of Religion*. It was essentially a sociological enquiry into the origin of religion and was less controversial than the *Dialogues*. It appeared in 1757.

At the present time, Hume is known mainly as a philosopher. But it should be emphasised that, during his own lifetime, his interest in history was as great as that in philosophy. Indeed, at certain periods during his life he was better known as a historian than as a philosopher. In a sense the two subjects were not divorced for Hume himself for, as he conceived it, the study of history was very largely the study of human nature, and the study of the latter was, in part, what philosophy was all about. It was his appointment to the Advocates' Library in 1752 which provided Hume with the first opportunity for serious historical research. The eventual result was the famous *History of England*, which appeared in six volumes between 1754 and 1762. These volumes did not appear chronologically, and this has led to the popular quip that Hume wrote history backwards.[9]

Apart from these major works in philosophy and in history, Hume was also a very productive 'essayist'. He wrote something in excess of forty-five papers or 'dissertations' during the course of his writing career. They covered a wide range of topics in politics, economics, aesthetics, human nature, topical social questions and religion. Many of these were controversial, particularly the essay *Of Miracles*, which is now best known as Part X of the *Enquiry Concerning Human Understanding*. It had originally been intended for inclusion in the *Treatise* but caution on Hume's part kept it out.

One further publication of Hume's should be mentioned. This was originally a thirty-two page pamphlet now generally known as the *Abstract*, which first appeared in 1740. It is a publication which stemmed from Hume's disappointment and indignation at the reception of the *Treatise* and in particular by the way in which it had been misunderstood by certain key reviewers of the period. The *Abstract* was an attempt to put things right by summarising some of the main issues of the *Treatise* and by directing attention to some of the principal philosophical goals of the work. One writer, commenting on the *Abstract* soon after its publication, evidently did not see things in quite such a laudable light. 'Some people', he says, 'having found that the *Treatise of Human Nature* of Mr Hume was a little too abstract, a brochure has been published to help them understand it.'[10]

Main characteristics of Hume's philosophy

It may be useful under this heading to look briefly at some of the standard labels that have been attached to Hume's thought through many years of intensive commentary. It would be foolish to suppose that his thought is precisely characterised by such labels, but they do serve as a rough 'signposting' of the directions in which Hume goes.

Empiricism

Of all the labels associated with Hume, empiricism is perhaps the most popular and the most accurate. Briefly, it is the view that sense-experience is the source of all human knowledge. It might be described as a 'look-and-learn' doctrine which has its analogue in the more precise looking and learning procedure involved in the scientist's use of the microscope. Indeed, it was a doctrine that went hand in hand with the rise of the 'new science' during the seventeenth century. John Locke (1632–1704), who was closely involved with the progress of this new scientific outlook through his connection with the newly formed Royal Society, is often regarded as the father of the school. The chief characteristic of the new science was its emphasis upon the experimental method. The correct procedure for the task of understanding any given phenomenon, it was argued, was to take apart, scrutinise, and perceive. This was to be contrasted with the attitude, prevalent until that point, of supposing that there could be some kind of intuitive, reasoned account of various natural processes. The philosophical school of empiricism, then, had its counterpart in seventeenth century science. In one sense, 'counterpart' is a misleading term here since what was essentially the same movement found expression in two distinct spheres.

In understanding what empiricism amounts to, it is also important to grasp its negative side; that is, to see what precisely it wishes to deny. Under this heading there is certainly one possibility which it strives to exclude and that is that there are ideas in the mind at its inception. The doctrine which held there were such ideas was known as innatism and it was one that Locke spent much time trying to refute. He saw its refutation as a necessary prelude to the enunciation of empiricism, whereas Hume was more inclined to see it as following definitionally from the statement and arguments for empiricism. We shall have a little more to say about this matter when we begin to discuss the details of Hume's empiricism. For now it is sufficient to note that if the empiricist creed is true, and all the materials of knowledge arrive from the workings of the senses, there can be no room for the view that there are ideas in the mind at birth.

The other doctrine which empiricism necessarily wishes to exclude is its traditional rival, known as rationalism. Rationalism has taken many forms, and it would be impossible to do full justice to it in the present context. However, perhaps its most notable characteristic is its insistence that the nature of what exists, or much of what exists, can be determined by human reason. Naturally, since empiricism holds that the nature of the world is discovered entirely by our senses, it cannot admit the validity of rationalism.

It will be perfectly correct, then, on the basis of what has been said above, to describe empiricism as anti-rationalist. But there is another, more specific, sense in which Hume in particular was anti-rationalist. It is a pervasive feature of Hume's philosophy to deny that reason has the important role in the conduct of our lives which we ordinarily suppose it to have. Hume was distinctive in holding that reason is much more a follower than a leader. We shall see in more detail what this means as we proceed on our excursion through Hume's thought. It will suffice to point out now that he saw human beings as creatures of habit and custom, governed by emotions (in a broad sense of that word) rather than by reason.[11]

Scepticism

The other claim regularly made about Hume's philosophy is that he was a sceptic. It would be misleading to suppose that Hume anywhere announces that he is a sceptic, any more than he announces that he is an empiricist. But at least one form of scepticism is the natural result of Hume's very consistent application of the empiricist creed, as described above. An example of this consistency is immediately seen in the anti-rationalism to which we have referred. The more one makes it obvious that human knowledge is founded upon the senses, the more one becomes committed to the view that the findings of reason are limited. But Hume's scepticism was more specifically extended to religious belief, to morality, to our knowledge of the external world, and even to knowledge of ourselves. We shall not begin to understand this until we see more clearly how his empiricism developed.

Before turning to the details of Hume's philosophy, one more introductory comment needs to be made. It would be a mistake to think of Hume as a dated philosopher, a kind of antique-piece having no relevance today. He should be seen rather as a forerunner of much that is important for contemporary philosophy, and particularly for the empiricist trend that still largely characterises the British philosophical outlook.[12] He has direct and vital links, for example, with the empiricism that was boldly proclaimed by Professor A. J. Ayer in the 1930s and that is now commonly referred to as logical positivism.[13] This is not to say that there is any precise equivalence in the details of the philosophy that was expounded in both cases. For example, Ayer does not have Hume's doctrine of impressions and ideas; nor does he have Hume's general psychological apparatus. But there is a broad common ground between them that finds its expression not so much in a set of doctrines and beliefs as in a certain attitude of mind. Thus, in both Hume as well as in such modern British philosophers as Ayer, Bertrand Russell, Gilbert Ryle and John Austin, there is the same distrust of, and impatience with, grand metaphysical schemes and pretentious theories of life and reality; there is the same striving for hard facts by careful, broadly scientific scrutiny; and perhaps the same modesty about the achievements of philosophy itself.[14] Philosophy is not there to tell us about ultimate truth, or to tell us how to lead our lives. It is rather, an analytic tool, like the instruments of the various sciences. Its purpose is to sift and clarify, to seek out hidden assumptions, and to make us aware of our prejudices. The decision about how to lead one's life is up to us as individuals. That is a personal decision which it is not the philosopher's business to make on our behalf. The philosopher's task is to help us to see more clearly what the facts are, or what they may be. That, then, is very much the message that came from Hume and that is echoed in his philosophical descendants.

If one were to ask, in the light of this message, just what is the point of reading what Hume had to say, then Bertrand Russell's famous words from his book *The Problems of Philosophy* are worth thinking about:

The man who has no tincture of philosophy goes through life

imprisoned in the prejudices derived from common sense, from the habitual beliefs of his age or his nation ... To such a man the world tends to become definite, finite, obvious; common objects rouse no questions, and unfamiliar possibilities are contemptuously rejected. As soon as we begin to philosophise, on the other hand, we find ... that even the most everyday things lead to problems to which only very incomplete answers can be given. Philosophy, though unable to tell us with certainty what is the true answer to the doubt which it raises, is able to suggest many possibilities which enlarge our thoughts and free them from the tyranny of custom. Thus, while diminishing our feeling of certainty as to what things are, it greatly increases our knowledge as to what they may be; it removes the somewhat arrogant dogmatism of those who have never travelled into the region of liberating doubt, and it keeps alive our sense of wonder by showing familiar things in an unfamiliar aspect.[15]

With these words in mind, we shall turn our thoughts to Hume's beginnings.

Notes

1. D. Hume, 'My own life', (1777), reprinted in Eugene F. Miller (ed.), *Essays: Moral, Political and Literary* (Indianapolis, Liberty Classics, 1985).
2. 'My own life', p. xxii.
3. For details about the nature of Hume's education as a student at Edinburgh University see M. Barfoot, 'Hume and the culture of science in the early eighteenth century', in M. A. Stewart (ed.), *Studies in the Philosophy of the Scottish Enlightenment* (Oxford, Clarendon Press, 1990). For an introduction to the cultural and intellectual context in which Hume flourished see D. Daiches, P. Jones and J. Jones (eds), *A Hotbed of Genius: The Scottish Enlightenment 1730–1790* (Edinburgh, Edinburgh University Press, 1986).
4. In 1745 Hume wrote a long letter to the Lord Provost of Edinburgh replying to the charges of scepticism and atheism made against him. This letter is reprinted in facsimile, together with an historical introduction, in Ernest C. Mossner and John V. Price (eds), *A Letter from a Gentleman to his Friend in Edinburgh* (Edinburgh, Edinburgh University Press, 1967).
5. 'My own life', p. xxxv.
6. 'My own life', p. xxxvi.
7. Letter dated 9 November 1763 to Adam Ferguson. See J. Y. T. Greig

(ed.), *The Letters of David Hume* (Oxford, Clarendon Press, 1969), vol. 1, p. 410.

8. E. C. Mossner, *The Life of David Hume* (Oxford, Clarendon Press, 1970), p. 124.

9. For an introduction to Hume's historical writing, see Nicholas Phillipson, *Hume* (London, Weidenfeld and Nicolson, 1989).

10. See Mossner, p. 124.

11. For an interpretation of Hume's philosophy which provides a different account of the role of reason in everyday life, see David Fate Norton, *David Hume: Common-Sense Moralist and Sceptical Metaphysician* (Princeton, Princeton University Press, 1982).

12. See H. H. Price, 'The permanent significance of Hume's philosophy', *Philosophy*, vol. 15, 1940; reprinted in A. Sesonske and N. Fleming (eds), *Human Understanding* (California, Wadsworth, 1965).

13. 'The views which are put forward in this treatise derive from the doctrines of Bertrand Russell and Wittgenstein, which are themselves the logical outcome of the empiricism of Berkeley and David Hume.' A. J. Ayer, *Language, Truth and Logic* (London, Gollancz, 1936), opening lines of the Preface.

14. Although in the Preface to the *Treatise*, Hume claims to 'propose a compleat system of the sciences, built on a foundation almost entirely new...', it is the science of man, 'laid on experience and observation', which is to provide that foundation (I., p. xvi). Hume here indicates his own inclination, and one characteristic of much British philosophising, to keep his feet on the ground rather than allow himself to get lost in flights of philosophical fancy.

15. B. Russell, *The Problems of Philosophy*, (Oxford, Oxford University Press, 1967), p. 91.

2. *Where does thought begin?*

(*Treatise*, Bk. I, Part I, Section I; *Enquiry*, Section 2)

The fact that human beings can think is something we very much take for granted, and indeed we often distinguish ourselves from other species by reference to this characteristic. But it occurs to some of us to wonder how this remarkable phenomenon is possible. It occurred to Hume, as it had done to his two immediate predecessors, Locke and Berkeley. His answer to this question forms the basis of his empiricist philosophy and, as we shall see, has far-reaching consequences.

That answer is not, of course, stated in physiological or neurological terms. Neither Hume nor any of his predecessors was concerned to say anything about, for example, the kind of brain-functioning that makes thought possible. What they were preoccupied with was the source of material for thought. The assumption was that, granted we have the ability to think, we need something to think *about*. Thinking cannot begin without objects to be thought about, any more than a pair of binoculars will function, despite their being in perfect working order, unless there are objects upon which to focus. That, then, was the sense in which the empiricists were asking how thought was possible.

Locke's answer to this question was a little simplistic, though not inaccurate. He asserted, quite straightforwardly, that ideas were the objects of thought and that these were received through the ordinary functioning of the senses. As Locke himself was later to acknowledge, the term, 'idea' is a very vague one, covering many different mental contents. Further discrimination was required, and this is what Hume's more refined position supplied. We shall now begin to look at the way in which Hume approached this central question.

He begins by introducing one general term to cover all the contents of the mind. They are to be called 'perceptions'. These perceptions resolve themselves into two distinct classes which he calls 'impressions' and 'ideas' (*T.*, p. 1; *E.*, p. 18). Since this distinction forms such an important foundation for the rest of Hume's thought it is essential to characterise it as precisely as we can.

Impressions

Impressions constitute, as one might put it, the master key to Hume's empiricism. Everything else stems from them. One useful way of getting to understand precisely what Hume was referring to by the term 'impressions' is to bear in mind that Hume saw a clear distinction between feeling and thinking. Impressions refer to feelings, in a broad sense, and ideas refer to thoughts. It is important to stress that Hume means feelings in the broad sense because he includes in the class three things we might ordinarily be inclined to distinguish. There is, first of all, the kind of feeling that is constituted by sense experience, as when I see a cyclist passing by, or smell a rose, or handle a knife and fork. Secondly, there is the more intense kind of feeling we have when touch sensations develop into pain or pleasure. Thirdly, there is that use of 'feelings' which refers to passions or emotions. It is this third sense of 'feeling' with which Hume will be more directly dealing in Books II and III of the *Treatise*, as well as in the Second *Enquiry*. We shall be returning to this use in due course. At the outset of the *Treatise*, it is the impressions of pure and direct sense experience that Hume most wishes to stress. It is primarily from here that the materials for thought, and thus for knowledge, stem.

Some further general features of impressions should be noted before we discuss the account of ideas. Firstly, Hume regards them as being, by definition, vivid and lively experiences (*T.*, p. 1). We shall have more to say about this below. Secondly, he sees the impressions from sense experience in particular as being 'original' or non-derivative. They are what freshly strike the mind, as one might put it; here the analogy of impressions being stamped upon a piece of soft wax suggests itself. Thirdly, impressions may be either simple or complex (*T.*, p. 28). Thus, my seeing the colour blue of a certain book, not having noticed its title or its texture, will constitute a simple impression; my view of Princes Street, with its shops, buses, cars, pedestrians, etc., from Edinburgh Castle will be a complex one. Fourthly, one must stress a negative characteristic of impressions, of which it is very easy to lose sight in giving an account of them. It is that Hume does not explicitly commit himself to the view that impressions are necessarily the impressions of physical things existing objectively beyond our minds. As he says at an early stage in the *Treatise*, impressions of sensation arise 'from unknown causes' (*T.*, p. 70). Already, then, we have an instance of Hume's very thoroughgoing empiricism and the scepticism that is consequent upon it. Hume simply cannot assume, without further investigation, that there is a physical world to cause our impressions for us.

Ideas

If, as we have said, impressions are construed as 'original' experiences, then ideas are to be seen as derivative or secondary. Hume describes them as faint images or copies of impressions (*T.*, p. 1). They are, therefore, by definition, associated with the faculty of memory, and every idea will be either a memory or a construction from elements which are memories. For example, the idea that I have of the colour of my book is a memory of the blue impression I had when I saw it. In this connection, it is very natural to think of the difference between actually experiencing a certain event on the one hand and, on the other, seeing a photograph or film of something previously experienced. The analogy is in fact a little more accurate than one might have supposed, since Hume, at this point and also quite frequently in the remainder of the *Treatise* and in the *Enquiry*, does seem to construe ideas as mental images.

Characterising the distinction

The way in which Hume distinguishes between impressions and ideas is already implicit in what has been said so far, but we must now formulate the distinction more clearly. The claim is, simply, that impressions are more lively, forceful and vivid experiences than ideas. In a paradigm case, the difference might be likened to that between, on the one hand, actually being present at a musical concert or a rugby match and, on the other, watching the same on television. Thus, what Hume has in mind is a distinction in degree and not a distinction in kind. The content of the two experiences is exactly the same, as one might expect, since Hume describes ideas as copies of impressions. The difference, then, consists only in the rather more colourful, lively character of impressions as compared with their counterparts. To use one of Hume's own examples from the corresponding section of the *Enquiry*, when a person feels the pain of excessive heat, or the pleasure of moderate warmth, that is an impression. But when he afterwards thinks about the sensation, or remembers it, that is an idea (*E.*, p. 17). *Thinking* about the sensation of excessive heat does not reach the force or vivacity of the original sensation. Hume puts the position elegantly in the same passage from the *Enquiry*:

> When we reflect on our past sentiments and affections, our thought is a faithful mirror, and copies its objects truly; but the colours which it employs are faint and dull, in comparison with those in which our original perceptions were clothed. (*E.*, p. 18)

One further point must be made. Hume allows that there will be certain situations in which the force and liveliness of an idea might almost be equal to that of an impression. He lists dreams, fevers, madness and highly emotional states as examples of such situations (*T.*, p. 18). The reverse may also be the case. Thus, our impressions may sometimes be so dull as to be indistinguishable from ideas. There is a potential inconsistency in Hume's thought here, and we shall have cause to return to it below.

The Empiricist Dictum

The feature of the impressions/ideas distinction to which we must now draw attention is perhaps its most important. It is the essence of the empiricist creed as Hume sees it. It is appropriate to refer to it as the empiricist dictum. It is simply the claim that there cãn be no ideas without impressions. Another way of putting it is to say that there can be no thoughts without sensations. It is a way of emphasising, through the terminology of impressions and ideas, that all human thought, and thus all human knowledge and belief, stems ultimately from sensory experience. It must also be made clear that it is not simply the conjunction of the two that matters, but also the precedence of the one over the other. That is, all ideas must be preceded and caused by impressions: the latter must occur before the former can do so (*T.*, pp. 4–5).

Hume concedes one curious exception to this empiricist dictum: it is mentioned at the end of Section 1 of the *Treatise* (pp. 5–6). He envisages a situation in which a person is acquainted with all colours and colour shades except for a particular shade of the colour blue. Let us suppose that this happens to be a shade that he has never met. It is nevertheless highly probable, Hume now admits, that this person will be able to imagine, that is, to derive an idea of, the missing shade under certain circumstances. Suppose, for example, he is confronted with a spectrum of shades of blue in which one particular shade is absent: he will surely be able to create an image of it for himself. This, then, would be, technically, an exception to the empiricist dogma on the ground that such a person would be in possession of an idea that had not been preceded by an impression – the person had not actually experienced the missing shade at any previous point. This counter-example is repeated in the *Enquiry* (pp. 20–21), but, in both cases, it is dismissed as being so exceptional as to be of no significance. Hume obviously had no intention of revising a general thesis for the sake of it.

Before beginning our assessment of the impression/ideas doctrine, there is one clarificatory point made which requires mention. It amounts to an anticipation, on his part, of the objection that there are surely many ideas that we can conjure up for ourselves by means of our imagination and such that they have no preceding counterparts in sensory experience. For example, I can imagine a winged horse carrying me over the roof-tops of London, but I have never actually witnessed or experienced such an event. Or, to use Hume's example from the *Enquiry*, I can imagine a golden mountain, though such an object has never been a subject of sensory experience (*E.*, p. 19; *T.*, p. 3). In short, the imagination has an almost unbounded ability to create such ideas, none of which appear to have experiential counterparts. Hume's answer to such cases will be predictable to anyone who has given the matter some thought. The response is to say that such cases are examples of complex ideas and that, although it is true that there is no counterpart in sensory experience for the complex as a whole, nevertheless the ingredients of such complex ideas do have precise counterparts in previous impressions. Thus, I may not have experienced a golden mountain or a winged horse, but I have experienced mountains and gold, and I have experienced horses and wings. My imagination simply puts these ideas together so as to form something more complex. In this way, then, Hume claims to preserve the general rule that *all* ideas are *ultimately* grounded in impressions: it is just that when it comes to complex ideas the one-to-one relation between them is lost.

Assessment of the impressions/ideas doctrine

There are three principal propositions involved in Hume's impressions/ideas doctrine, and we shall look at each of them in turn. They are, firstly, that there are no ideas without impressions; secondly, that there are no ideas without *corresponding* impressions; and thirdly, that impressions and ideas are to be distinguished intrinsically in terms of their relative forcefulness or vivacity.

Considering the first of these propositions, we must remind ourselves again that Hume really has simple ideas in mind. He has already conceded that complex ideas are not necessarily preceded by complex impressions and that they may be constructed by the imagination out of simpler ones. He has also held that this fact is not incompatible with the general doctrine that all ideas are *ultimately* based upon impressions. But now, even if we confine ourselves to the one-to-one relationship of simple ideas to simple impressions, can we happily accept it as universally true? Can we accept, that is, that all simple ideas must, of necessity, be preceded by sensory experience? The view may well be true and indeed we may feel naturally drawn towards it, but, from a more formal point of view, can Hume compel us to accept it?

Let us consider what arguments Hume offers in support of it. Basically he has two arguments. The first appears in an appeal to the standard procedure for teaching children the meanings of words. If we want to get a child to acquire the meaning of the word 'orange', that is, to have the idea of orange, we would proceed by *showing* him an instance of this colour. It would be absurd to proceed in any other way (*T.*, p. 5). In other words, an impression has to be induced before an idea can be present. But although our immediate intuitions may be entirely in accord with those of Hume, it cannot be said that the argument is conclusive. Strictly speaking, it only shows that we regard such a method as the most effective means of producing the relevant idea in the child; but the most effective teaching method is not necessarily the *only* method by which the idea can be produced. The argument may also indicate an *assumption* on our part that that is the only way in which we can get a child to have an idea of orange; but, again, this does not show that the assumption is correct. It remains a possibility that such an idea can be produced without the help of impressions.

Hume's second argument consists of what he calls 'another plain and convincing phenomenon' (*T.*, p. 5). It is that, where the senses are obstructed in their operation such that no impressions can be had, there are no ideas either: 'A blind man can form no notion of colours; a deaf man of sounds' (*E.*, p. 20). Again, the argument is, strictly speaking, deficient. If the facts are correct, they will show only that ideas *normally arising from these sources* have been prevented. The argument will not demonstrate the universal thesis Hume wants, namely that no ideas whatever can arise without sensory input. Essentially the same comments can be applied to Hume's other persuasive illustration from the same context, namely that 'we cannot form to ourselves a just idea of the taste of a pine-apple, without having actually tasted it' (*T.*, p. 5).

What has to be said about both of the above arguments is that the psychological claims upon which they are based are, to say the least, dubious. In order to make this point clear we need to remind ourselves once again that, certainly at this point in the *Treatise* and *Enquiry*, Hume is using the term 'idea' to refer to a mental image or picture. Now the psychological claim is that, in all the cases he has considered, no such entity is to be found. But the point to be made against him is that there is no way in which he can be justified in making such a pronouncement. One may ask how Hume can be sure that the child has no mental image of orange before being shown an instance of it. One must ask whether the blind man has no colour images and the deaf man no auditory images. And do we really know that the person who has never tasted pineapple has not 'internally' experienced that taste? Hume could only be justified in making the pronouncement he does make about these cases if the thesis he was propounding were a logical one.[1] That is, he would be justified only if it were to be part of the meaning of the term 'idea' that it was the sort of thing that had to be preceded by an impression, just as it is part of the meaning of being a square that it has four sides. In that case, one could automatically *infer* the absence of an idea from the absence of an impression. But the necessary correspondence of impressions with ideas is the very proposition that Hume seeks to establish, on an empirical basis. He cannot, therefore, allow the matter to be settled beforehand as a matter of logic. As things stand, it is possible that the blind man should have in his mind, at various times, what we would be happy to call images of colour. So long as this remains a possibility, the case for Hume's universal thesis (no ideas without impressions) has not been established.

What may be the case – and this may be the truth that Hume was misleadingly trying to capture – is that the blind man may not *know* that he has experienced colour sensations, and the deaf man may not *know* that he has had internal experiences of sound. We can imagine a situation in which a person, blind from birth, suddenly gains his sight and, upon having various colours pointed out to him, exclaims 'If that is what it is to see colour then I had colour sensations during my blindness'. Contemporary philosophy would be inclined to put the general point in the following way. In the sense in which Hume is here using the term 'idea', the class of people to whom his examples refer may well have had ideas without impressions, that is, without sensory experience. But what they lacked in their respective areas is what we should now call a *concept*. Thus, while the blind man may have *images* of colour during the period of his blindness, he lacks a *concept* of colour. He does not know what colour *is*, in the important sense that he is not able to identify instances of it. Some people would draw the analogy with certain kinds of animal experience in order to explain the distinction. A cat or dog may have an image of a table in its mind when confronted by one, but it would be false to say that it knows what a table *is*.

What we must say, then, is that, had Hume been using the term 'idea' to mean a concept, the impressions/ideas doctrine might have had a greater ring of truth about it. It would amount to the more respectable empirical thesis, echoed by many today, that without a world of sensory experience and a common language by means of which the objects around us are given identifying descriptions, concept acquisition would be impossible. Perhaps, indeed, that is what Hume dimly saw but was prevented from expressing by the restricting psychological vocabulary he inherited from Locke.

It must not be supposed, however, that such a charitable modification of Hume's thesis would completely defend the universal claim that there can be no ideas without previous impressions. Even if Hume's ideas are interpreted as concepts, there would be no automatic agreement that they must always be dependent upon sensory experience. Hume did not give any serious attention to the theory of innatism, which held that certain ideas or concepts are present in the mind at birth. He probably thought that Locke's famous attack upon it had completely dislodged it.[2] But the doctrine has undergone something of a revival in recent years through the work of Noam Chomsky.[3] Chomsky's principal interest is in language acquisition and, more generally, in the nature of language. The particular claim for which he has earned a reputation is that language is such an extraordinarily complex activity that it is impossible to explain its acquisition entirely by reference to a straightforward empirical learning process. He therefore holds that acquiring a language requires innate assistance. Chomsky himself, at one stage, saw this as providing some support for the traditional innatism that Locke was so concerned to attack. There is a great deal more detail involved in Chomsky's position to which it is impossible to do justice here. But it has been the subject of considerable discussion for many years and, since its outcome has, potentially, a direct bearing upon Hume's impressions/ideas doctrine, it was important to draw attention to it at this point. After all, if it is true that we *are* born in possession of certain concepts, then, depending on what the having of them amounts to, this may falsify the claim that all ideas (meaning concepts) must be preceded by what Hume calls impressions.

Finally, in our consideration of the first of the three propositions which characterise Hume's doctrine, we should remind ourselves again that he himself concedes a counter-example to the general dogma that there can be no ideas without impressions. This was the curious case of the missing shade of blue, mentioned above. Some writers have taken a strict line over this concession. Professor H. A. Prichard, for example, in a series of lectures on the theory of knowledge delivered in the late 1920s and early 1930s, had the following remark to make about the missing shade of blue:

> This is, of course, just the kind of fact which should have led Hume to revise his whole theory. It is really effrontery on his part and not mere naiveness to ignore an instance so dead against a fundamental doctrine of his own.[4]

Professor Norman Kemp Smith, on the other hand, takes a more casual view, holding that 'Hume might easily have accounted for the phenomenon'.[5] We must content ourselves with two remarks. Firstly, in view of Hume's strong insistence on the universal claim, albeit an empirical claim, that there can be no ideas without impressions, there is certainly something straightforwardly inconsistent about a carefully worked-out counter example. The inconsistency is made more emphatic by the fact that Hume recognises it to be a genuine exception. But, secondly, despite Hume's acceptance of it as genuine, there is reason to agree with Kemp Smith's verdict that Hume could have coped with it. It is not so much that it is hardly worth altering a general thesis for one exception, which is very much the line Hume himself adopts. It is rather that the character of the phenomenon itself does not clearly run counter to the essential emphasis of Hume's doctrine. That emphasis really consists in the claim that, ultimately, there can be no ideas without impressions. His example does not, strictly, disobey this principle since, presumably, Hume would argue that, without sensory experience of other colours and particularly of other shades of blue, the missing shade could not be envisaged. It is not an admission of innatism, nor is it a claim that the idea was, as it were, produced out of a hat. It is perhaps nothing more than the concession that the natural powers of the mind are a little more enterprising than he had allowed for.

Continuing our assessment of the impressions/ideas doctrine, we shall look at the second of the three propositions characterising it, as set out above (p. 18). This is the claim that there are no simple ideas without *corresponding* impressions. It is important to stress this feature of Hume's account because it highlights an aspect of his psychological apparatus that we may find unacceptable. This feature can be tracked down by reflecting on the fact that if ideas are to be faint copies or images of impressions, then an impression has to be 'something' present to the mind in the first place. That is, there has to be an original picture to be copied. Indeed, Hume explicitly acknowledges this in a passage that occurs in Part 11, Section VI. In some well-known words, he has the following to say:

> We may observe that 'tis universally allow'd by philosophers, and is beside pretty obvious of itself, that nothing is ever really present with the mind but its perceptions or impressions and ideas, and that external objects become known to us only by those perceptions they occasion. (*T.*, p. 67)

This passage actually suggests that Hume held a view of perception known as representationalism. It is a theory that holds that the external world is not known directly, but only through the medium of ideas. But what is of immediate interest from the quotation is the view we have mentioned, namely, that impressions are mental entities that Hume regards as being present to the mind in sensory experience.

The comment to be made upon this view concerns Hume's psychology. Can we really accept that sensory experience always involves these 'presentations' to the mind? Certainly we can give some sense to the notion of the mind being presented with 'pictures'. It sometimes happens, for example, in vivid imaginings, in day-dreaming, in reminiscing, and in dreaming itself. We know what it is to be lost in reminiscence such that we would describe ourselves as being entirely occupied with the images floating before our minds. But few of us would be happy to accept that such mental entities are necessarily involved in all sensory experience. When we see an orange, a book, a bicycle or a carnival, can it plausibly be said that such images are occurring? Had Hume been faced with the question he might have replied that the mental presentations in which impressions consist are not necessarily the kind of experiences to which we have just referred. The trouble is that if they are not those kinds of experiences, and yet *are* still the kind of entities of which ideas are faint copies or images, it is difficult to see how Hume can give them any intelligible content. If ideas are to be, in any sense, pictures or representations of them, the theory seems to demand that impressions be the kind of thing which can be pictured or copied, and it is not clear that this makes sense.

Of course if it had been established by Hume that there is no external, physical world – a view for which his predecessor Berkeley was famous – the position might have been very different. The known absence of a physical world would make it plausible, perhaps inevitable, to hold that our perception of so-called physical things was really the perception of sense data, or, in other words, that all of human experience consisted in the having of some kind of images or mental presentations. But, just as Hume could not, certainly at this point, assume that there *was* a physical world beyond our perceptions, so, by the same token, he could not assume that there was not. And if he cannot assume the latter, then the possibility remains that in sensory experience we simply perceive physical objects directly. While that possibility remains open, there is no automatic route to the view that impressions are 'presentations' to the mind, things actually there to be copied by ideas.

These, then, are some of the difficulties that emerge, granted Hume's psychological vocabulary, from the claim that ideas are faint copies of impressions that exactly correspond to them. However, it must not be supposed that the empiricist creed itself is thereby put in jeopardy. The heart of Hume's empiricism is a claim that need not be clothed in the vocabulary of impressions and ideas. It is, essentially, that sensory experience (however this is to be analysed) is the basis from which all human knowledge and belief proceeds. Ideas, meaning more generally thought (however this in turn is analysed), consists of reflections upon the more basic experience.

Moving on to the third of the propositions characterising the impressions/ideas doctrine, we are now dealing with Hume's criterion for distinguishing the two. This criterion was outlined above (p. 16) and is simply that impressions are more lively, colourful experiences than ideas. The view is that there is no difference in content, only a difference in vivacity. One is tempted to put it by saying that an impression is an experience in technicolour, whereas an idea is one that occurs in black and white only.

The major criticism of this distinction is one that has become commonplace in successive commentaries on Hume.[6] It is the obvious one that, if the difference is *only* one of degree and nothing more, then a very vivid idea seems to transform itself into an impression, and a very dull impression seems to become an idea. Surprisingly, Hume admits that there will be certain rare occasions in which this may occur, but he casually dismisses the fact as being of no significance (*T.*,

p. 2). But it is indeed significant. Upon this distinction hinges the general issue of whether, on any particular occasion, the mind is receiving new material from its primary source or whether it is involved in its secondary activity of reflecting upon, remembering or imagining. To know whether I am having an impression rather than an idea is tantamount to knowing that I am genuinely sensing or genuinely feeling some passion or emotion. It would be in contrast to thinking about sense material or emotions, either by means of memory or by imagination.

What is more, the occasions on which an impression might be as dull as an idea and vice versa are probably much more numerous than Hume supposes. This makes it doubly important that the criterion for distinguishing them should be absolutely clear-cut and dependable. Consider the following type of situation, for example, that is far from being uncommon. Suppose that I am standing at a bus stop and a cyclist ambles past on an old upright bike. I notice the fact without finding it in any way remarkable. That would have been an impression, according to Hume's scheme. But now suppose that, ten minutes later, riding on the bus, the thought of the cyclist passes through my mind again and, as it does so, I suddenly realise that the person upon the bicycle was Margaret Thatcher. It hardly needs saying that the thought would become, as one might put it, illuminated. It becomes vivid, to use Hume's word, and obviously more vivid than the original experience of seeing the cyclist had been. It follows that, if we adhere to Hume's claim that the only difference between impressions and ideas is in respect of their force and vivacity, the experience I had while riding on the bus was a sensory one, while the bus stop experience was not. But that is contrary not only to our own intuitions but also to what Hume had intended. We have already said that such a phenomenon is not uncommon; and therein lies the difficulty for Hume's way of making the distinction between impressions and ideas.

Let us now undermine two tempting thoughts. It is possible to suppose that Hume could have formulated the distinction by saying that impressions are those experiences that occur *before* ideas, especially since Hume does stress the fact that they appear in that order. But it is easy to see that this is not a viable way out. First, even though Hume's account of impressions and ideas sometimes suggests that they occur in discrete pairs, this can hardly be the case, and Hume could not possibly have thought that it was the case. It is simply not true that every time we have an impression it is immediately followed by an idea. Some impressions are never followed by ideas. Human experience often consists of long periods of successive impressions, when we are using our senses over a long stretch, for example. Images (that is to say, Hume's 'ideas') of these impressions may or may not occur. That depends on whether we reflect upon our experience or not. In any case, when they do occur, it need not be immediately after the impression or impressions. Therefore, the whole notion of human experience being neatly divided into successive pairs of perceptions such that the first in any pair is designated an impression and the second an idea is a misconception.

Secondly, if the distinction between impressions and ideas were to be made entirely in terms of the temporal priority of impressions over ideas, there would no longer be any reference to the qualitative difference between feeling and thinking. And it was just that qualitative difference which Hume tried to capture in terms of degrees of vivacity.

The other avenue that needs to be closed off at this juncture is the following. It is sometimes thought that the most effective way for Hume to have made the distinction between the two kinds of perception would be to say that impressions are sensory experiences of the world, whereas ideas have no immediate contact with the external world. But there are two reasons why this will not do either. Firstly, it has to be stressed that the class of impressions is not confined to sensory experiences alone. There are impressions of sensation, but there are also impressions of reflection (*T.*, pp. 7–8). The latter class consists mainly of passions and emotions. But even if we were to confine ourselves to impressions of sensation, the distinction could not be made in this way since it presupposes the existence of an external world, an observation that was made above (pp. 15 and 24). Hume, being the consistent empiricist that he was, could not presume the existence of an external physical world. Sensory experience does not in itself carry such an assurance. Therefore, the distinction could not be made out in those terms.

It is tempting to suppose that, if the distinction cannot be so put, it can at least be formulated more tentatively, though along the same lines. Thus, why can we not say that impressions of sensation are those that *appear* to stem from an external world, that they are those that have the 'feel' of being thrust upon us? Now there is no doubt that something of this kind does justice to the position Hume wishes to hold. A variation on the position is provided by those commentators who say that Hume is really trying to formulate a distinction between the 'given' and our thoughts about the given, where 'given' presupposes nothing about an external world.[7] But, for both versions, the essential difficulty remains. We are left with a distinction but without a reliable criterion for drawing it. In other words, how can we know when we are presented with the 'given', as opposed to a figment of our imagination? We have therefore travelled full-circle, because it was precisely this issue that the criterion of force and vivacity was designed to settle for us. That it does not perform this function adequately is the essential criticism of Hume.

But, when all is said and done, it is important not to overdo the criticism of Hume we have been exploring. Certainly, within the confines of his own psychology, there are difficulties. Principally, he has provided us with no reliable means of identifying impressions and ideas for what they are. But if the criticism is that he has provided us with no means of deciding when we are confronted with an external world and when we are not, it assumes a less serious tone. Hume differed from his predecessor, Descartes, in this respect, that while the latter was obsessively concerned to produce an infallible guarantee of knowledge, the former was not.[8] It is a feature of Hume's general philosophical position that he was prepared to settle for far less. Indeed, this readiness was dictated by his view that knowledge, in the strict sense, was unavailable in many areas of human life. Belief, well- or ill-founded, was to be its substitute. Therefore, although Hume thought that we could never be in doubt about the identity of a perception – that is, deciding whether it was an impression or an idea – he nevertheless allows that, in any strict sense of knowledge, we cannot *know* that there are external, physical objects corresponding to our impressions. The criticism we have been exploring, then, constitutes an attack upon the psychological scheme that Hume offers us, and the confidence with which he offers it. It is not an attack upon the claim that impressions necessarily represent the external world to us, for that is not the claim that Hume made. His more detailed discussion of this precise issue is to be found in Section II, Part IV of Book 1 in the *Treatise* and in Section XII of the *Enquiry*.

We shall conclude this chapter with one further comment upon Hume's method of distinguishing impressions from ideas. We saw that it amounted to a difference in degree, such that impressions are more vivid and forceful perceptions than the latter. We also saw that the distinction corresponds to the distinction between thinking, on the one hand, and feeling, on the other. At times, Hume seems concerned to stress this difference. He does so in the example from the *Enquiry* that was mentioned above (p. 16) where he says that there is a considerable difference between feeling the pain of excessive heat and afterwards merely thinking about it (*E.*, p. 17). Now these features of Hume's distinction, taken in conjunction, seem to suggest the following picture. At its extremity, feeling will run into thought; and thought, at its extremity, will run into feeling. We are, after all, presented with a continuous sliding scale from impressions to ideas and vice versa, with no cut-off point to mark any difference in kind between them. Therefore, to make the point again, the picture encourages us to think that, somewhere in the middle of this scale, feeling can merge into thought and thought into feeling. The question we must raise is whether we find this an acceptable implication. Many would hold that feeling is one thing and that thinking or thought is another. They are entirely different mental activities, and therefore there can never be a point at which one simply merges into the other. And, indeed, granted what we have already recorded, that Hume himself wished to stress the difference between them, one wonders whether he really saw the implication of his distinguishing procedure for impressions and ideas. (It must be mentioned also that there is further evidence for the view that Hume saw and wished to emphasise a clear difference between the two categories. This centres upon his famous dichotomy between the work of reason, on the one hand, and the work of feeling or sentiment, on the other, in his analysis of morality. (The issue will be discussed in Chapter 12.)

However, having raised the matter as something that might strike us as counter-intuitive, it is important to realise that certain strands in contemporary philosophy may be seen as supporting such a view. That is, there may be some support for the view that thought and feeling are not essentially different categories of human experience and that they may indeed be seen as part and parcel of the same phenomenon. At least one contemporary view, for example, holds that to be perceiving something (that is, generally, to be using one's senses) is nothing more that to be thinking about it or having the capacity to think or talk about it.[9] Consider the following analogy: the statement that glass is brittle indicates how the glass can be expected to behave under certain specifiable conditions. In a similar way, the statement that someone is seeing, hearing or feeling something may be seen as a claim about what the person can be expected to say if challenged or again, what he can be expected to say to himself, that is, think. So, too, in the case of an emotion like jealousy (to take one of Hume's impressions of reflection), an analysis in terms of thought can be provided. To be jealous of someone is tantamount to thinking of that person in certain negative ways, imagining the person disadvantaged or deprived of something, or seeing oneself in a position of control over him, and so on. It would be quite wrong to suppose that this is necessarily a correct view of what feelings and sensory experiences consist in. But the mention of it does serve to put our criticism of Hume into perspective.

Having now seen the doctrine that lies at the heart of Hume's philosophising, the doctrine that explains how the material for thought and belief is derived, we must now turn our attention to Hume's account of the mechanics of thought. It must be borne in mind, as we proceed, that the impressions/ideas doctrine is not merely an account of the source materials for knowledge and belief, though it is certainly that. It also functions as Hume's testing apparatus for the intelligibility of certain key views about the world, about the human mind and about God. We shall see the working of this apparatus as we proceed.[10]

Notes

1. For a discussion of the status of the empiricist dictum see James Noxon, *Hume's Philosophical Development* (Oxford, Clarendon Press, 1973).
2. John Locke, *An Essay Concerning Human Understanding* (1689), edited by P. H. Nidditch (Oxford, Clarendon Press, 1975), Bk. 1, chs. 2–4. For a discussion of Locke's arguments against innatism, see J. J. Jenkins, *Understanding Locke* (Edinburgh, Edinburgh University Press, 1983), ch. 1.
   In the final paragraph of Section 1 of the *Treatise*, Hume comments that the arguments against innatism 'prove nothing but that ideas are preceded by other more lively perceptions, from which they are derived, and which they represent' (*T.*, p. 7). In a footnote to Section 2 of the First *Enquiry*, Hume claims that the great controversy over the doctrine of innatism was largely due to failure to distinguish different senses in which it may be said that ideas are innate (*E.*, p. 22).
3. Noam Chomsky, *Cartesian Linguistics* (New York, Harper and Row, 1966); *Reflections on Language* (London, Fontana, 1976). For a critical discussion of Chomsky's views on language see G. P. Baker and P. M. S. Hacker, *Language, Sense and Nonsense* (Oxford, Basil Blackwell, 1984); also Alexander George (ed.), *Reflections on Chomsky* (Oxford, Basil Blackwell, 1989). There is a collection of useful material on the philosophical problem of innatism in S. Stich (ed.), *Innate Ideas* (Berkeley, California University Press, 1975).

4. H. A. Prichard, *Knowledge and Perception* (Oxford, Clarendon Press, 1950), p. 177.
5. Norman Kemp Smith, *The Philosophy of David Hume* (London, Macmillan, 1949), p. 206.
6. See B. Stroud, *Hume* (London, Routledge, 1977), p. 29; J. Bennett, *Locke, Berkeley, Hume: Central Themes* (Oxford, Clarendon Press, 1971), section 46. For a defence of Hume which presents an alternative interpretation of the doctrine of ideas and impressions, see S. Everson, 'The difference between feeling and thinking', *Mind*, vol. xcvii, 1988. See also R. P. Wolff, 'Hume's theory of mental activity', *Philosophical Review*, vol. 69, 1960, reprinted in V. C. Chappell (ed.), *Hume* (London, Macmillan, 1966).
7. See, for example, D. G. C. MacNabb, *David Hume: His Theory of Knowledge and Morality* (Oxford, Basil Blackwell, 1966), p. 26.
8. See R. Descartes, *Meditations on First Philosophy* (1641), especially the first meditation, in *The Philosophical Writings of Descartes*, translated by J. Cottingham, R. Stoothoff and D. Murdoch (Cambridge, Cambridge University Press, 1985), vol. 2.
9. D. M. Armstrong, *Perception and the Physical World* (London, Routledge and Kegan Paul, 1961), especially ch. 3. For a discussion see J. Nelson, 'An examination of D. M. Armstrong's theory of perception', *American Philosophical Quarterly*, vol. 1, 1964.
10. On the relation of Hume's methodology to contemporary philosophical discussion, see David Pears, 'Hume's Empiricism and Modern Empiricism', in D. F. Pears (ed.), *David Hume: A Symposium* (London, Macmillan, 1963) and reprinted in David Pears, *Questions in the Philosophy of Mind* (London, Duckworth, 1975). See also A. J. Ayer, *The Central Questions of Philosophy* (Harmondsworth, Penguin Books, 1976), especially chs. 1 and 2.

3. How does thought proceed?

___

(*Treatise*, Bk. 1, Part 1, Sections iii–iv; *Enquiry* Section 3)

Under this heading, we shall be examining Hume's account of the mechanics of thought. In the last chapter, we explained and discussed how the mind receives the materials for thought. But human thought, according to Hume, is a process that proceeds on certain basic principles and with the help of certain natural capacities or powers. In thought we move from one thing to another. We 'reason', we 'argue', we form expectations and beliefs on the basis of which we act and react. One of Hume's aims, in both the *Treatise* and the *Enquiry*, is to explain this movement of thought, as one might describe it. Seeing the fireman shovelling coal into the furnace of a steam locomotive is one thing: understanding how the vehicle moves is another. So, one might say, seeing how impressions enter the mind is one thing: seeing how they 'move' is another. We must begin by looking at the two principal tools of the mind that are jointly responsible for the progress of thought. These are our ability to remember and our ability to imagine.

Memory and Imagination
These two faculties are discussed in the *Treatise*, Book 1, Part 1, Section III, and in Book 1, Part III, Section V. Their operation has already been alluded to by Hume in his account of impressions and ideas. It will be recalled that, while impressions are the given data of the senses, ideas are the faint copies of these and therefore at all times involve the memory of them. Imagination comes into play when the simple copies of impressions are put together to form more complex ideas.

For Hume, then, both memory and imagination involve the having of images. But this immediately presents a problem: how are we able to distinguish those images we want to call memory images from those we think of as images of the imagination? If we think that remembering essentially involves the having of images, this problem looks inescapable. There must, it seems, be some special characteristic of the images we have in remembering by which we are able to tell that we are remembering and not imagining.

There is one thing we need to be clear about straight away. The question which Hume attempts to answer is the question of how the subject himself is able to pick out certain of his experiences as experiences of remembering as opposed to imagining. What is it about memories that marks them off from the deliverances of the imagination? It is *not* the question of what makes a memory experience a genuine or correct memory. It is important to be clear about this, since Hume himself did confusingly suggest, only to dismiss, a possible answer to the problem which might indicate that he really was concerned to answer this latter question also. Hume does indeed suggest in the earlier of the two sections mentioned above that what distinguishes memory from the imagination is that the images in memory reproduce the order of the events remembered, and are in that respect tied down, whereas the imagination is not so restricted. Now it seems obvious that the sequence of memory images will only reproduce the original order of experiences if it is a *correct* memory of such events. Nevertheless it will become clear that what Hume is fundamentally seeking are the distinguishing marks of memory *experiences*, quite apart from whether these experiences are correct memories.

In any case, he saw quite clearly that this whole suggestion must be rejected. It is impossible, he said, to recall our past impressions and compare them with our present ideas to see whether the original sequence of events is preserved. He might also have noted that many of our memories are not memories of sequences of events, but of objects or people, and we would be at a loss to explain what makes these experiences memories by Hume's criterion. Furthermore, even where we do remember a sequence of events, we are not in the least bound to remember them in the order in which they occurred. We may, for example, remember the blow which ended the boxing match before going on to recall other incidents in the fight, so that the order of our ideas is different from the original order of events; but we are genuinely and correctly remembering, nevertheless. But, in addition to all this, it really does look as if Hume has attempted to answer a question which cannot be his central concern. He cannot be construed as attempting to answer the question of how we can know when our memory impressions give us *knowledge*. He is concerned, not with knowledge, but with a particular sort of *belief*. That this is so becomes clear on inspection of Hume's other suggestion about what distinguishes memory from imagination, a suggestion which he does not reject, and which cannot possibly be construed as any sort of answer to scepticism about memory.

Hume's main answer to the question, what distinguishes memory from imagination, is that the ideas of memory are easily identifiable by reference to their greater forcefulness and vivacity. 'When we remember any past event', he says, 'the idea of it flows in upon the mind in a forcible manner; whereas in the imagination the perception is faint and languid, and cannot without difficulty be preserved by the mind steady and uniform for any considerable time' (*T.*, p. 9). This is the suggestion we must now consider.

It is at once clear that this suggestion is open to the very same kind of objection we encountered when considering the general doctrine of impressions and ideas in the previous chapter. The objection is that there will be many occasions on which the images of imagination will be quite as strong, forceful and vivid as those of memory. If, then, the present criterion is the only one at our disposal, we should be committed to regarding such images as genuine cases of memory, and that can hardly be acceptable. There is certainly no denying that the faculty of imagination is capable of producing very vivid experiences. Indeed, we are sometimes capable of frightening ourselves by the figments of our imagination. Are we then remembering on such occasions?

Two further points should be noted. The first is that, within the confines of his own psychology, Hume is walking a tightrope. We have already seen, in Chapter 2 above, that Hume distinguishes between impressions and ideas in terms of relative forcefulness and vivacity. In the present context, he is distinguishing between realms of ideas, between memory and imagination in the very same terms. But, that being the case, we seem to be faced with a psychology that requires us to decide that a certain image, or series of images, is vivid and forceful enough to count as a memory but not sufficiently vivid and forceful to count as an impression, that is, a sensory experience. It is doubtful whether we are as psychologically discerning as this doctrine seems to demand. We shall see the same situation arising when we come to discuss Hume's account of belief.

The second point to note is a comment on both of the criteria for distinguishing between memory and imagination that we have mentioned. They both assume that remembering and imagining necessarily consist in the having of images. This was a point we noticed when discussing the general character of impressions and ideas, but it needs to be stressed here also. An obvious objection to this claim is that there are many cases of remembering, and also of imagining, which do not consist in the experience of imagery. There is, for example, what is often called factual memory. I can remember the date of the Battle of

Hastings, I can remember that the first moon landing occurred in 1969, and I can remember that Aberdeen is 130 miles or so north of Edinburgh. Contingently, there may be images associated with these rememberings, but imagery is certainly not an essential part of their nature. It is true that the activity of imagining is more intimately involved with the having of images than memory is, but here too it is possible to think of examples where images are absent. I can imagine what it would have been like if the Labour party had won the last general election. This may mean only that I can formulate the kind of acts that I believe would have been passed in Parliament. Again, I can imagine the conflict in Margaret Thatcher's mind when confronted by the Argentinian invasion of the Falkland Islands, but this may be only to say that I know the kind of issues on which her thoughts were dwelling. In neither case does the mention of images form a necessary part of the description of the mental scene.

Now of course it is possible to say what, indeed, some philosophers have said, that memory in a strict sense must involve images, and that imagination, in a strict sense must do so also.[1] The senses of remembering and imagining that we have highlighted are extended or attenuated uses of the concepts. I see no justification for such a move. Quite apart from anything else, it would render a person who was devoid of mental imagery – and apparently there are such – incapable of either imagining or remembering, and that cannot be an acceptable implication.

We have seen that Hume's suggestion, that what distinguishes those experiences we call remembering from imagining is the force and vivacity of the images we have, cannot stand. One additional reason why this won't do is that even if it were the case that memory always involves the having of images and that these images were always more vivid than those of the imagination, it would still be totally puzzling why it should be the case that the mere fact that an image has a certain degree of vivacity should suggest that it is an image of something in the *past*. It is obvious that, whatever else memory is, it is a matter of thinking of something we take to have happened or existed in the past, and it is quite clear on reflection that thinking of something as past is one thing and the having of images of a certain degree of vivacity is quite another. It is this flaw in Hume's account of memory that Russell tried to rectify in his book *The Analysis of Mind*. Russell accepted the idea that memory involves having images, but suggested that what distinguished memory images from others were two factors: they are characterised by a feeling of familiarity, and they are characterised by 'feelings giving a sense of pastness'.[2]

This certainly looks to be an improvement on Hume's account, but it might seem that it is still open to the following criticism. There remains, it might be felt, something curiously artificial about this suggested criterion of memory, an artificiality it shares with Hume's suggestion. It is as if the process begins with a person being in a state of complete ignorance about the character of a certain train of images, and then setting out to determine whether they are images of memory or of imagination. But this misrepresents what typically happens on a psychological level. It is certainly sometimes the case that a series of images passes before our minds quite involuntarily and such that we wonder about their status. 'Am I remembering?', I may ask myself on such occasion. But more characteristically there is no 'neutral' set of images awaiting a label in this way. They *are* already labelled or branded by virtue of the intention with which they are invoked. I 'set out' or 'resolve' to remember or to imagine, as the case may be. In the ordinary course of events, I do not discover that what I am engaged in doing is remembering, any more than I discover that what I am doing is calculating or fitting together the pieces of a jigsaw. Of course I may 'catch myself' doing any of these things, but this would not be a two-stage process in which I first discover that I am doing something and then determine what it is that I am doing. To catch myself doing one of them is at the same time to know what it is that I am doing. It is in this sense, then, that both Hume and Russell provide us with a misleading account of what goes on psychologically when a person remembers.

The fundamental flaw in both Hume's and Russell's account of memory lies in their shared assumption that memory *essentially* involves the having of images. If we accept that this is what memory is, there seems no escape from the suggestion that I am first of all confronted with a set of images and then have to determine whether these images have a certain character. But in fact images are incidental to remembering. I remember what I had for breakfast this morning. That is, I can recall what I had for breakfast, and am able to tell anyone who has any interest in the matter. I may, in doing so, have all sorts of vivid imagery of the breakfast table, but that is entirely incidental. The occurrence of such images is not what remembering consists of, nor is the occurrence of such images an essential component of memory. In remembering something, I normally know *that* I am remembering,[3] just as in consciously intending to do something I normally know *that* I have that intention. In neither case do I inspect a set of images and infer from their character what my mental state is.

Association of ideas (*Treatise*, Book I, Part I, Section IV; *Enquiry*, Section IV)

A further – and extremely important – feature of Hume's account of the mechanics of thought, of the way in which thought proceeds, is his description of the way in which ideas associate with one another. He is not referring to a deliberate act of the mind, whereby it actively puts certain ideas together. He is, rather, directing our attention to a natural phenomenon among our ideas, 'a gentle force, which commonly prevails' (*T.*, p. 10). Towards the end of Section IV, he describes this force as 'a kind of attraction' and compares it with the force of gravity which holds between physical objects in the natural world.

Hume must not be credited with the first statement of the doctrine. John Locke had already singled it out for attention.[4] But it was Hume, more than Locke, who saw the significance of the doctrine in explaining the nature of thought. Hume was also more attentive to the phenomenon in that he mapped out the principles in accordance with which it seemed to proceed. Locke merely recorded it as a fact about the working of the mind without exploring it further.

The topic arises fairly naturally in the course of Hume's thought. It follows the section (I, II, III) in which he has been discussing the distinction between memory and imagination. One of the things he had been concerned to say in that context, as we have already seen, is that, while the activity of memory is restricted somewhat by the order of the impressions from which it derives, imagination is unrestrained. The imagination is at liberty 'to transpose and change its ideas' (*T.*, p. 10). But, having drawn this contrast, Hume is then anxious to stress that the connections between ideas in imagination are not so loose that they become just a matter of chance. And it is to counter any temptation to suppose this that he outlines his principles of association. There are three such principles.

Firstly, if one thing resembles another in my experience, then, whenever the idea of the one arises, it tends to invoke the other. Thus if I see a photograph of Edinburgh Castle, and I am already familiar with it, this will tend to produce memories of it. Secondly, if one thing is situated near to another in space or time, it will similarly tend to invoke the thought of that other whenever perceived. Anyone who knew the Mary who had a little lamb would presumably be subject to this kind of association. Finally, there is association based on cause and effect. The bee that is the cause of the painful sting will naturally be associated with that painful effect in any subsequent thought about it.

Hume does not explain how it is that ideas associate in accordance with such principles. He is happy to accept the phenomenon as a brute fact. They are 'original qualities of human nature which I pretend not to explain' (*T.*, p. 13). But, casual as his treatment of the subject seems to be, both in the *Treatise* and the *Enquiry*, Hume does attach a great deal of importance to it. This is something that will become evident when we come to discuss in detail his account of causality in chapters 4 and 5. It is also evident from the way in which Hume describes the principles of association in the *Abstract*, the pamphlet in which Hume summarises the main doctrines of the *Treatise*. He tells us there that, if anything can justify his being called an 'inventor', it is the use he makes of the doctrine of association.[5] Indeed, he concludes the *Abstract* with the claim that the three principles of association outlined are so all-pervading in explaining the progress of human thought that they deserve to be called the 'cement of the universe'.[6] There could not be a much stronger claim on behalf of their importance.

One question that needs to be raised about Hume's account of association is whether Hume is right in suggesting that there are three *distinct* modes of association. As we shall see in the next chapter, for Hume to say that one thing is the cause of another is just to say that 'all objects *similar to* the first are followed by objects *similar to* the second' (*E.*, p. 76). That is to say, the notion of causality embraces that of resemblance and is not independent of it. Again, Hume tells us that a cause is contiguous with its effect, both in time and space. Even though he came to allow that not all causes and effects could be contiguous in *space*, since some causes and effects are mental, and mental events are not situated in space, it is clear that all causes are contiguous in *time* with their effects, and all non-mental causes and effects are contiguous both in time and space. In short, the notion of causality embraces that of contiguity and is not independent of it. Of course, it is true that two items may resemble each other, and in consequence be associated together in the mind, without being causally connected; and it is also true that two items may be contiguous, and in consequence associated together in the mind, without being causally connected. But it is *not* possible for two objects to be causally connected without their being *contiguous*, or without their *resembling* other pairs of contiguous objects. Perhaps it was the recognition of how the relations of resemblance and contiguity are included in the notion of causality which led Hume to say that 'of the three relations ... this of causation is the most extensive' (*T*., p. 12).

Hume's account of causality may seem to give rise to another difficulty in relation to what he says about association. As we shall see in the next chapter, Hume offers another definition of cause which is rather different from the one quoted above. A cause, he tells us is 'an object followed by another, and whose appearance always conveys the thought to that other' (*E*., p. 77). Now Hume is quite clearly saying here that to say that one thing is the cause of another *is* to say that the one thing is associated with the other in our minds. And if that is the case, then it cannot be right to say that the relation of causality *explains* this association. What has gone wrong?

A full understanding of this issue must wait on our discussion in the next chapter on Hume's conception of causality, but we can briefly indicate the answer to this puzzle here. Hume does indeed insist that whenever we come to judge that one thing is the cause of another all we have actually perceived is that the one thing is regularly followed by the other. This relation of 'constant conjunction' is, so far as Hume can see, all that causality objectively is. But it is because A is thus constantly conjoined with B that we come to associate them together and to *think of A as necessarily connected to B*. We all think that if A is the cause of B then A is necessarily connected in some way with B. This idea, Hume says, is in fact groundless. It is the result of the associative link between A and B which is established in our minds. What explains this link is the constant conjunction of A and B in our experience; and constant conjunction is all that causality objectively amounts to. There is, then, no inconsistency in Hume's position. But we must now turn to a detailed account and examination of Hume's views on the centrally important issue of causality.

Notes

1. ' ... memory of past sensations seems only possible by means of present images' (B. Russell, *The Analysis of Mind* (London, George Allen and Unwin, 1921) Lecture IX, p. 159).
2. *The Analysis of Mind*, p. 163.
3. To say this is not to deny the need for a discussion of more complex cases involving memory and imagination. See J. O. Urmson, 'Memory and imagination', *Mind*, vol. 76, 1967. For recent discussion of memory and epistemology, see Norman Malcolm, 'Three lectures on

memory', in Norman Malcolm, *Knowledge and Certainty* (New Jersey, Prentice-Hall, 1965); Jonathan Dancy, *Contemporary Epistemology* (Oxford, Blackwell, 1985), ch. 12.
4. John Locke, *An Essay Concerning Human Understanding*, Bk II, ch. XXXIII, section 18.
5. *An Abstract of a Treatise of Human Nature* (1740), reprinted in *A Treatise of Human Nature*, second edition, revised by P. Nidditch (Oxford, Clarendon Press, 1978).
6. *Abstract*, p. 662.

4. *What do we mean by cause and how do we reason from experience?*

(*Treatise*, Bk. I, Part III, Sections II–VI, XIV and XV; *Enquiry*, Sections IV,V, and VII)

The wording of the title of this chapter draws our attention to two topics that have occupied a position of central importance in the history of philosophy since Hume's time. They are generally known as the problem of causality and the problem of induction. The former can best be summarised, at least for the purpose of an introductory paragraph, as the problem of how it is that something comes to be designated a cause. The latter is the problem of how, if at all, we can rationally justify our judgements either about future events or about present events of which we are not witnesses. The two topics are intimately linked in Hume, for a reason that can be simply stated. It will be spelt out in more detail as we go along. The reason is this: Hume believes that the majority of our judgements about unseen events or about future events are based upon our knowledge of causal sequences. It therefore follows that any discussion of the problem of induction will inevitably involve a discussion of causality.

Why causality?

It has already been said that the topic of causality was an important one for Hume. Indeed, many philosophers would hold that Hume's thoughts on the topic were his most significant contribution to philosophy. But why should the topic be so important to him, and, for that matter, to philosophers generally? In order to answer this question, we shall have to say something about its genesis within the progress of Hume's thought. At the beginning of Chapter 3 we saw how, after Hume had discussed the contents of the mind, namely, impressions and ideas, he then went on to discuss the 'mechanics' of the mind. This was the programme of outlining various mental powers or capacities and the principles upon which they operate. In that connection, we looked at memory and imagination and at the three principles of association. In a sense, the introduction of causality constitutes a continuation of this same general theme. To put the position somewhat naively, Hume looks at the way in which the enquiring human mind produces the various factual claims that it does. His examination of the topic is more complex in the *Treatise* (Bk I, Part III, Section I; Bk. III, Part I, Section I) than it is in the *Enquiry* (Section IV), perhaps because in the former work he was still working towards a considered conclusion.

At the beginning of Section IV of the *Enquiry* Hume distinguishes two classes of propositions formed by the mind (*E.*, p. 25). The one class is the result of a reasoning process that is quite independent of conditions in the world. It consists of propositions that are the result of comparing one idea with another such that the very act of comparing yields certain implications. Just for this reason, he calls them 'relations of ideas'. The paradigms for such a class of proposi-tions are to be found in the spheres of geometry, algebra and arithmetic, and it is from this area that Hume draws his illustrations. It is the mere operation of thought, independently of conditions obtaining in the world, that will tell us that in any right-angled triangle the square of the hypotenuse is equal to the sum of the squares of the other two sides. It is, again, the mere operation of thought that tells us that three times five is equal to the half of thirty. These are the sort of truths that would now be known as 'analytic' or as 'a priori', and Hume regards them as yielding knowledge claims that are immune to doubt. It is a mark of their having this status that, for any given proposition of this class, its contradictory will be inconceivable. How does one begin to create, in one's imagination, for example, the idea of a square that does *not* possess four sides?

The other class of propositions comprises what Hume refers to as 'matters of fact'. They are nothing more than the findings of the senses, or propositions based on the findings of the senses. It is therefore of their essence that they refer to conditions in the world. 'The picture on the book in front of me is of David Hume', 'The sun is beginning to penetrate the mist', 'My door is ajar and producing a draught' would all be examples of such propositions. We would now refer to them as contingent or empirical statements, and it is a feature of them that facts they describe could always be other than they are. Hume put this by saying that 'the contrary of every matter of fact is still possible; because it can never imply a contradiction' (*E.*, p. 25). It is raining now, but it did not have to be, and I can easily imagine its not doing so. But the geometrical figure of a square that has four sides necessarily has four sides, and that could not have been otherwise. This truth was expressed above, by saying that the contradictory of such propositions was inconceivable. What needs to be said about matters of fact, on the other hand, is that their contradictory is always conceivable.

Having forged this distinction between two classes of propositions, Hume concentrates on the second of the two classes, matters of fact, or empirical propositions. Furthermore, it is upon a particular sub-class of these that he centres his attention. We can delineate them in the following way. Certain of the factual statements that we make are straightforward reporting of present-tense sensory experience. I see the book in front of me, the picture on the wall, and hear the sound of the traffic outside my room. But there are other claims about the world that are not direct reportings in the same way. One might say about them that they are indirect, or that they are 'inferences'. I receive a letter from a friend; the envelope has a Bristol postmark, so I 'infer' that the friend is in Bristol. I hear, in the distance, the regular sound of the fog-horn, and I remark that there is a mist at sea. And it is in relation to these more indirect factual claims that Hume begins to impress upon us the significance of the causal relation in our reasoning about the world. What he actually asserts is that in the case of those judgements that go beyond the immediate testimony of the senses we are employing causal reasoning (*E.*, p. 27). Once one recognises that such judgements are very extensive, covering an awful lot of human reasoning, one can readily see why Hume saw causality as being so influential. Quite simply, it permeates so much of our thinking and reasoning about the world that we must seriously wonder whether we can do without it.

Having thus isolated the route by which the topic of causality enters both the *Treatise* and the *Enquiry*, we must now try to disentangle the features of Hume's particular contribution to the topic. The general aim must be to see why that contribution is regarded as so distinctive and how Hume's thoughts on the topic presented the challenge that they did. But that is something that is not easy to do. This is partly because very few of us have scrutinised what we normally mean by a cause. It might therefore be of some help to outline some assumptions which a cursory survey of our thinking about causality will probably yield. Firstly, there is some vague tendency to think that a cause is something that can be readily identified for what it is at first glance, so to speak. Perhaps another way of putting the point is to say that even those causes with which we are newly-acquainted are thought of as being immediately recognisable for what they are; it is to say that they somehow exhibit themselves as causes, even on first view. Secondly, there is a tendency, similarly vague, to suppose that a cause is something having within it the power to bring something else about. Thirdly, and very closely related to the previous point, we tend to think in terms of some transference of power taking place whenever an effect is brought about by its cause. All three of these assumptions are, in one way or another, scrutinised and subsequently challenged by Hume. We must now try to summarise his position.

The key to understanding Hume's approach to the topic is to be found, once again, in the impressions and ideas doctrine which we discussed in Chapter 2. One of the important features of that doctrine is that we cannot have an idea without an impression. That particular claim needs to be expanded a little at this point in order to understand how Hume proceeds. Strictly speaking, what Hume means is that it is not possible to have an idea that can be taken as a reflection of how things are unless there is an impression from which it can be seen as stemming. It is as though Hume wants to say that, without a corresponding impression, an 'idea' is simply unintelligible. As he himself puts it, ''tis impossible perfectly to understand any idea, without tracing it up to its origin, and examining that primary impression, from which it arises' (*T.*, pp. 74–5). The thought seems to be that unless we can point to what an idea picks out in our experience, it is doubtful that the idea has a clear meaning: the presence of an impression renders an idea perspicuous (*E.*, p. 22). Granted this, the impressions and ideas doctrine becomes a testing procedure for meaningfulness or intelligibility, and that is how it operates in the case of the idea of causality.

Therefore, in the *Treatise* at least, Hume's first move is to look for the impression that provides the source for the idea of causality. That, in turn, means looking at those things in experience that we standardly call causes in order to see whether they possess some one quality that marks them out as such. Do we have an impression of some one quality the possession of which renders something a cause? Is there one quality in common to heating water, hammering a nail, switching a light on and an insult's causing offence? The answer is obviously in the negative. There is nothing common to all those things we call causes that is an object of sensory experience.

Yet it is equally plain to Hume that there is no a priori knowledge of causes, a point that is given more immediate emphasis in the *Enquiry* version. We are told, quite emphatically, that a person with no experience of the behaviour of natural phenomena would be quite incapable of identifying a cause (*E.*, p. 27). No inspection of the intrinsic qualities of an object will reveal what effect it may produce. In the Garden of Eden Adam could not have inferred from first seeing water that it could suffocate, or from seeing fire that it could burn. These things have to be learned from experience. With the extensive and detailed knowledge of the world that we have, there is some danger of our losing sight of this fact. But then we have to remind ourselves of those learning contexts from the past in which we have had to be taught, or have had to discover for ourselves, the way in which some object will behave. In either case, what we learn will be dependent upon experience, on observation of the behaviour of the natural world. It is not possible for us to 'read off' an effect from a mere scrutiny of an object in isolation.

Hume's progress in the analysis so far, then, amounts to this. When we survey the causal sequences with which we are acquainted, we find that there is no single discernible quality which all causes possess, such that they can be so designated. On the other hand, as we have seen, there is no a priori knowledge of causes: we cannot pick out a cause independently of experience. The next move must therefore be to return to the drawing-board. That means returning to the causal sequences with which we are already acquainted. The object must be to pick out any general features that they exhibit. The supposition that there is some one quality that all causes possess has already been discarded, but there may yet be certain ascertainable general characteristics of causal sequences. Hume discovers three such characteristics. The first is that a cause is always situated near to or next to its effect, both in time and place, a characteristic normally referred to as contiguity. It sometimes appears that a cause is, temporally or spatially, distant from its effect, but Hume thinks we shall always discover intervening links upon closer scrutiny, such that the principle is sustained (*T.*, p. 75). The second characteristic to which Hume refers us is that of the priority in time of the cause over the effect. It amounts to the claim that a cause always occurs before its effect (*T.*, p. 76). Hume admits that this claim may be disputed and does provide an argument to support it. We shall consider this in due course. Meanwhile, he feels that contiguity and the temporal priority of the cause, though essential to the causal relation, are not sufficient in themselves to characterise causal sequences. *A* can be contiguous to *B* and also precede *B* without being its cause. The missing element, says

Hume, is that of necessary connection (*T.*, p. 77). That is to say, when we survey those sequences in our experience we call causal, we suppose, rightly or wrongly, that the cause is necessarily connected with its effect. We suppose that, granted the presence of a cause, its effect *must* follow. On Hume's view, another way of putting this same point is to say that we regard the cause as possessing a kind of power to bring about its effect. An exaggerated view would be to think of the cause as the process of giving birth to something, thus suggesting its necessary connection with the effect. It is, then, this particular ingredient in the analysis of causality that most occupies Hume in both the *Treatise* and the *Enquiry*, and it is to this that we shall be returning in due course. Firstly, however, we must make some brief comments upon the two other features of the causal relation that are mentioned by Hume.

We have seen that Hume was quite happy to list contiguity as one of the essential ingredients of the causal relation. In fact, he should have had some reservations about doing so. Not all of the things we regarded as standing in a causal relation are next to each other, either in time or place. It is true that many of the counter-examples we are tempted to give may be accommodated by Hume's claim that, in those cases where there appears to be causality at a distance, we shall, if we look closer, discover an underlying sequence of contiguous events. Thus it is initially tempting to say, for example, that the effect of hot sunshine in melting a piece of wax is causality at a distance – and, in this case, at a great distance. But it is possible for Hume to claim that, in actual fact, a clear continuity is provided by the rays of the sun, stretching continuously from the wax to the sun itself. A row of collapsing dominoes stretching from Edinburgh to London would be a more picturesque example of the truth to which Hume is alluding. But it is not at all clear that the moon's effect upon the tides can be explained in the same way. Nor is it clear that my anger or indignation, caused by the report of distant atrocities, can be similarly explained. The distinction between the mental and physical looks to present a problem here. To be sure, if one is a physicalist, holding that all causality necessarily takes place on a physical level, then the problem does not arise in the same way. But if one holds, as many people do, that mental events are both essentially different from physical events and at the same time are causally related to them, one is bound to hold that there is a fairly decisive objection to Hume's contiguity require-ment. Mental events, by their nature, have no location in space. The neurologist, for example, does not expect to reveal little thinkings or intendings when he opens up the brain. This is not because he thinks his instruments are inadequate to the task but because he thinks there is a conceptual impossibility involved. Mental events are just not that kind of thing. But if mental events have no spatial location, then it is, to say the least, difficult to see how they can be described as spatially contiguous to the physical events that they sometimes cause, or are caused by.

However, though it is perfectly appropriate to underline this difficulty for the thesis that cause and effect are always contiguous in time and place, it would be wrong to suppose that Hume himself was entirely unaware of the problem. Hume does actually warn us, in the passage in which the contiguity requirement is discussed (*T.*, p. 75), that further thought may lead us to revise it. A footnote refers us to Part IV, Section V of the *Treatise*. There, Hume is primarily involved in discussing the nature of the soul and whether it can be seen as something in which perceptions can 'inhere'. This in turn leads him to wonder whether one can intelligibly speak about a 'local conjunction' between mental and physical states. In other words, is it ever possible to speak of a mental state as being spatially contiguous with a physical state with which it is supposed to be related? He immediately denies the possibility. He asserts, as a maxim, 'that an object may exist, and yet be nowhere' (*T.*, p. 235), and he illustrates this claim by reference to mental events. His point is simply that it never makes sense to say of a mental event that it has any particular place: 'A moral reflection cannot be placed on the right or on the left hand of a passion ... '(*T.*, p. 236).

It is obvious from these remarks, therefore, that Hume is well aware of the general difficulty to which we have referred. That is, he clearly sees the logical difficulty involved in any attempt to describe a mental event as being spatially near to a physical event. Whether he was equally aware of the problem when specifically discussing the contiguity condition is another matter. The most reasonable conclusion at this point is that it is unlikely that Hume saw spatial contiguity as being a necessary condition of the causal relation, even though he is popularly thought to have held this view.

The temporal priority condition – the second of the three characteristics mentioned above – is one that Hume lists with greater conviction (*T.*, p. 76). Indeed, he produces what he evidently thinks of as a convincing argument in support of it. The argument is somewhat compressed, but the following would appear to be a fair summary of it. It actually proceeds by way of an attack upon another line of thought, said to be well-established both in physics and in human psychology. It is a view that stresses the role of a cause as a sufficient condition. On this view, a cause will be something that, once present, will automatically entail the existence of the effect. What is more, it will entail its simultaneous existence. The reasoning behind this is conceptual in character. If we were to suppose that there is a lapse of time between the presence of the cause and the coming about of the effect, then it follows that what we were tempted to regard as the cause could not truly have been so. That is to say, it could not have been the sufficient reason for its effect; something else was required in order to produce that effect. As soon as that something else is present, the effect is also automatically present. It is therefore clear that any genuine cause must be simultaneous with its effect.

Hume's response is as follows. First, he underlines the point that the conclusion of the above argument is indeed that all causes are simultaneous with their effects. If a cause is capable of existing prior to its effect, the argument claims, it cannot be *sufficient* for that effect. If it were sufficient for that effect, the effect would come into being at the very time the cause occurs. But, Hume claims, this view has the absurd implication that there would be no such thing as the causal sequence of events over time, as we know it. If a cause is always simultaneous with its effect, and that effect is, in turn, simultaneous with its effect, and so on, then the concept of succession can get no foothold. All would be co-existence, and time would collapse into a single moment. It is the evident absurdity of this position that compels us to say that a cause must precede its effect, according to Hume.

It has to be said that this is a very strange argument on Hume's part. Let us look at the famous 'maxim' to which he refers us and which he sees as constituting an argument against the priority condition. It amounts to the claim that if there is any interval of time between the existence of A and the coming into existence of B, then A could not truly have been a cause of B; some other intervening event would have been required to constitute its cause. By its exponents this was seen as supporting the view that, at least sometimes, the cause is contemporaneous with its effect. Hume responds by claiming that the argument is untenable since it is committed to the absurdity that all causes will be similarly contemporaneous with their effects. But he appears to have got it wrong. If the maxim concerned is correct, what it will show is not that cause and effect have to be simultaneous but that there will always be some overlap between them. That will be compatible with the claim that cause and effect are sometimes contemporaneous events, since there may be occasions on which the overlap is total. But it will also allow for those occasions on which, although there is no time-lapse between the completion of the cause and the beginning of the effect, the latter nevertheless still continues after the cause is complete. Thus, for example, a red ball in a game of snooker may continue on its course around the table after the white cue-ball has hit it and become stationary itself. Many sequences will be of this kind. The important thing to note about them is that, while they comply with the requirements of the maxim, as set out by Hume, they do not have to be cases of simultaneity, even though they may sometimes be so. It therefore follows that the maxim does not result in the absurdity that Hume envisaged. From that it follows, in turn, that Hume has not actually demonstrated that a cause must always precede its effect. The maxim, if it is correct, will continue to show that the simultaneity of cause and effect is possible.

It is only fair to say, however, that, although Hume claimed to be able to 'establish' the priority condition by means of the argument we have now discussed, he did end up with certain reservations (*T*., p. 76). That is perhaps as it should be, at least on the basis of our intuitive experience. But he might have been even more ready to surrender the claim as a necessary condition had he been more aware of the fact that states as well as events can be causally related. Thus the tension of the door-spring is causally and simultaneously related to the state of the door being kept ajar; the movement of pistons in a car engine is similarly related to the motion of the car; the revolution of pedals on a bicycle keeps the wheels turning, and so on. We certainly think that we are legitimately talking about the operation of causes in such cases, but it would be difficult to construe them as coming before their effects.

It must also be mentioned that some philosophers have speculated about what is known as backward causation.[1] If precognition were an established fact, for example, then it would present at least a *prima facie* case for saying that here the cause, far from preceding its effect, was actually succeeding it. Precognition would involve knowing or perceiving an event that had not yet come about. But then my knowledge of such an event could only be explained by reference to a causal relation between that future event and my present perception of it. The cause, in other words, would be in the future, that is, after its effect, my present experience. On the analogy with present-tense perception, just as it is the presence of the chair in front of me that explains my seeing it, so it must be the existence of some event in the future that explains my knowledge of it.

Obviously, a great deal more needs to be said both about simultaneous as well as backward causation. But enough has already been said to show that Hume should have had many, and more readily-conceded, reservations about the priority claim. But we must now turn to the third characteristic of causal sequences as we know them that Hume had delineated for us. This is what he called 'necessary connection' and, as we saw above, what Hume had in mind in using this term was our ordinary belief that effects are in some way *produced* by their causes. It has already been said that, for Hume, the idea of necessary connection constitutes the most important aspect of his analysis of causality. To repeat the point, this is partly because he saw that the relations of contiguity and priority, while they may be essential to something's being a cause, are not sufficient in themselves. If we did not feel that A and B are necessarily connected, we would not regard them as being causally related. But there is another reason why the idea of necessary connection so much occupies Hume's time. It stems directly from the doctrine of impressions and ideas that had been set out at the beginning of both the *Treatise* and the *Enquiry*. When discussing that doctrine, we singled out one of its most important features. That amounted to the claim that there cannot be an idea without an impression. In the present context, that particular feature of the doctrine becomes highlighted since it presents Hume with a challenge that he cannot easily evade. He is faced with a situation in which, very clearly, we do have an idea of causes being necessarily connected with their effects. As an empiricist, surveying the character of our experience, he was hardly in a position to deny the fact. But then his own doctrine required him to seek the impression from which such an idea could come. That was to become a search that was not easily completed and perhaps, as we shall see, not satisfactorily resolved.

The search begins in a negative way, both in the *Enquiry* (Section 7) and in the *Treatise* (Book 1, Part III, Section XIV), though the latter work tells a more complicated story. We must try to provide a summary that will do justice to both works. Let us bear in mind, once again, what it is that Hume is doing. He sees the idea of a necessary connection between cause and effect as being the predominant feature of causal sequences. Indeed, he often uses the words 'necessary connection' synonymously with the term 'causality'. His next move, then, is to search for the impression from which this very important idea is derived. As we have seen, our ordinary experience of causal sequences will only yield contiguity and priority. Where, then, does the idea of necessity come from? The answer to this question takes a little longer to arrive at in the *Treatise* than in the *Enquiry*. In the former work, he first explores two ways in which necessity enters into our thinking about cause and effect. This is intended to clear the ground a little by eliminating certain avenues of thought.

One of the two possibilities is expressed in our conviction that every event must have a cause.[2] Hume has little difficulty in showing that, while this is certainly an ingrained attitude in our approach to natural phenomena, there is no way of demonstrating that this really is the case (*T.*, p. 79). The only way of demonstrating the truth of such a proposition would be by showing that it follows from the very meaning of the term 'event' that every event must have a cause. Patently, this does not follow. It is possible to provide a complete analysis or definition of an object or event without mentioning the fact that it was caused. What is more, there is no contradiction or absurdity involved in supposing that some event, X, was not actually caused. It may be, psychologically, difficult to believe that there could be such an event. But that is not the same as to say that there is a contradiction in conceiving of it. An analogy makes the point clear. There *would* be a contradiction involved in trying to think of a square that did not have four sides. The concept of a square *requires* that it have four sides; that is the defining property of a square. It is not similarly required of any object or event that it must have been caused. Of course, as Hume points out (*T.*, p. 82), if one is speaking of something that is specifically designated as an effect, then it does follow that it had a cause, for the simple reason that an effect is defined as that which is caused. But this is a trivial, verbal matter that bypasses the real issue at stake, which is in Hume's words whether, 'whatever begins to exist must have a cause of existence' (*T.*, p. 78). Hume is happy to conclude that the proposition 'every event has a cause' is not a necessary truth.

A similar argument is deployed against the demonstrability of the second possibility. The first of these possibilities was that the concept of necessity might enter into our thinking about cause and effect on a very general level. It concerned the proposition that every event must have a cause, where the 'must' indicated our assumption about necessity. The second possibility, then, is simply a more particular version of this. It is the view that some particular event, X, is necessarily caused by some particular event Y. This would be to say that it could not have been caused by anything other than Y. Hume's response is essentially that, just as no inspection of an object or event will tell us that it had to be caused, so it is the case that no inspection of it will tell us that it had to be caused by Y in particular. Nor again will any scrutiny of Y tell is that it must have X as its effect. One might put Hume's point in relation to both of these possibilities in the following way: each object has its own nature and, in order to be what it is, contains no necessary link to any other object.

The position at which Hume has arrived at this point in his exploration, then, is as follows. We do have an idea of causes and effects being necessarily connected together. But this cannot be logical or conceptual necessity. That is, it is not part of the concept of an object that it must be caused by something in particular, nor indeed that it must be caused by anything at all. Hume must therefore look elsewhere for the source of the idea of necessity which we ascribe to causal sequences. Before following him in this task, it will be appropriate to make one or two brief comments.

Although it has not been made clear so far, Hume actually uses two arguments which he never clearly separates to support his claim that causes and effects are not logically linked together. The first of these, the one that we have emphasised most, states that there is nothing in the nature of any one object that necessarily implies the existence or coming into being of another and that, only if this were to be the case, would the one be logically connected to the other. His other argument, though certainly present in the *Treatise* (*T.*, p. 80), is more obviously present in the *Enquiry*. It is the claim that if cause and effect were conceptually or logically tied together, either on a general or on a particular level, there would have to be an absurdity or 'contradiction' involved in conceiving things to be otherwise (*E.*, pp. 29–30). This is what was implied on our analogy with the square, above. It would be contradictory to suppose that a square could have more or less than four sides. Therefore, it necessarily has four sides. There is no corresponding absurdity involved in the claim that an object or event might not have been caused, or caused by this particular thing, and therefore there is no similar necessity in this context.

Both of these supporting arguments against logical connection require to be treated with a little caution. It needs to be said about the second test of logical necessity that it depends upon the purely human propensity to 'conceive' of this or that state of affairs. That we are not able, on any particular occasion, to conceive of an alternative state of affairs may reflect not on what is actually logically possible but on the limitations of our own psychology. It may be an accidental fact about us that we cannot conceive of a situation, X, but that is not to imply that X is a logically impossible state. Hume, and those of his generation, might have found it quite impossible to imagine a physical body having no weight. It would certainly have been wrong to conclude, on this basis, that a weightless physical body was a logical impossibility. Space travel has now made this evident to us.

It must also be pointed out that it would be just as unwise to conclude from the fact that we *do* seem able to imagine some particular state of affairs that that state of affairs is logically possible.[3] Time travel is something that is imaginable in a way; nevertheless, there is good reason to suppose that the whole idea is logically absurd. I can imagine being Julius Caesar, but many philosophers would reject the claim that I might actually have been Julius Caesar. In general, the claim that what we seem able or unable to imagine is a sure guide to what is logically possible is one which needs to be treated with the greatest caution.

The other test for logical connection emphasises what we may call the 'self-contained' nature of any and every object around us. Nothing intrinsically belonging to the nature of X or Y or Z entails any reference to an object outside itself. Therefore there can be no such thing as a logical or 'conceptual' link between two things we call cause and effect. There is a strong temptation, when faced with this view, to argue that many objects or states do necessarily require a reference to some other object or state in order to identify them for what they are. This seems to be particularly true when we are talking about an object's properties and where these properties appear to be causal in character. For example, we identify a telescope as an instrument that enables us to see distant objects, or to see them clearly. Here, it seems as though the description of the instrument contains, intrinsically, a reference to some other state of affairs to which it is causally related. Examples of this kind, of which there are many, seem to belie Hume's claim that no description of an object necessarily links it with some other object.

But one needs to be careful. We can certainly claim that nothing can be called a telescope unless it brings distant objects closer to us, just as nothing can be deemed to be heat unless it affects its surroundings as heat does – causing water to boil, wood to burn, and so on. But this is a matter of how we have chosen to define the word 'telescope' and the word 'heat'. Whether some particular object or phenomenon that we have before us actually has the effects which would justify its being called a telescope, or entitle it to the label 'heat', remains a purely contingent matter. We can certainly say, 'If the phenomenon before me has certain specified effects, I must call it "heat"'; but we *cannot* say 'This thing in front of me necessarily has those specified effects'. The necessary connection is a purely *linguistic* one, a matter of how we define the relevant terms. What we will not find, if Hume is right, is a logically necessary connection, not just between concepts, but between *objects or states of affairs in the world*.

The quest for logical connection is not quite finished at this point. In the *Treatise* (Bk I, Part III, Section XIV), and in the *Enquiry* (Section VII, Part I), one further avenue is explored. The thought here is that, though the experience of external objects does not provide us with the idea of necessary connection, perhaps internal, psychological experience will do so. Hume considers in particular those cases in which, by virtue of the act of volition on my part, I can bring about the movement of some part of my body, or, alternatively, I can bring about some further activity of mind. Both possibilities are dismissed, on the basis of three arguments, that are drawn out more fully in the *Enquiry* than in the *Treatise*.

The first of these arguments concerns the relation of mind and body in particular (*E.*, p. 65). Basically, it reminds us that the relation between mind and body is, and always has been, a mystery to us. It is therefore unlikely to provide us with any insights into the nature of necessary connection. In appealing to this area of human experience, the hope would be that the experience of willing a limb to move will itself, by its very nature, reveal a necessary connection with its effect: that it affords us a privileged view of the transaction that takes place between mental act, considered as a cause, and the physical movement, considered as its effect. This it evidently does not do; we simply do not know 'the secret union of soul and body'.

Secondly, we only discover what we can and what we cannot will by actually trying (*E.*, p. 65). For example, on a physical level I discover that I can will my arm to rise or my leg to move but that I cannot move my heart, lungs or liver. Similarly, on the mental level, I can decide to think out my route to Birmingham or to dwell upon a financial problem, but I cannot decide to feel sad or grieved, at least in any genuine sense of these emotions. That being the case, it is not possible to 'read off' from my willing what *must* be the result of it. Our experiences on a mental level, in other words, are not essentially different from our experience of the behaviour of physical objects in the world. We have to learn by experience what conjunctions there are among physical objects such that we can expect the one upon the occurrence of the other. It is in a similar way that we learn what we can and what we cannot achieve by willing. Essentially the same point is made by considering a case of sudden paralysis (*E.*, p. 66). Here, it is often the case that the patient realises that he cannot move his leg only after he has actually tried to do so, that is, willed himself to do so. Hume's point is that these 'trials' would be quite needless if there really were a necessary connection between the willing and what is willed; for then an inspection of the character of the willing would itself reveal whether such actions would follow as their effects or not. It would be something we should know a priori.

The third argument amounts to this. The findings of anatomy make it obvious that we could never seriously expect to be able to 'read off' the result of willing from the act of willing itself. The reason for this is that what is immediately brought about by my willing to raise my arm, for example, is not, strictly, the raising of the arm but the operation of certain nerves and muscles – or perhaps something 'still more minute and more unknown' (*E.*, p. 66). The raising of the arm is therefore indirectly brought about by the putting into operation of something about which we have no knowledge. In other words, the real transaction, the necessary connection – if there is such a thing – remains utterly mysterious to us and is certainly not revealed in the act of willing. Physiology shows us, then, that the search for the source of the idea of necessary connection in this domain is doomed to failure.

One comment needs to be made about these arguments before we move on. They bring out, admirably well, Hume's quite widespread tendency to confuse issues of logic with issues of psychology. The first of the three arguments considered above dwells upon a matter of psychology. There, Hume tells us that we do not have any experience of the transaction of power from the exercise of willing. Now, as a matter of psychological fact, it is possible to dispute this claim. Many of us would claim to have the experience of 'bringing something about', especially in those cases which involve pushing or pulling heavy objects. So, for one thing, the psychological facts he quotes are questionable. But, even if the psychological claims were acceptable, they miss the point. Hume's avowed concern is with necessary connection, where this means logical necessity. Therefore, even if we did regularly have the experience of power that is involved in 'bringing things into being' by our willing, we should still not be able to 'deduce' the effect from such an act. No matter how detailed a description we may provide of the act of volition itself, considered as a cause, it will tell us nothing about the nature of the effect. It is this central, logical point that Hume brings back into focus in his second argument. As we have seen, his point there is that we have to discover, by actually trying, what our various acts of will can bring about. We cannot read it off from the nature of those acts themselves. Such information will be the result of an empirical and not an a priori investigation.

In these three arguments, then, we have a curious mixture of logic and psychology. We have seen how the reference to the psychological facts is unsatisfactory. Nevertheless, the central, logical point that Hume wishes to make is firmly established in the second argument; and, indeed, this is all he needed in order to proceed.

At this stage, then, Hume is happy to conclude that, though the idea of necessary connection is very much part of our concept of causality, we certainly cannot mean any kind of logical connection. With that thought, one might say that the negative part of Hume's quest for the source of that central idea is over.[4] But the source, in the form of an impression from which that idea can be derived, has to lie somewhere. The impressions/ideas doctrine insists on that. The alternative would be to say that when we speak of necessary connection in our reference to causes and effects we are speaking nonsense, and Hume is not finally prepared to say that, even though he does raise this possibility in both the *Treatise* and the *Enquiry*. The next part of our programme, then, will be to trace out and examine Hume's claim that we are not, after all, simply talking nonsense when we employ the idea of necessary connection. Since we have already come some distance and covered much detail in depicting the negative side of Hume's account of causality, it will now be in the interests of clarity to resume the discussion in a new chapter.

Notes

1. See the symposium, 'Can an effect precede its cause?', *Proceedings of the Aristotelian Society*, supplementary volume, 1954. See also J. L. Mackie, *The Cement of the Universe*, (Oxford, Clarendon Press, 1974), ch. 7.
2. For a discussion of Hume's treatment of the causal principle in relation to his commitment to the methodology of natural science, see James Noxon, *Hume's Philosophical Development* (Oxford, Clarendon Press, 1973), part 3.
3. For a consideration of the relationship between imagining and conceiving see Peter Carruthers, *Introducing Persons*, (London, Routledge, 1986), especially pp. 95–6. See also J. Bennett, *Locke, Berkeley, Hume*, section 58.
4. For a detailed analysis of various strands in Hume's analysis of causality see J. L. Mackie, *The Cement of the Universe*, ch. 1; also the essays by J. A. Robinson and Thomas Richards in V. C. Chappell (ed.), *Hume*, and Galen Strawson, *The Secret Connexion* (Oxford, Clarendon Press. 1989).

5. *What do we mean by cause?*
The source of our idea of necessary connection

───

(*Treatise*, Bk I, Part III, Section XIV; *Enquiry*, Section 7)

By the end of the last chapter it had become evident that the idea of necessity was the single most important aspect of Hume's enquiry into the nature of causality. In following Hume's thoughts on the matter, however, it also became apparent that this important ingredient could not be derived from sense experience of the world. Nor could it be derived from the workings of our minds. To use his own language, we do not have an *impression* of power, efficacy or necessary connection from these two sources. Nevertheless, such an idea does come about, and Hume looks more closely at the conditions under which it does so. What he notices is that the relevant idea comes into being after we have had repeated experience of A's and B's going together. To talk of A's and B's going together in this context is to refer to the fact that they fulfil the other two conditions of causal sequences laid down by Hume: they must be successive and contiguous. One might say, therefore, that Hume had now discovered a further feature of causality, namely, constant conjunction.

But it is a further feature in a very peculiar sense, of course, and that is what we must now try to analyse. Hume asserts, again and again, that there is no impression of necessity in any one instance of A being followed by B. They are conjoined but not connected (*E.*, p. 74). And that must remain true no matter how many times they are seen together. If there is no connection between A and B in themselves, then no amount of repetition will change the situation. The scene that I see through my office window will be the same, no matter how many times I change the glass in my window, and provided it is always the same kind of glass. Mere repetition, then, will not in itself create something that was not already there in the first instance. Yet it remains the case that, somewhere along the line of observed repetitions, an idea of A and B being necessarily connected is generated. How is the trick done?

Hume's answer is that the relevant idea is really the result of a purely psychological phenomenon. What happens is that, as a result of repeated exposure to the same kind of conjunction, the mind is conditioned to expect B upon the occurrence of A. Hume most often puts it by saying that there is a 'determination' of the mind to expect one upon the occurrence of the other (*T.*, p. 165). In practice, this takes the form of our seeing A as being necessarily connected to B. The conditioning is such that, whenever we see an A, we feel it *must* be followed by a B, and that whenever we see a B, we feel that it *must* have been preceded by an A. Here, at last, is the source of that necessity for which Hume has for so long been hunting. It is a 'psychological' necessity that we somehow transfer to things beyond the mind in such a way that events themselves seem to 'have' it or possess it. As Hume rather quaintly puts it, '... the mind has a great propensity to spread itself upon external objects, and to conjoin with them any internal impressions which they occasion ... ' (*T.*, p. 167).

However, the story is not yet complete. We have already made it clear that the source of the idea of necessity has to be in the form of an impression. The original impressions/ideas doctrine had stipulated that every idea has to be preceded by an impression, and Hume happily concedes this in the present context. Where is the impression, then, from which the idea of necessity in particular derives? There is only one answer open to Hume. He has to say, and does say, that it is the determination of the mind that constitutes the required impression. One's immediate thought, when confronted by this claim, is that an impression, as originally defined, is simply not that kind of thing. There is a quite popular tendency to think of Humean impressions as being solely related to the sense experience of supposedly external objects. In fairness to him, however, it must be emphasised that he had also talked of a second class of impressions which were labelled impressions of reflection (*T.*, pp. 7–8 and p. 165). The impression of necessity that we have now tracked down falls into that second class. In that respect, it is in the same class as the 'passions' or emotions to which Hume turns his attention in Book II of the *Treatise*. The search for necessity is now at an end.

Hume offers two definitions of the notion of cause in one and the same paragraph of the *Treatise*. According to the first definition, a cause is 'An object precedent and contiguous to another, and where all the objects resembling the former are plac'd in like relations of precedency and contiguity to those objects, that resemble the latter'. It is probably because Hume saw that this definition says nothing about the crucial notion of necessary connection that he immediately added the following amended definition:

> A CAUSE is an object precedent and contiguous to another, and so united with it, that the idea of the one determines the mind to form the idea of the other, and the impression of the one to form a more lively idea of the other. (*T.*, p. 170)

Taking stock

The search may have ended as far as Hume was concerned, but there is more to be said. Some of the following comments are internally related to Hume's psychology, but there are other, more general features of his account to which we shall later proceed.

There is one initial remark that must be made in order to put Hume's overall account into perspective. It has to be stressed that Hume's way of handling the topic of causality was not the only way in which it could be done. His was very much an empiricist approach and, moreover, it was an empiricism that was wedded to a particular psychology. That psychology was, as we saw, very much centred upon the doctrine of impressions and ideas. It was a doctrine according to which there could be no ideas without impressions and in which impressions figured as mental contents that were complete and intelligible within themselves. It is therefore important to contrast this empiricist approach with that of Hume's famous successor, Kant.[1] The latter saw the situation quite differently. He held that Hume's account of empirical experience was over-simplified. There could be no such thing as 'experience' except in so far as the mind brought certain in-built concepts to bear on it, which Kant entitled 'categories'. Without such activity on the part of the mind, there would be, not 'experience', but only bare sensation. And among those concepts, with which the mind must be equipped independently of experience, was that of causality. On the Kantian view, Humean psychology had the cart before the horse in some important respects. In the case of causality in particular, Hume went off on a wild-goose chase, searching for the impression from which the idea of cause could be derived. What he should have realised was that the very search itself already presupposed the a priori existence of the idea. The concept of cause was one of a small number of basic concepts that must be regarded as part of the structure of the mind itself if 'experience' was to be possible. You cannot derive the concept of cause from experience because it was already presupposed by experience. The whole enterprise of searching for an impression of causality or necessary connection that would come ready-made, requiring no synthesising on the part of the mind, was misconceived. Indeed, the account of psychological necessity that Hume finally comes up with might be seen as offering some support for Kant's view, if only because it is very difficult to identify just what it is that Hume's search has isolated.

Let us see if we can pin-point what is suspicious about the 'impression' of necessary connection with which Hume finally presents us. We can concede to him, as mentioned above, that the impression with which we are dealing is one of reflection and not of sensation. That is to say, it is a second-level impression: it is not directly derived from sensory experience but is generated in the mind as a reaction to sense experience. In this respect, it is rather like emotions such as anger, grief or joy. Anger is not something that is directly given in sensory experience, but is the mind's reaction to something, or a series of things, that is so reflected. To that extent, then, the analogy between emotions, considered as impressions of reflection, and the impression of necessary connection is nicely sustained. They are both second-level reactions. But the difficulty for Humean psychology is that, once one begins to analyse precisely what the impression of necessity amounts to, it seems to dissolve into nothing. To see the force of this comment, we have to remind ourselves that when Hume talks of impressions he means events or episodes in consciousness. They are to be seen as experiences or non-physical happenings. They constitute a 'something' to which one can introspectively point. This view of impressions is clearly reinforced when Hume begins to discuss the nature of human passions and emotions in Book II of the *Treatise*. Anger, grief, sadness, joy, pride, shame and any other we care to mention are 'happenings' in the mind. They are events in consciousness which are *experienced*, or *felt*. The question we must put to Hume is: can we regard the putative impression of necessary connection as at all comparable, something which is experienced as an event in consciousness? We may initially suppose that Hume's 'determination of the mind' is precisely that, but further reflection ought at least to weaken this assumption. In fact, it should be clear that when Hume talks of the determination of the mind to pass from the impression of the cause to the idea of its attendant effect he is merely describing the succession of perceptions in the mind. The events in consciousness are, first, the impression of the cause and, second, the idea of its effect, and this succession is a regular feature of our experience. But, whatever Hume may suppose, there is no *further* event in consciousness, called the 'determination' to pass from the first to the second. All we experience are the two 'perceptions', regularly occurring in that order. There is no *additional* 'impression' or experience at all, and therefore nothing answering to the term 'impression of necessity'.

Hume's failure to locate the impression of necessity means that he has no way of avoiding his own interim suggestion that we may have to conclude that terms such as 'necessary connection', 'power', 'efficacy' and 'production' are *meaningless*, since they pick out nothing in our experience – there is no impression that answers to these terms (*T.*, p. 162, and *E.*, p. 74). The story about the 'determination of the mind' is put forward as an answer to this challenge, but it is an answer that fails. Hume's quandary can be put in the following way. The upshot of his analysis of causality is that necessity is not an objective feature of either mental or physical sequences that we experience.[2] All we witness is constant conjunction. But he does want to hold that an impression of necessity is nevertheless generated in the mind and is projected on to things external to it. This is intended to be both an account of the origin of the idea of necessity as well as an explanation of why we regard causally related events as being necessarily connected. How-ever, if, as we have argued above, the impression of necessity that he claims to locate simply disappears as a Humean impression, then he has no more than constant conjunction at this level either. The idea that A is necessarily connected with B is explained by reference to the fact that whenever we *think* of A we automatically *think* of B, and that is just another conjunction. As a mere constant conjunction, it cannot possibly ground or in any way explain our belief that there is something more to causality than constant conjunction, viz., necessary connection.

Having shown that there are difficulties for Hume even within the context of his own psychology, we must now look at some of the more general problems that are suggested by his account. We can begin with the 'constant conjunction' requirement. This is a particularly promin-ent feature of Hume's treatment of the topic, and he repeats it many times. The requirement has been criticised from two angles. First, it is quite usual to find commentators arguing that we can often designate something as a cause without having had experience of its constant conjunction with some other object or event.[3] It is tempting to suppose, for example, that on the first occasion on which a person breaks a sheet of glass by throwing a stone he will immediately realise that the throwing of the stone constitutes the cause. No experience of its regularly occurring would seem to be required.

Now there may be an important point to be made against Hume on this score, but, in fairness to him, it must be recorded that he does have an answer to at least some cases of this kind. He certainly concedes that '... not only in philosophy, but even in common life, we may attain the knowledge of a particular cause merely by one experiment ...' (*T*., p. 104). However, he does not regard this as an exception to the claim that experience of constant conjunction is required. Essentially, he wishes to hold that the 'one experiment' only has the appearance of being singular. In reality, what is happening is that we implicitly recognise it as a particular instance of a regularity with which we *are* already acquainted. Thus, for example, the person who strikes a match for the first time may immediately identify the act of scraping the match on the box as being the cause of the ensuing flame. Hume's point is that he is enabled to do this by virtue of his more general experience of friction – that, in its turn, being reducible to his experience of particular conjunctions. The principle that governs our behaviour in such cases, whether we explicitly acknowledge it or not, is 'that like objects, placed in like circumstances, will always produce like effects' (*T*., p. 105).

Hume's response is not entirely acceptable. We have only his word for it that all cases of 'first-time recognition' of a cause conform to the match-striking example considered above. What, for example, is the more general principle that governs the child's reaction on first putting his finger in the fire? It certainly seems proper to say that he identifies the fire as the cause of his pain, but it is difficult in this case to locate the more general regularity of conjunction that lies behind it, and upon which the 'like objects, like effects' principle can operate.[4]

There is, too, another slightly worrying element in Hume's response to the 'single experiment' kind of case. He allows the designation of something as a cause, in these cases, 'provided it be made with judgement, and after a careful removal of all foreign and superfluous circumstances' (*T*., p. 104). What is worrying about these words is that they suggest a much more reflective, and therefore rational, approach to the identification of causes than his general account allows. It is a feature of that account – something that Hume himself is, at other times, at pains to emphasise – that the business of picking out causes or effects is very much a matter of conditioning. It is the effect, upon our minds, of the observation of repeated conjunctions, in such a way that the mind is channelled in a certain direction. In essence, it is the view that the identification of causes is a non-rational affair. Yet here we are being told that it is possible to identify a cause after only one experience of conjunction, provided we use our judgement and eliminate irrelevant details. This is not to make a point directly against Hume's constant conjunction requirement; it is simply to record what looks like an inconsistency in his analysis of causation.

We must now discuss the other angle from which the constant conjunction requirement has been attacked. What we have just considered is the criticism that this requirement is not fulfilled in all cases of coming to identify causes. But it has further been claimed that, even in the case of established causes, we often allow that it is not fulfilled. Throwing a stone at the sheet of glass will usually cause it to shatter, but it does not always do so; strong coffee is usually a stimulant, but it is not always so; vigorous exercise will usually cause fatigue, but not on every occasion. There are many such examples, and, therefore, as one writer puts it, 'there seem to be many cases of causality that are not cases of constant conjunction'.[5] Yet, if constant conjunction is a necessary condition of something's being a cause, according to the Humean analysis, how can such examples be explained?

Hume's answer is to be found, not immediately within the sections on causality but, rather, within the context of his treatment of liberty and necessity, both in the *Treatise* and the *Enquiry*. His thoughts in that area are very much a product of his analysis of causality, and we shall be dealing with them below, in Chapter 8. What is important in the present context is the reference he makes there to the concept of 'contrary causes'. This is just another way of describing intervening causes, and refers simply to the interruption of an established regularity by factors of which we may not be aware. One of his own examples well illustrates what he means (*Enquiry*, Section VIII, p. 87). A 'peasant', confronted by the sudden stopping of his clock, will be happy to suggest that the mechanism has simply failed to operate. An experienced clockmaker, on the other hand, will be able to explain that it was the presence of a piece of grit in the mechanism that had caused the breakdown. The point that is effectively made by means of this illustration is that the constant conjunction requirement has not been infringed: it simply appears that way, granted ignorance of certain crucial facts about the situation. Another way of putting the point in relation to this example is to say that, *all other conditions being equal*, there is a constant conjunction between the mechanism and the displaying of the time. When other conditions are not equal, this is tantamount to saying that the conjunction has not been adequately specified. The mechanism, minus the piece of grit, *is* constantly conjoined with the displaying of the time: with the piece of grit, it is not. In the same way, if we carefully specify the conjunction between vigorous exercise and the ensuing fatigue, it will emerge as a conjunction that is constant. In this case, we would have to say that, for example, granted vigorous exercise and provided the person concerned has not been given artificial stimulants, etc., then fatigue will invariably follow. To put the position in brief, Hume's point is that the kind of cases we have considered only appear to be infringements of the constant conjunction requirement because we have not fully spelt out the conjunction concerned.

If we are to be charitable to Hume, then, these thoughts, drawn from his section 'Of liberty and necessity', may be construed as an answer to the objection we considered. That objection was, basically, that it did not seem to be the case that constant conjunction was a necessary condition of causal sequences. In addition to construing it as an answer to this objection, one may also see it as an attempt tidy up this particular feature of his account of causality. Hume has often been criticised for talking as if constant conjunction always occurred between one event and another, or one object and another, as though the conjunctions occurred independently of surrounding circumstances. In other words, he has been criticised for over-simplifying the conditions under which one thing can be said to be the cause of another. More positively, it is false to suppose that A can be seen as the cause of B in total abstraction from the context in which the sequence of A followed by B occurs. And it is precisely this that his talk of 'contrary causes' in essence acknowledges.

Let us try to spell this out more clearly. If we consider again our example of the sheet of glass that is shattered by the throwing of the stone, it will become obvious that the breaking of the glass is dependent not simply on the throwing of the stone but on other factors as well. For example, the glass will have to be of a breakable kind and not too thick; the stone must be over a certain minimum weight, must be thrown in a particular direction, and with a certain minimum force; strong wind and other possible impediments must be absent; and the glass must be sufficiently supported to allow the stone to exert the pressure required to break it. The absence of one or more of these factors will prevent the usual result. It was precisely this consideration that led John Stuart Mill to argue that Hume's account was far too simple. A truly scientific account of cause would require us to mention all such factors on all occasions. The sum-total of these individually necessary conditions is sufficient to produce the result, in this case, the breaking of the glass. Therefore, strictly speaking, it is the sum-total that constitutes the cause. The implication is that to single out the mere throwing of the stone in this context can only be arbitrary.

It has been said above that Hume's talk of 'contrary causes' can be seen as an attempt to accommodate just this thought. But, in a way, this is to be over-charitable to him. He was apt to conceive of such causes as being occasional and active interference in an established pattern of things. Perhaps what he had not fully grasped is the way in which causal sequences are dependent upon a set of static conditions. Physical objects, chemical substances, air, gases, and the various relations that hold between these things, all have or exhibit enduring qualities. Fire will not burn without the presence of oxygen, for example. These enduring qualities of things provide the framework within which causal sequences take place, and they are as essential as any other factor we care to mention. These, then, are the conditions that the concept of 'contrary causes' fails to capture. We are talking here about the difference between the piece of grit that stops the mechanism and, on the other hand, the enduring properties of the metals that compose its parts. What must be said at this point, then, is that Hume's talk about 'contrary causes' is perhaps a tacit acknowledgement, on his part, that the act of spelling out the cause of something is a little more complex than his account had originally suggested. But his failure to take into account what we have called the enduring qualities of objects suggests that he did not fully comprehend that complexity.[6]

We must now look at the other side of the coin. We have just been considering the constant conjunction requirement in the light of the popular criticism that it is not a necessary condition of causal relations. Our next move must be to examine the equally popular complaint against Hume that, even where there exists a universal conjunction between A and B, we do not always pronounce the one to be the cause of the other. The point can be illustrated by means of hypothetical examples. Country people are apt to say that the closing-up of a fir-cone is a sign of rain. Even if there really exists a universal conjunction between these two events, it is obvious that no one would suppose that the former is the cause of the latter. Again, to borrow an example that has been prominent in this area, it may be the case, regularly and without exception, that the sounding of a certain siren at five o'clock in Glasgow is followed by a general exodus of workers from a factory in Liverpool. Would anyone suppose that there was a causal relation between the two events? Perhaps even more relevant, because it clearly also satisfies the contiguity requirement, is the case of the traffic lights that turn from green to amber and then to red. Here we have constant conjunction, together with succession and contiguity; but we see no causal relation between these events – we do not think the flashing of the amber light causes the red light to come on.

However, despite the quite striking character of these examples, it is far from clear that they constitute a justified criticism, at least of the spirit of Hume's position. In order to do justice to the spirit of Hume's position one needs to bear in mind some significant words from the *Enquiry* version of the notion of causality. There, in Section VII (p. 76), after reiterating the first of the *Treatise* definitions, Hume produces what he obviously thinks is a piece of alternative wording for it. His words are 'Or in other words where, if the first object had not been, the second had never existed'. In fact, the two forms of wording are not synonymous: 'All A's are followed by B's' makes a different claim from 'If not-A, then not-B'. But what it concerns us to note here is that the alternative form implicitly suggests an empirical testing procedure for genuine causality. What it implicitly tells is is that, if we find ourselves in doubt as to whether A really is the cause of B, we should try removing or preventing A in order to see whether B still occurs. If B continues to occur, then this means that A was not the cause; and we know that A *is* the cause of B if B now fails to appear. Effectively, this is the test we apply, hypothetically or otherwise, in the case of the fir-cone, the factory workers and the traffic lights. It is precisely because we know that the second event in each of these pairs would have occurred in the absence of the first that we do not regard the one as the cause of the other.[7] It is because we have a pretty fair idea, without actually going to investigate, that the workers will issue from the factory in Liverpool whether or not the siren sounds in Glasgow that we never entertain the idea that the former might be the cause of the latter. (That the two events are not spatially contiguous is also, presumably, a contributory factor.)

Taking this significant bit of wording from the *Enquiry* into account, then, seems to do more justice to the Humean position. It is, in any case, in keeping with the empiricist emphasis of that position. It is also worth mentioning that, at least from one angle, the wording we have singled out is not really an additional feature, suddenly tacked on in the later work. One might well construe it as stating a test of whether two events are indeed constantly conjoined. To discover, by artificial means or otherwise, that B will occur without A is, technically speaking, to show that A and B are not constantly conjoined: they may have gone together up until this point, but the sequence has now been broken. In so far as the wording is construed in this way, it can be seen simply as a more thorough way of stating the conditions for testing whether the constant conjunction requirement has been satisfied.

Notes

1. Immanuel Kant (1724–1804), *Critique of Pure Reason* (1781). For an introduction to Kant's philosophy, see S. Körner, *Kant* (Harmondsworth, Penguin Books, 1967); R. Walker, *Kant* (London, Routledge and Kegan Paul, 1978).

2 Hume does not deny that there may be objective properties of objects and connections between events which we do not experience (see *T.*, p. 168), but he maintains, consistently with his empiricist stance, that we have no clear idea of such features of things. For an interpretation of Hume which emphasises this aspect of his thought about causality, see Strawson, *The Secret Connexion*.

3. See J. Hospers, *Introduction to Philosophical Analysis* (London, Routledge and Kegan Paul, 1967), p. 290.

4. Hume himself clearly recognises that a child needs only one experience of being burnt by the flame of a candle to ensure that he will be careful in future not to put his hand near any candle (*Enquiry*, p. 39).

5. Hospers, p. 290.

6. See J. L. Mackie, *The Cement of the Universe* pp. 34–6 for a discussion of the distinction between conditions and causes.

7. For a discussion of the role of counterfactual conditionals in the analysis of causality, see *The Cement of the Universe*, chs. 2 and 8. See also E. Sosa (ed.), *Causation and Conditionals* (London, Oxford University Press, 1975).

6. *Is it rational to be guided by experience?*

(*Treatise*, Book I, Part III, Sections II-VI; *Enquiry*, Sections, V and IX)

Hume did not use the term 'induction' in his discussion of arguments based upon experience. But he did very effectively formulate a view about such arguments which generated the problem of induction as we know it. The view arose quite naturally out of his analysis of causality which we have considered in the two previous chapters, and indeed is implicitly a part of that analysis. To put Hume's view in a nutshell, and therefore at its most provocative, he held that no argument that is based on experience can ever be rational. Granted this view, and granted also that Hume put the point very persuasively, the problem of induction has been essentially that of exploring whether or not Hume's claim is well-founded.

The way in which the problem of induction arises out of Hume's analysis of causality can be briefly stated. Hume holds, as we have already seen, that, once we move beyond the realm of immediate sensory experience, a high proportion of our judgements employ causal reasoning. We proceed by way of saying that because X was the cause of Y in the past, then it will be on this occasion too. But Hume shows that, though this appears to be a rationally based inference on our part, it is not really a case of inference at all. There is no objective necessity in events such that we can read off an effect from its cause, or vice versa. What binds events and objects together is to be found in the realm of psychology. It is a habit of the mind that develops as a result of constant exposure to the conjunctions we see around us. To say that there is no objective necessity to be found in objects and events in themselves is just another way of saying that things could always be other than they are. The conjunctions that have held in the past may not hold in the future. No matter how regular our experience of such conjunctions may be, they do not in themselves yield a reason for believing that things will continue in the same way. X has caused Y on every occasion until now, but it may not do so tomorrow.

Granted, then, that most of our everyday judgements based upon past experience make reference to causal sequences, and granted that our judgements about causes are not rationally based, it follows that these judgements from experience are not properly described as rational. In other words, Hume is claiming that, in a strict sense of 'evidence', we have no evidence for saying that X will cause Y in the future. Hume's conclusion is put very forcefully in the *Enquiry*, Section IV: 'I say, then, that, even after every experience of the operations of cause and effect, our conclusions from that experience are *not* founded on reasoning, or any process of understanding' (*E.*, p. 32).

One minor point should be clarified at this stage. Hume speaks as though *all* experiential judgements that go beyond immediate sensory experience make an appeal to causal sequences. Strictly speaking, this is to overstate his case. In at least some cases, the kind of conjunction upon which we base our judgement is not an example of causality but, rather, an example of a thing and its properties. For example, a stone has the property of sinking in water, though this property is not, in any strict sense, causally related to the stone. Similarly, wax has the property of melting in the presence of heat; and swans are, by and large, white in colour. However, what is important to note is that, though these are not, strictly, cases of causality, they remain cases to which Hume's general claim is applicable. Causal or not, they are cases of conjunction to which no objective necessity attaches. They could always be other than they are. We simply cannot *infer* from the fact that stones have always sunk in water in the past that they will continue to do so. Our conviction that they will do so reflects the way in which our minds have been conditioned: it does not reflect the possession of 'evidence' for the claim.

So it turns out that Hume's general point applies not only to causal conjunctions but also to conjunctions which we would not regard as causal. In short, his claim is that we can never be in possession of evidence for the view that nature is uniform in its operation, whether we are thinking of future events or simply those events that are in the present but beyond the reach of our senses.

We have from Hume, then, a very bold and far-reaching claim that seems to undermine the confidence we normally place in our ability to 'reason' from experience. It is therefore little wonder that philosophers have been so preoccupied with the issue since Hume's time. We shall now take a closer look at what Hume tells us.

In the first place, in the face of such a challenge, one is tempted to ask how exactly Hume supports his claim. The immediate answer to that is that, in one sense, he does not see it as needing support. He sees the situation as one in which he is simply exposing or making explicit the way in which the mind works in relation to judgements from experience. Once that has been done, he thinks that it will be immediately clear to any thinking person that such judgements are not based upon reason or evidence. What will be revealed, if we scrutinise our psychology closely enough, is that there is a mechanism which allows the mind to make a jump from past experience to future experience without the intervention of reason. This policy of exposure, as one might call it, is reinforced by a further move on Hume's part. He invites us to consider what would have to be the case if the jump that the mind makes were genuinely a rational inference, and then tries to show that this could not possibly be the case. Briefly, his position is as follows. If the jump from observed to unobserved were dictated by reason, then we should have to proceed upon the principle that 'instances of which we have had no experience, must resemble those, of which we have had experience, and that the course of nature continues always the same'(*T.*, p. 89). But how could such a principle ever be established? In order to be an item of knowledge, in any strict sense, that is, an analytic truth, it would have to be deducible from some further idea. For example, it is deducible from the idea of a square that it has four sides: the idea of a square *compels* us to say that it has four sides. But the idea of regular sequences from the past does not compel us to say that the future or the unobserved will be the same. Of any regular conjunction that has held until now, it is always possible for us to conceive of its not holding on some further occasion, and indeed many of the conjunctions we have been acquainted with *have* ceased to hold in just this way. Therefore, using Hume's 'conceivability' criterion, the principle that the future must resemble the past cannot be analytically derived.

Nor, Hume maintains, can it be empirically derived. The supposition would be that we can use the fact that A has always been succeeded by B in the past to support the conclusion that it must continue to do so in the future. But Hume's general response to this, expressed more clearly in the *Enquiry* (p. 36), is that this would be reasoning in a circle. In order to allow past conjunctions to count as evidence for the proposition that the future will resemble the past, we would have to presuppose the truth of that very proposition. An analogy helps us to make Hume's point clearer. In order for the bearing of acorns to count as evidence for a tree's being an oak tree, one must first *know* that the bearing of acorns truly characterises an oak tree. It is in the nature of what we call 'evidence' that it can only be such in the light of a more basic piece of knowledge already possessed. To use another analogy, if the doctor did not already know that the presence of spots of a certain kind and distributed in a certain way were symptoms of the disease we know as 'measles', it would not be possible for him to use their presence as evidence of the disease. In the same way, then, Hume argues that unless we already *know* that the future will conform to the past, we cannot use the past as evidence for any claim about the nature of the future. We do not in fact know the proposition that the future will conform to the past to be true: therefore the past does not constitute evidence for our beliefs about the future.

As we have seen, then, Hume's immediate answer to the question of how we can support his general position on inductive reasoning is that it does not require independent support. All that is required is to expose the way in which we proceed, psychologically, when we 'reason' from experience. We shall then see that it is not really a case of reasoning at all. That would be his immediate answer. But one other strand needs to be considered. Both in the *Treatise* (p. 176) and in the *Enquiry* (p. 104), Hume includes a section entitled 'Of the reason of animals', the basic message of which is intended to support his claim about induction. One might therefore see this as constituting further support for his general position. His argument, in both of these sections, is quite simple. It is a matter of common consent, he argues, that animals learn from experience and that, in many ways, they are as efficient in reacting to their environment as we are. Indeed, Hume might have argued, there are many contexts in which there would be no discernible difference between animal behaviour, based on experience, and human behaviour similarly based on experience. But we certainly would not wish to describe animal behaviour as a case of 'reasoning' or 'inferring' or 'deducing' that the future will be like the past. There is no acknowledged 'premise' upon which the animal proceeds, either explicitly or implicitly. In that sense, Hume argues, the behaviour of animals is not properly a matter of reason or the understanding. They evidently manage on the basis of a spontaneous habit of the mind that is set up by conditioning, by exposure to regular conjunctions in their experience. By implication, then, Hume's rhetorical question to us is this: why should we suppose that anything more is required to explain comparable human behaviour? As Hume says in the *Treatise* version of the argument – though perhaps overstating his case – 'To consider the matter aright, reason is nothing but a wonderful but unintelligible instinct in our souls ...' (p. 179).

We have now outlined Hume's position on induction. To reiterate the thrust of that position, emphasising its two main aspects, one can put it in this way: not only can we never *know* that the future will resemble the past, but it can never be 'reasonable', in a strict sense, to *believe* that the future will resemble that past. As we have already made clear, this has been a main area of philosophical discussion ever since Hume's time and the topic has attracted volumes of literature.[1] Our present task must be simply to hint at some of the main avenues of attack upon Hume.

One popular criticism of Hume is that he operates with a somewhat restricted account of 'reason' or 'understanding'. It is only on the basis of such a restricted account that he can possibly argue that judgements from experience are not a matter of reason. The point is often made by means of a contrast. Thus, it might be quite plausible to hold that when I jump out of the path of an oncoming vehicle, what I do is certainly based upon experience and it would be implausible to suppose that my action was a matter of reason. This is the kind of action which we are happy to call instinctive and unthinking. Animals are capable of this kind of response, as Hume himself saw, and so are very young children when they learn by bitter experience not to put their fingers near the fire. But to be contrasted with this is the kind of action that essentially depends upon reflection on our part. The boy who 'calculates' that his girl-friend is not going to turn up at the cinema where he has arranged to meet her is a case in point. He may *reason* that, being the kind of person she is, having the kind of characteristics she does have, it is highly unlikely that she will keep the appointment. Surely, it is argued, this is a case of reasoning from experience and, in the light of it, Hume's position is bound to be counter-intuitive.

The point is sometimes reinforced from a negative point of view. Suppose, for example, that a person tells us that he is going to ignore the way in which some particular thing or person has behaved in the past in relation to some present decision he is about to make. He decides, perhaps, that he wants to build a boat out of lead. Confronted by such a decision, do we not want to say that here is the epitome of irrational behaviour? If we were teaching a child what it is to be irrational, that would be just the kind of decision to which we would draw his attention. Yet Hume's philosophy seems to tell us that we cannot legitimately describe such behaviour as irrational. Again, this renders his position counter-intuitive.

This criticism in a certain sense misses its target, but it is important because it serves to make clearer the kind of position Hume is presenting us with. Hume would not deny that when we actively reflect upon the characteristics of things and persons around us, we are using our reason and behaving as rational beings. He would probably also concede that, in that respect, we are to be distinguished from animals. His point would be that the judgement we make on the *basis* of such activity is not itself rational. The judgement which consists in our saying, in respect of some particular sequence, that the future will be like the past is more properly described as a function of how we *feel*: it is not something that we can rationally infer. A similar position emerges from Hume's treatment of moral judgements which we shall be discussing in Chapter 12, and it is instructive to compare the two contexts. Hume argues that, in the case of moral judgements, although reason functions as the agent that discovers facts for us – that is, purely empirical facts about people and the world – it does not tell us what we ought to do. He holds that there is no jump that *reason* can make from what *is* the case to what *ought* to be the case. When we arrive at a decision about what ought to be the case, we are, essentially, expressing how we *feel* about the situation. That, then, is precisely Hume's point about induction. Nothing about the facts we discern concerning past uniformities will tell us, or indicate to us, that things will continue in the same way. The belief that things will so continue is a conviction that has been established in us as a result of exposure to such uniformities. In short, then, Hume's response to the criticism we have considered is to concede that reason is certainly involved in the collection of, and reflection upon, facts concerning regular conjunctions. What he wishes to deny is that the crucial step which the mind makes from those facts to a judgement concerning the future or the unperceived is a matter of reason. The criticism may therefore indicate that Hume has not properly isolated which putative function of reason he is referring to, but it does not show him to be wrong.

Essentially the same criticism as the one we have just considered is sometimes to be found in another form, but it is worth mentioning since it reveals a distinctive angle on the problem. It is often put in the form of an attempted trivialisation of Hume's position. All Hume is really telling us, it is argued, is that inductive reasoning is not deductive reasoning. It does not follow from this that the former is an inferior kind of reasoning. We must not suppose that inductive reasoning is a pale copy of deductive reasoning, such that the former is constantly striving to be the latter and always failing. As John Hospers says, that would be like blaming a dog for not being a cat.[2] Just as cats and dogs are not on the same scale of comparison, so deductive and inductive reasoning are not on the same scale. Therefore it cannot be acceptable to condemn the one for not matching up to the other.

Again it is instructive to see how Hume can intelligibly respond to this second version of the criticism. His response would be that it is not as though there is something called inductive reasoning that can be seen as failing to measure up to something else called deductive reasoning. Rather – and to put it bluntly – there simply is no such thing as inductive reasoning, except loosely so-called. More precisely, the jump from past experience to future experience is not a product of the reasoning part of the mind. Just as morality, according to Hume's picture of things, is something that is more properly felt than judged, so our expectations with regard to the future are felt rather than judged. As Hume himself says (*T.*, p. 103), 'Thus all probable reasoning is nothing but a species of sensation'. In short, Hume's stance would be that he makes no attempt to draw a comparison between two things aspiring to the same label, such that the one comes out as inferior to the other. Rather, he is asserting that, in the one case, what we usually take to be a case of reasoning is really something quite different, and that we shall see that this is true if we look at the matter closely.

Had Hume been pressed harder upon this issue, he might have continued in the following way. The temptation to suppose that there really is something called inductive reasoning stems from our conflating two distinct things. We have already had cause to comment upon them separately. Because we evidently use our reasoning capacity to reflect upon our experience, comparing this event with that, judging them to be similar or dissimilar, etc., we very naturally suppose that the jump from these events to as yet unwitnessed events is all part and parcel of the same process. We fail to see that when we make that jump we are in fact doing something that is quite different in character. Hume's views about our moral judgements once again illustrate his point more clearly. When we witness one person robbing another, it is certainly true that our reasoning faculty is at work. It is this faculty which collects the facts together for us and informs us that what we are observing constitutes what we know as robbery. Now it is very natural for us to suppose that the judgement that what we are witnessing is morally wrong is also involved in this reasoning process.

Most of us do indeed suppose this. Hume, however, maintains that the judgement that the action is wrong cannot be established by a process of reasoning. There is nothing about the situation we know as robbery, provided we describe it in neutral terms, that compels us to say that it is wrong. The judgement that it is morally wrong is an expression of how we feel about it. Nevertheless, our feelings about it are so intimately connected with the information that reason puts at our disposal that we fail to distinguish the two things. The same, then, is true in the context of induction.

We must now turn to a criticism of Hume that is not guilty of conflating the two distinct activities we have outlined above. It is essentially an attempt to show, contrary to what Hume says, that the principle that the future will resemble the past can actually be established on an empirical basis. That being possible, it then argues that the fact that A has always been followed by B in the past does indeed justify the claim that A will be followed by B in the future.

We saw above that it is part of Hume's case that any attempt to establish the principle of induction on an empirical basis is bound to be circular. We cannot use the past as evidence for the character of the future unless we already know that it constitutes such evidence, and that is the very question at issue. But the present objection to Hume uses a slightly different line of argument. It says that we need not presuppose the truth of the principle of induction at the outset. We simply regard it as a hypothesis to be either confirmed or not. As things turn out, however, the principle gets confirmed in a large majority of cases. In other words, what had been futures in the past were revealed later on to be in conformity with the past, just as the hypothesis had said. The situation is, then, that we have ample evidence that the future resembles the past; our predictions have been regularly fulfilled in this respect. Moreover, the soundness of this argument is supported by the consideration that this is precisely the way in which science itself proceeds, namely, by positing a hypothesis and systematically seeking confirmation of it.

Unfortunately, plausible as this may sound, it will not do as an answer to the problem as Hume saw it. The problem simply breaks out again at a slightly higher level.[3] Although the suggested solution to the problem talks of 'pasts' and 'futures' and the way in which the latter resembles the former, what one has to stress is that these 'pasts' and 'futures' are themselves in the past. The jump from what has thus occurred in the past to what may occur in the future as it is viewed from now remains one for which we cannot have evidence. And the reason why it is something for which we cannot have evidence remains exactly the same. Nothing about the way in which past futures have conformed to past pasts compels us to say that things will go on in the same way.

We must now turn to a response to the problem of induction which really consists in saying that the whole issue was misconceived from the start. Such a response was canvassed, for example, by P.F. Strawson in his book *Introduction to Logical Theory*.[4] The line adopted by Strawson, and by others, is to attempt to demonstrate the inappropriateness of a request for the justification of inductive reasoning. Strawson proceeds by way of a useful analogy.[5] It is inappropriate to ask whether the law, or the legal system, is itself legal because no intelligible answer can be given to that question. Individual actions, decisions and judgements can be described as legal or illegal because there is a system or framework of law in terms of which such descriptions make sense. But, outside of that framework, there is nothing that would allow us to make judgements of legality on the system as a whole. Similarly, then, it might be said that there is a 'practice' of proceeding inductively in daily affairs and, within the confines of that practice, there are right and wrong ways of doing it. But just as it is idle to wonder whether the legal system itself is legal, so it is idle to ask whether our inductive practice is rational. Let us now try to assess the weight of this criticism.

In the first place, the analogy, though a challenging one, does not seem to be quite perfect. So long as one retains the term 'legal' then it certainly seems to be absurd to ask whether the law itself is legal. But, in a more general sense, it does make sense to ask whether such a system is justified. We might wonder, for example, whether the particular system we have should be radically altered and proceed on different general principles. We might even wonder whether we should have a legal system at all. At all times we shall presumably be governed by a higher order principle to the effect that any legal system is there to serve the interests of society. As we shall see in Chapter 12 below, Hume himself argued that the system of justice exists only because of its usefulness to society. So in that general sense it seems to be intelligible to ask whether the legal system is justified.

But, independently of the accuracy of the analogy itself, the point that is being made by means of it may well be applicable to the case of inductive reasoning. That is to say, we may wish to hold that it is pointless to ask whether inductive procedures can be justified since there exists nothing over and above such procedures by reference to which they can be judged correct or incorrect. And this position is made even more plausible if one accepts what was argued above, namely, that it is a mistake to suppose that induction should emulate deduction. Provided deductive reasoning is not used as the yardstick for inductive reasoning, then it does indeed seem fruitless to seek a criterion of correctness that lies beyond the latter.

Having said so much, however, at least one interpretation of Hume would indicate that the criticism does not apply to him, even though it may be of relevance to other treatments of the topic. If Hume is to be understood in the way in which we have interpreted him above, he might be construed as holding a position essentially similar to that of Strawson. Hume has shown us that the so-called principle of induction cannot be known a priori and he has also shown us that it cannot be empirically derived. That, surely, is a way of demonstrating that there is nothing beyond the practice of reasoning inductively that can guarantee the correctness of it. On this view, it is not as though Hume is saying, as some commentators assume, that here is a way of proceeding in human affairs that is very suspect, and that our practice stands in urgent need of justification. Rather, he is saying that no justification is possible; let us not embark on a wild-goose chase. More positively, let us accept it as a matter of psychological fact that we do proceed inductively in our encounters with people and the world and, indeed, that it could not be otherwise.

With these sketchy comments upon the problem of induction and the way in which it arises naturally out of Hume's treatment of causality, we must now begin to look at the way in which the major topic of cause and effect permeates other aspects of Hume's philosophy. The first of these aspect is Hume's treatment of the nature of belief.

Notes

1. For a collection of recent essays, together with a useful bibliography, see R. Swinburne (ed.), *The Justification of Induction* (Oxford, Oxford University Press, 1974). See also Karl Popper, 'Conjectural knowledge: my solution to the problem of induction', in K. Popper, *Objective Knowledge* (Oxford, Clarendon Press, 1971); D. C. Stove, *Probability and Hume's Inductive Scepticism* (London, Oxford University Press, 1973); Dancy, *Contemporary Epistemology*, ch. 13.
2. Hospers, *Introduction to Philosophical Analysis*, p. 257.

3. This point is made by B. Russell, *The Problems of Philosophy* (Oxford, Oxford University Press, 1967), ch. 6.
4. P. F. Strawson, *Introduction to Logical Theory* (London, Methuen, 1952), ch. 9, pt. 2.
5. Strawson, p. 257.

7. What is it to believe that something is the case?

(*Enquiry*, Section V, Part 2; *Treatise*, Book I, Part III, Sections VII, VIII)

The question posed by the title of this chapter is one that deserves a place in any book that seeks to consider some of the central questions of philosophy. There is some evidence that Hume himself eventually saw the topic in this way. In the Appendix to the *Treatise*, for example, he describes the nature of belief as being 'one of the greatest mysteries of philosophy'(*T.*, p. 628) and admits to 'considerable difficulty' in providing an analysis of it. However, so far as the order of events is concerned, in both the *Treatise* and the *Enquiry*, the topic is introduced not on its own merit but because it is a natural corollary of the thoughts that had preceded it. In the treatment of causality and induction, one of Hume's more prominent findings was that, as a result of regular exposure to the various conjunctions we encounter in experience, the mind comes to have certain expectations about future or unseen experience. It is to this that Hume refers when he talks about the habit of mind to pass from A to B, having seen A and B conjoined regularly in the past. But at this juncture the thought occurs to Hume that the state of mind that we describe as the expectation of B is what we standardly call 'believing'. In situations in which we expect, or 'infer', and predict in this way, we are actually believing that something will be the case. One might say, then, that the notion of belief has crept into Hume's analysis of causality and induction almost by the back door.

Having recognised that the state of mind involved is a case of belief, Hume was immediately faced with a problem. It is to his credit that he was able to delineate this problem for future philosophers. It is true that Hume's particular version of the problem is captured in the terms of his doctrine of impressions and ideas but, as we shall see subsequently, the problem exists even outside that context. We must now try to see the problem as Hume saw it.

We must start by emphasising that when one has an expectation of an event or state of affairs on the basis of past experience, this must involve having an idea of that event or state of affairs. We would perhaps put this by saying that there must be something that is envisaged. Since this is the believing state that Hume has located, then belief is, in some sense, the having of an idea. For Hume, this will normally mean having an image. The problem, as Hume saw it, is that we have ideas about all sorts of things that do not amount to beliefs. I can think of a Constable painting hanging on my study wall without believing that it actually hangs there. To use one of Hume's own examples, I can think of Caesar dying in his bed without actually believing that he died in his bed (*T.*, p. 95). It is the difference between believing that something is the case and, on the other hand, 'entertaining a thought about something'. Hume characterises it as the distinction between believing something and imagining something. Since in both cases it will be true to say that we have ideas before our minds, what is it that constitutes the difference? There was Hume's problem.

Having stated this problem, he was quick to point out that the difference between these two activities does not lie in what is believed in or thought about. Whether the Constable painting does actually hang upon my study wall or not, the content of my thought or belief about it will be precisely the same. To say of the object of some thought of mine that it does actually exist adds nothing to the nature of that thought. Hume therefore concludes that the difference must lie in the manner of thinking rather than in the object thought about. In particular, it must be the case that when one believes something, the internal state of envisaging a certain state of affairs is much more vivid than the activity of merely thinking about that state. The difference between believing and imagining, then, is located in the greater degree of vivacity and forcefulness of the former over the latter. As Hume puts it in the *Enquiry* version: 'I say, then, that belief is nothing but a more vivid, lively, forcible, firm, steady conception of an object, than what the imagination alone is ever able to attain' (*E.*, p. 49). The same thought is reiterated a little later in the same work, when Hume tells us 'It is evident that belief consists not in the peculiar nature or order of ideas, but in the *manner* of their conception, and in their *feeling* to the mind' (*E.*, p. 49).

That being Hume's analysis of belief, one question immediately presented itself: how does an idea acquire the extra vivacity and forcefulness required to convert it into a belief? Hume's answer was clear enough, and was set squarely within the confines of the impressions and ideas doctrine. The extra vivacity stemmed from a 'present impression'. Indeed, this reference to its origin forms a part of Hume's official definition of belief in the *Treatise* version. There, he tells us that an opinion or belief may be most accurately defined as 'a lively idea related to or associated with a present impression' (*T.*, p. 96). What Hume means by this may be illustrated in the following way. Suppose that my neighbour's car has a distinctive engine-note, and suppose that I have come to associate this with his arrival home. Now it is certainly possible for me to think about these two things, to reflect upon them, or to tell others about them, and so on. None of this amounts to my believing that he has arrived home. But if I happen to hear the characteristic engine sound on some particular occasion – that is to say, have an impression of it – this will give rise to my *believing* that my neighbour has actually arrived home. The current impression lends some of its vivacity to the associated idea. What was merely an idea has been converted into a belief without any change in content: it is simply the manner of conceiving that has changed; the idea *feels* different.

Can we believe it?

Having now seen what Hume's account of belief amounts to, we can perhaps begin to see why, in the Appendix, he expresses reservations about it. There are indeed a number of problems that remain unresolved. We must now try to formulate them. The first of them concerns the scope of his definition. One's initial reaction is that surely it is not the case that all beliefs are the result of a present impression in the way specified. For example, I now believe that three nines are twenty-seven and, if I work it out, that three twenty-sevens are eighty-one; but there seem to be no present impressions with which such beliefs are associated.

Now, in fairness to Hume, it should be said that, although his wording in both the *Treatise* and the *Enquiry* suggest that he is giving an account of belief per se, he is in fact doing something far more restricted. Specifically, he is providing us with an analysis of those beliefs that result from our experience of past conjunctions. In terms of the distinction between two different classes of propositions, outlined in Chapter 4 above, Hume is speaking about the beliefs that arise in the realm of 'matters of fact', as opposed to 'relations of ideas'. One of Hume's commentators makes it clear that he is referring to what should be called empirical beliefs.[1]

There are some who would argue that the restriction of Hume's account to empirical beliefs is not really a restriction at all. They might argue that, outside the realm of empirical propositions, there is simply no room for the concept of belief to operate. On Hume's view of the matter, if one is outside this realm, one is necessarily in the domain of 'relations of ideas'. It is a characteristic of beliefs formed by the activity of discerning relations between ideas that they are intuitively or demonstratively known. As Hume had originally conceived of them, the truths discerned by these means could not be otherwise. But, it is argued, what is believed could always be otherwise and, therefore, belief does not belong in this area. It is, essentially, a characteristic of matters of fact that they could always be other than they are, and this is the home of belief. According to D.G.C. MacNabb, this is the view that Hume is, rather badly, trying to formulate near the beginning of Section VII of the *Treatise* version.[2]

But, if this *is* Hume's view of the matter, it is not readily acceptable. Certainly it is true that, within the class of analytic or necessary truths, if I really know something to be the case, there is no room for doubt, and the truth concerned could not be other than it is. But this is something that must follow analytically from my *knowing* the proposition. It does not exclude the possibility that, working within the field of necessary truths, I can have doubts about the correctness of the entailments I have deduced and thus *only* believe that something is the case. Complex arithmetical calculations would presumably fit the bill – 'I *believe* I've got the sum correct: I'm not absolutely sure.' If all this is true, then we seem to have legitimate cases of belief that are not the result of a 'present impression'. This means that, if we are to accept Hume's analysis of belief at all, it can only be in relation to empirical beliefs. If it is agreed that the believing state of mind also occurs in relation to necessary truths, one must reiterate the initial reaction that Hume's account seems to be arbitrarily restricted.

In any case, and more importantly, even within the realm of purely empirical beliefs of the kind to which Hume has referred us, there seem to be beliefs that are not dependent upon the occurrence of a present impression. Internal reflection upon contingent matters of fact can often produce a belief without there being any impression to provoke it. Suppose I wish to borrow a certain book from my university library, but I reflect upon the fact that it is currently being recommended to a large class of students. I may then come to believe, quite firmly, that it is absent from the library shelves and that it will not be worth my while to pay a visit to the library. This would surely be a clear case of reasoning on the basis of my experience of past conjunctions. Just by virtue of being an example of 'armchair' reflection, there seems to be no evidence of a relevant 'present impression' that could impart its vivacity in the required sense.

The talk of vivacity must also lead us to wonder about the precise status of belief within the confines of Hume's impression/ideas doctrine. To see the kind of difficulty Hume is confronted with here one needs to emphasise that, for Hume, belief lies clearly in the field of ideas rather than impressions. It is precisely because belief consists in the having of ideas that the difficulty of distinguishing it from imagination had arisen. It is true that he sometimes refers to it as a 'sentiment' or 'feeling', thus suggesting that it is an impression, but, in general, he is very careful to describe it as a very vivid or forceful *idea* rather than an impression. This can only be because impressions are associated with *feeling* and ideas with *thought*; and opinions and beliefs belong firmly in the field of thought. This view is in fact expressed very clearly in the Appendix (*T*., pp. 625–6), where Hume explicitly rejects the possibility that belief might consist in an impression. As he says in that context, 'there is nothing ever enters into our conclusions but ideas, or our fainter conceptions'(*T*., p. 625).

Now if we emphasise this aspect of Hume's analysis of belief, what emerges is that belief is clearly an idea, but it is no ordinary idea because then it would not be possible to distinguish it from the ideas of imagination. It is therefore described as being an extra-vivid idea, more colourful, more forceful. At the same time, as we have just seen, its vivacity is not sufficient to make it an impression. It is thus evident that Hume has drawn a very fine line between ideas and impressions, and one wonders what criterion could prevent us from mistaking the one for the other, especially when one bears in mind that on the official doctrine the distinction between impressions and ideas is only one of degree. The difficulty will arise for all cases of belief on this theory, if only because, by definition, all beliefs are very vivid ideas. What prevents them from being impressions, that is, *feelings*?

What seems to be happening here is that Hume's psychology is preventing him from saying clearly what he has correctly perceived. His emphasis on the claim that belief is essentially an idea, not an impression, is surely Hume's way of recognising that it is a cognitive state. To believe something is to hold that it is the case, whether one has good grounds for doing so or not. Some would put this fact by saying that belief is essentially propositional in character. In this respect, then, it is intrinsically different from feelings or sensations which are neither cognitive nor propositional. Certainly it is true of many of our feelings or emotions that they are directed at some object, and, mostly, we know what that object is. But we do not wish to say that our feelings or emotions are capable of being true or false, if only because there is no proposition involved that could be so. We can thus say that there is a difference in kind between feelings or emotions and beliefs and that that is almost certainly what Hume was attempting to capture, especially in the Appendix passage. But, as we have now seen, the impressions and ideas doctrine gets in the way of this claim and prevents Hume from being able to formulate it clearly. If the distinction between impressions and ideas is one of degree only, then we have no ground for distinguishing between very vivid ideas and impressions; these ideas will just *be* impressions.

While speaking about the way in which Hume's psychology gets in the way of his philosophical insights, it is also appropriate to make a further, mere general, comment. One can put the point by saying that Hume's account of belief is too psychological. Just by virtue of being a lively idea, it is necessarily an *item* on the mental scene; it is an episode or occurrence in the mind. That, in turn, means that the final and decisive criterion for saying that a person believes something is whether he has had such an internal 'experience'. This seems contrary to the facts as we know them. We do not, in general, suppose that, in order to decide whether some other person believes something, we have to be supplied with this piece of information. If we are hesitant about ascribing a belief to someone, we might indeed seek verbal confirmation from him, but, again, we do not suppose that this is necessarily the report of such an internal occurrence. The point is not that, in our ascriptions of beliefs to people, we can get on very well without reference to such reports: it is, rather, that, in most cases, we feel there is nothing there to report *about*. What Hume takes to be an item in the mental world is really no such thing. To say that someone believes something is, at least very often, to say something about the way in which he behaves. His belief finds expression in his actions and reactions, in the kinds of thing he has a tendency to do or to refrain from doing.[3] If, as a result of hearing a noise, I come to believe that there is an intruder in my house, this belief will be expressed in any of a number of standard ways. I may pick up an implement with which to defend myself from attack; I may go searching around the rooms; I may telephone the police, etc. We would say that that kind of behaviour *constitutes* my believing that there was an intruder in the house, without remainder. That is, there need have been no mental experience at all of the kind that Hume speaks of. The account of my belief will have been exhausted by this reference to the kind of behaviour I indulge in. It is not to be denied, of course, that my behaving in this way may have been accompanied by certain feelings, for example, fear, anxiety, or hostility, but it hardly needs saying that such feelings would not have been constitutive of my belief. Indeed, these feelings would have the status of accompaniments even on Hume's account of the matter.

That, then, is what is meant by the claim that Hume's account of belief is too psychological. It can also be brought out in the following way. A person can often discover that he holds a certain belief by reflecting upon the course of his behaviour or by having his attention drawn to aspects of his behaviour by someone else. He might come to recognise, for example, that he believes X to be an untrustworthy person because of the kind of things he has said to X or because of the kind of assignments he has refrained from entrusting to X, etc. The claim that one has a certain belief is grounded on observation of one's behaviour, rather than upon the discovery, through introspection, of the kind of inner experience depicted by Hume.

Still concentrating on the strongly psychological character of Hume's account, there is a further aspect of it which is at odds with our normal concept of belief. Hume stresses, in both works, that he is unable to give a definition of belief, other than saying that it is a very vivid and forceful idea. In his further reflections upon the subject in the Appendix, for example, he tells us that, although it is the manner of the conception that distinguishes belief from imagination, he is lost for words when it comes to delineating this 'manner'. He appeals to the reader to consult his own experiences (*T.*, pp. 628–9). In the *Enquiry*, the tone is even more emphatic. We are told that to attempt a '*definition*' of belief would be very difficult, if not impossible (*E.*, p. 48). Again, the reader is referred to his own experience. The problem is this: if it really were the case that there is no way of defining belief, it is difficult to see how the concept could have entered the language. Yet, clearly, it is a part of the language: we do claim to be able to teach people the meaning of the word 'belief' and get them to use it appropriately. And what this must surely indicate is that belief is something much more public than Hume allows. This, in turn, must further support the contention mentioned above, that belief is standardly to be found expressed in external behaviour, including verbal behaviour, rather than in a unique state of mind that lies beyond description. Once more, one must reiterate the claim that Hume's account of belief is far too psychological.

We must now comment upon a provocative-sounding remark made by Hume in the *Enquiry* version of the matter. There, he asserts that belief 'is an operation of the soul ... as unavoidable as to feel the passion of love, when we receive benefits; or hatred, when we meet with injuries' (*E.*, p. 46). It is further described as 'a species of natural instinct, which no reasoning or process of the thought and understanding is able either to produce or to prevent' (*E.*, pp. 46–47). One must not deny that there is an element of truth in what Hume says, especially if one restricts one's attention to the empirical beliefs, based upon regular past conjunctions, with which he is mainly concerned. This is often the area in which one wishes to talk about being 'conditioned' by experience in such a way that one cannot help forming certain beliefs. If I see Professor X emerging from the library day after day at the very same time, I shall very likely come to believe that he will emerge at the same time today also. One might well wish to describe it as a situation in which I simply 'fall into' the belief without being able to do much about it. But the question must be whether, even in this area of empirical beliefs, the situation *has* to be like this. Is believing *just* like falling in love, or being overcome with pride or jealousy? Most people would agree that we cannot help falling in love: it is something that 'happens' to us. But it is not clear that empirical beliefs just 'happen' to us, at least not all of the time. To begin with, belief is best described as a cognitive state, as we noted above, and as Hume seemed to acknowledge in the Appendix passage to which we referred. Belief is to be cashed in terms of ideas, not feelings or sensations. As such, it often has to do with 'conclusions', to use Hume's own word, and conclusions are usually the result of *thought*. So, to repeat the point, certainly some of our beliefs may be states we simply 'fall into' as a result of a kind of conditioning. But on other occasions it is the active reflection upon the character of our experience that leads us to believe something. Suppose that I specifically wish to speak to Professor X and I begin to wonder where I might encounter him. I reflect upon the fact that he emerges from the library at a certain time every day and I form the belief that that is where I am most likely to meet him today at that time. That is surely a case of dealing in the coinage of ideas and reflection, and 'conclusions'. It is not the coinage of emotions and, for example, helplessly falling in love. Or suppose that I want to get hold of a copy of a first edition of one of Bertrand Russell's early philosophical works. I reflect upon the fact that books of this kind are to be found at Bookseller X rather than Bookseller Y and come to believe that the former is the one most likely to have it in stock. This, again, is surely a legitimate case of reasoning from experience, thus being an empirical belief belonging squarely in the category mapped out by Hume. But one would hardly describe it as a species of natural instinct that is as unavoidable as falling in love.

It may be argued in Hume's defence that the objection is not accurately targeted. It may be said that of course it is true that, in some cases, we do deliberately reflect upon the direction of our experience and that this does indeed mark a difference from being 'conditioned' by it. What is important, it will be said, is that the end-product is of the same character in both cases. That is, by 'conditioning' or by deliberate reflection, I simply cannot help the last step of falling into believing that such-and-such is the case, willy nilly. This may therefore seem to bear out Hume's claim that it is a species of natural instinct and that it is unavoidable.

However, the matter is not as simple as this. One has to recognise that Hume is actually making a very strong claim at this particular point. As we saw from the second of the two quotations listed above, he holds that the psychological situation is such that 'no reasoning or process of the thought and understanding is able either to produce or to prevent it' (*E.*, p. 47). But, on the most obvious account of 'reasoning' or 'understanding', this is clearly false. To return to our example, I may reflect and thus come to believe that Professor X is going to emerge from the library at a certain time, but may then be informed that Professor X has been elsewhere on this particular day. To take this fact into account is surely to reason about or understand something in the required sense; and my belief is altered or suspended on the basis of it. This is surely representative of a large number of cases in which belief is altered, suspended or dissipated as a direct result of empirical reasoning. And that these are clearly cases of reasoning must surely be admitted, if only because they are cases in which one fact is brought into relation with another or others: they are standardly cases in which we put two and two together. If we grant the validity of such examples, it does not seem possible to defend Hume in the way mentioned above. That is, it does not seem plausible to say that, whether or not the antecedents of belief are unavoidable, certainly the end-product of coming to believe is unavoidable. The evidence seems to show that it is both avoidable and alterable. None of this is to be taken to imply that what we believe is a matter of *choice*, or of what we *will*. But to accept this is not to accept that no process of reasoning can affect what we believe.

We have been critical of Hume's treatment of the topic of belief, but we must not lose sight of the philosophical significance of his general project. The question that Hume was centrally asking is one that remains squarely within the philosopher's view today. It was the question of how we distinguish the believing state from the purely 'thinking' or imagining state. One can put it by asking what it is that constitutes a belief as opposed to a mere thought. Or again, what is it to believe that something is the case as opposed to simply 'entertaining the thought' that something is the case? Now one of the things we have made very clear in the course of the present chapter is that Hume went wrong in attempting to give a purely psychological answer to this question, and thus he produced distortions in the concept of belief that we find unacceptable. That does not alter the fact that there was a genuine question to be answered, and indeed it is still not clear that we have a satisfactory answer to it. Hume was certainly right in thinking that the question presented a real problem and that it was one of the 'greatest mysteries of philosophy'(*T.*, p. 628). It was to Hume's credit that he saw this.

There is something further in Hume's analysis to which we have not so far done full justice. It is that, despite the strong psychological emphasis, there are certainly some signs that he was beginning to see the connection between belief and behaviour. In the Appendix, for example, where Hume returns to the topic, he provides us with an 'insertion' for the main work. The new passage ends with the assertion that beliefs are 'the governing principles of all our actions' (*T.*, p. 629). The same words are repeated in the *Enquiry* (*E.*, p. 50). There is at least a hint here that, in addition to any intrinsic psychological difference there may be between belief and imagination, beliefs are also distinguished from imaginings by virtue of their motivating influence upon behaviour.

Finally, although the claim must stand that Hume's account is too psychological in character, one must not thereby suppose that there is nothing at all on the mental side to be explained. It may be that it is to a person's behaviour, both verbal and non-verbal, that we turn for the strongest evidence of his beliefs, but many would deny that this could be the whole story. F.P. Ramsey, for example, formulated a theory of belief which held that beliefs are 'maps' by which we 'steer'.[4] The theory has been taken up and developed in recent years by D.M. Armstrong.[5] If one presses the map analogy, what comes out of it is that there must *be*, in some sense, a map if one is to steer by it. This inevitably suggests that belief must be a tangible mental 'something' if it is to provide a guide to conduct. However, Armstrong is anxious to make it clear that the analogy is not to be taken quite in this way. He wishes to avoid Hume's 'mental occurrence' view but without being committed to the other extreme of holding that belief can be analysed entirely in terms of behaviour. The result is the attempt to construe belief as a 'state' or 'frame' of mind. It is to be seen as a kind of 'imprinting' upon the mind for which an appropriate analogy would be Plato's example, in the *Theaetetus*, of the imprint made by a seal upon a piece of wax.[6] The imprint may be strong or weak and may last for a long or a short time, and these are features of beliefs as we know them. The 'imprint' upon the mind is a metaphorical description of what it is that constitutes the 'state' of believing. The net result will be a 'navigating' effect upon one's behaviour. One's behaviour will be, either consciously or unconsciously, channelled in certain directions.

The point to make, then, after this brief glimpse of one strand of thought in contemporary philosophy, is that perhaps Hume's treatment of belief was not entirely misguided. He did at least grasp the fact that there is something 'mental' to be explained. He tended to concentrate upon this to the exclusion of other aspects of the concept, and he certainly underrated the behavioural aspects of belief, but the account was not completely off-target. What is more, he was able to formulate an important question that has continued to trouble philosophers.[7] This is the question, seen above, of how one distinguishes between simply thinking about something, on the one hand, and believing it, on the other. Armstrong's account acknowledges the importance of this question and tries to answer it by showing how the state of mind that constitutes belief may be distinguished from mere thinking just by virtue of the effects it has upon behaviour.

Notes

1. See D. G. C. MacNabb, *David Hume: His Theory of Knowledge and Morality*, (Oxford, Basil Blackwell, 1966) p. 74.
2. MacNabb, p. 74.

3. For an account of belief along these lines, see G. Ryle, *The Concept of Mind* (Harmondsworth, Penguin Books, 1968), pp. 128–30.
4. F. P. Ramsey, 'General propositions and causality', in D. H. Mellor (ed.), *F. P. Ramsey: Philosophical Papers* (Cambridge, Cambridge University Press, 1990), p. 146.
5. D. M. Armstrong, *Belief, Truth and Knowledge* (Cambridge, Cambridge University Press, 1973).
6. Plato, *Theaetetus*, 191b–195b, translated by J. McDowell (Oxford, Clarendon Press, 1973).
7. For a collection of essays on this topic, see A. Phillips Griffiths, *Knowledge and Belief* (London, Oxford University Press, 1967). See also H. H. Price, *Belief* (London, George Allen & Unwin, 1969); D. Davidson, 'Thought and talk', in D. Davidson, *Enquiries into Truth and Interpretation* (New York, Oxford University Press, 1984).

8. *Are our choices free?*

(*Enquiry*, Section VIII; *Treatise*, Book II, Part III, Section I)

To the question posed as the title of this chapter, Hume's answer is that in one sense they are and in another sense they are not. We shall now have to work out in detail how he arrives at such an answer. The topic occurs as Section VIII of the *Enquiry*, thus following on closely from his treatment of causality. In the *Treatise*, however, it does not emerge until the third part of Book II. The reason for this need not concern us since the argument is essentially the same in both versions. It is only worth noting that, since the topic is so closely related to that of causality, the order of discussion in the *Enquiry* is more natural.

One of the things that has been made evident by Hume's account of cause and effect, perhaps contrary to our expectations, is that the world is a very regular and law-governed place. Things do not happen haphazardly: there is a 'uniformity observable in the operation of nature, where similar objects are constantly conjoined together' (*E.*, p. 82). Of course it is part of Hume's thesis that there is nothing intrinsically necessary about this uniformity. Nevertheless, it is contingently there and we make predictions about how things will behave on the basis of such uniformity. This having emerged, it was quite natural for Hume to wonder whether human behaviour was characterised by the same kind of regularity and whether it allowed for the same kind of law-like descriptions. If this were to be the case, then much of what we say about physical object behaviour would also be applicable to the behaviour of human beings. Thus one of the things we commonly think about physical objects and events is that they are the results of causes that have preceded them, such that, once a particular cause obtained, a certain effect would automatically follow. And we normally think of this situation as one in which the effect is 'governed' by its cause such that no other outcome is possible. Is it possible, then, that human activity must be viewed in the same terms?

That roughly is the route by means of which Hume arrives at the topic of liberty and necessity. Having arrived there, he eventually concludes, as we have seen, that we are both free and determined, though from different points of view. Before examining the details of his position, one or two general points should be noted. In the first place, the terms 'liberty' and 'necessity' are normally regarded as mutually exclusive. People are either free or determined, but they cannot be both with regard to the same actions. In addition, most people would vigorously resist the claim that our actions are determined. In relation to these commonly held assumptions, Hume holds (a) that the terms are *not* mutually exclusive and (b) that there is nothing unacceptable about regarding human beings as determined or 'necessitated'.

Hume also maintains that people can be brought to recognise the truth of the above two propositions by exposing our everyday assumptions and tracing out their implications. This particular theme is more explicit in the *Enquiry* version than in the *Treatise*. As he says in the former work:

> I hope, therefore, to make it appear that all men have ever agreed in the doctrine both of liberty and necessity, according to any reasonable sense, which can be put on these terms; and that the whole controversy has hitherto turned merely upon words. (*E.*, p. 81)

It follows from this, then, that what Hume ultimately presents us with is something that is often described as a 'reconciling' thesis.[1] Freedom can be reconciled with determinism. In contemporary philosophy this position is known as compatibilism. As we shall see, its success depends upon being able to forge a viable notion of human freedom within a completely deterministic framework. Hume was not the first to formulate such a doctrine. A version of it had already appeared in Hobbes[2] as well as in Locke and Leibniz.[3] If there is anything distinctive about Hume's account, it is perhaps in the persuasiveness with which he puts his case. We shall now move directly to what he has to say.

Determinism

Starting first with the deterministic aspect of the picture, Hume tells us that necessity or determinism in the sphere of physical objects is something that we already acknowledge to be present. According to the Humean scheme what that means is that we acknowledge that physical objects and events are *caused*. When we say that something is caused, we actually *mean* that it is necessarily connected with that which preceded it. Each object or event is determined or necessitated by its cause, and that is how determinism gets into the picture. Of course it must be stressed that Hume, consistent with his previous thought, is not speaking about any objective necessity in events themselves. Our ideas of necessity and causation arise from observation of constant conjunction between instances of A's and instances of B's, and the mind is led to infer the one upon the appearance of the other. The two important factors involved here are, as we saw above, constant conjunction and the habit of mind. That, then, is what necessity or determinism amounts to in the sphere of physical objects, and Hume claims to have established our acknowledgement of it.

His next move is to assert that if we now concede that the two crucial factors just mentioned are also present in the case of human behaviour, then that will be to admit that it is determined in precisely the same way. The onus is therefore on Hume to show that these factors are in fact present, thus clinching the thesis. Clinching the thesis in this way is not something Hume finds particularly onerous. Basically, it is merely a matter of drawing our attention to the acknowledged 'uniformity among the actions of men' (*E.*, p. 83). 'The same motives always produce the same actions'(*E.*, p. 83). In human nature we have constant conjunctions that are every bit as comparable to the conjunctions we find in the physical world – conjunctions between human motives and human actions. We know, for example, that jealousy produces a certain pattern of behaviour, that love produces another, and malice another. Further, there is the same inference of the mind from the one to the other. From a certain pattern of behaviour, we infer the presence of jealousy as a motive; and from the known presence of jealousy, we infer that certain kinds of behaviour will emerge. And the thesis extends more widely to include not just human motives but more general human reactions. Thus, most rational people can be relied upon to walk on the pavement and not in the middle of the road. Drivers can be relied upon to stop at a red light, and so on. And again, our reliance, our expectations, and the determination of our minds in all these contexts are based upon the observation of constant conjunction.

So, Hume argues, there are discernible patterns in the behaviour both of physical objects and of human beings; the two cases are parallel. Therefore, all things are caused and all things are determined. That the two spheres are comparable is, he thinks, indicated by the way in which 'natural' and 'moral' evidence for the truth of determinism cement together. By the former he means evidence from the behaviour of physical objects and events in the world around us; by the latter, the evidence from human motivation. He has a rather telling example to illustrate this point (*E.*, p. 90). Standardly, a prisoner in jail will be convinced of the impossibility of his escape and his conviction will stem from two sources which bear equal weight. He will know that, all other conditions being equal, the walls and bars that surround him will resist any attempt to break them down. But, equally, he will know that the character of the jailer is such that, except under special conditions, he will not open the doors and let him out. What this is meant to indicate, then, is that, even given our ordinary way of thinking we rate the necessity of human motives and the actions that follow them as being equal in status to the necessity of physical events. Further, Hume wishes us to notice that, in both cases, the necessity stems from the experience of the respective conjunctions. We know the character and disposition of jailers and how they are related to a certain kind of behaviour. Similarly, we know the nature of iron bars and concrete walls and the kind of properties they exhibit. It is in this way, then, that natural and moral evidence cement together and thus seem to bear out Hume's claim that we rate the determination of the one as being on a par with that of the other.

But is it possible that the example of the prisoner is an isolated one that happens to favour Hume's position? Some would argue that there are in fact very good grounds for supposing that human behaviour is radically different from that of physical events. It is precisely this objection that Hume himself recognises and tries to counter. He clearly formulates the grounds on which the objection is based. In short, the argument is that human nature is capricious. People are known frequently to act out of character. Their behaviour is not always predictable. And this is often the reason given for saying that human action is therefore not governed by causes in the way that physical objects and events are. Hume succinctly summarises the objection thus: 'Necessity is regular and certain. Human conduct is irregular and uncertain. The one, therefore, proceeds not from the other'(*T*., p. 403).

Hume's response is to reassert that the two spheres are perfectly parallel and that causes operate regularly in both of them. However, what happens is that this fact is often disguised from us by the operation of additional, interfering causes of which we are unaware. Hume often refers to them as 'contrary' causes. His point is best illustrated by an example that appears in the *Enquiry* and not in the *Treatise*. A peasant would typically be mystified by the stopping of a clock or watch. His reaction would be to say 'that it does not commonly go right'(*E*., p. 87). However, we recognise that this is obviously an expression of his ignorance concerning watches. An expert, upon examining the watch, would be able to tell us that there is no real irregularity in the operation of the usual mechanical forces: it is just that, for example, a grain of dust has interfered with their working.

Just as we commonly acknowledge the operation of these contrary or interfering causes in the physical sphere, so we should similarly acknowledge their presence in the case of human conduct. To employ another of Hume's examples, a man may be known to have a very pleasant disposition such that one would expect him to chat amiably when met in the street. One day, however, he is unexpectedly bad-tempered and rude. But that does not show that his behaviour was uncaused. For example, it may turn out that, on that particular occasion, the man had a severe toothache.

The general point which Hume wishes to establish, therefore, is that whenever we feel inclined to say that a causal sequence is not uniformly fulfilled or that some cause has ceased to produce its usual effect, we shall discover that there was some interfering cause at work. And to discover this is effectively to show that the original causal sequence remains intact. Thus, to flick the switch will normally cause the electric light to come on. We do not claim that the sequence has failed to be uniform if, for example, the light bulb has expired. A useful way of putting Hume's point is to say that the statement of any causal sequence will implicitly include the clause 'other conditions being equal'. If it turns out that all other conditions were not in fact equal, this does not reflect upon the regularity of the sequence. And what Hume clearly wishes to emphasise is that this general point applies equally to both spheres. Thus to talk, as we do, about the capriciousness of human behaviour is just a sophisticated way of expressing our ignorance of concealed or contrary causes. In that respect, it is no different from the peasant who is mystified by the stopping of the watch. Hume is thus confident that his original claim has been sustained; all things, including human actions, are caused and therefore all things, again including human actions, are necessary. They are necessary in that peculiar sense of 'necessity' that Hume has spelled out for us in his main account of causality.

Freedom

Explaining what Hume means by necessity in the realm of human conduct is the difficult part of the story. To say what he means by liberty is, in many ways, the easier part, and we shall now turn to that.

It amounts to no more than the claim that we are free or at liberty in so far as we follow our own desires, inclinations and wishes, and manage to implement our own decisions. Hume's own words from the *Enquiry* are worth quoting:

> By liberty, then, we can only mean *a power of acting or not acting, according to the determination of the will*; that is, if we choose to remain at rest, we may; if we choose to move, we also may. (*E.*, p. 95)

What is more, this is a liberty that belongs to everyone 'who is not a prisoner and in chains'.

In the *Treatise* version, Hume uses the terms 'spontaneity' and 'indifference' to give us a clearer idea of the kind of freedom he is talking about. The liberty of spontaneity is what we have just outlined and what every person has, potentially. It is the freedom that consists in acting without any external constraint. It is to be contrasted with action at the point of a gun, for example, or actions performed under physical pressure of various kinds. The liberty of indifference on the other hand, is, an absolute liberty in human action meaning essentially action which is uncaused. For Hume, we do not and cannot have this kind of freedom. However, it is important to see what it *would* consist of since this will throw further light upon the kind of liberty we do have. Action that was uncaused would be action that was just a matter of chance, and, according to Hume's thinking, there is no such thing as chance. Talk about chance is just a way of revealing our ignorance of the causes which do obtain (*T.*, p. 404).

What we enjoy, then, is the liberty of spontaneity within a context in which all things are caused. Once we recognise that the liberty of indifference is unattainable and would in any case be undesirable we shall see that the former kind of freedom is what we should settle for and indeed seek to attain. A simple example well illustrates Hume's position. Let us imagine Margaret Thatcher voting in an election. It will be true to say of all her relevant actions in this context that they will be caused, and therefore that they have the kind of necessity that Hume analysed in his account of causality. Her actions will be predictable for that reason, and, in particular, we know that she will vote Conservative. Now, obviously, since all these established causes are at work, she does not have the liberty of indifference. Nevertheless, on Hume's view she does have what it concerns us all to have, namely, the liberty of spontaneity. This is guaranteed by the fact that, for example, nobody actually forced her to go to the polling booth; nobody thrust a pencil in her hand and dragged it across the ballot paper. Her actions were the outcome of her own unconstrained deliberations. These actions were caused and therefore determined by those deliberations, but they were not unfree for that reason. It is precisely in that sense that Hume's is a reconciling thesis and is commonly termed 'compatibilism'. We must now take stock of what has been offered us.

Taking stock

One thing must be immediately obvious to anyone acquainted with what Hume had to say about causality and induction. In order to make the present claim that all human action is determined or necessitated, Hume has to be able to show that all actions are caused, but, strictly, even according to his own thinking, there is no way in which he can establish this. It is not analytic that every event has a cause. Using Hume's own criterion, there is no contradiction involved in conceiving of an event that was not caused. Nor can one establish empirically that every event must be caused. That would run into the problem he has so explicitly formulated: we can never be rationally justified in moving from known instances to unknown instances. Even if we could know that all events to date were caused, this could not guarantee the universal claim that all events must be caused. In fact, however, we are not in a position to know that all events to date have been caused. And it is precisely on this point that Hume's thesis seems to be particularly question-begging. In response to that kind of doubt, his position, both in the *Enquiry* and in the *Treatise* is perfectly clear and equally dogmatic. All actions that *appear* to be uncaused or a matter of chance are dismissed as cases of ignorance on our part. In the earlier work, for example, he tells us that 'what the vulgar call chance is nothing but a secret and conceal'd cause' (*T.*, p. 130). He becomes even more emphatic in the later work: 'It is universally allowed that nothing exists without a cause of its existence, and that chance, when strictly examined, is a mere negative word ... ' (*E.*, p. 95). Whether it is in fact 'universally allowed' is just the question at issue and Hume has no right to assume that it is. Admittedly, there will be cases where the ascribing of an event to chance turns out, after closer scrutiny, to be mistaken, as in the case of the watch that inexplicably stops. But can we assume that all such cases will fall into the same category?

It seems worth saying, then, that Hume's claim that all events are caused, and thus determined, is not one that he has substantiated. Not only has he failed to justify it, but the claim also seems to run counter to some of the important aspects of his account of causality and induction. However, let us grant, for the moment, that Hume is correct and that the only kind of freedom we can intelligibly talk about is the freedom of spontaneity. What we must now do is to unpack this concept a little more in order to decide whether it is capable of satisfying the demands we make upon the concept of freedom. Is the freedom of spontaneity ultimately all that we want?

In order to shed some further light on this question, it will be useful to look at Hume's position from a slightly different angle. Essentially Hume is saying that, while all actions are certainly caused, nevertheless it is possible to see some causes as constraining while others are not. It is only when a cause constitutes a restraint upon conduct that we shall see our freedom as impaired. His thesis is, in other words, a way of emphasising that the distinction that should concern us is not that between caused and uncaused action: it is between caused action that is constraining and caused action that is not. To revert to a previous example, nobody has any objection to saying that Margaret Thatcher's voting in an election, and voting Conservative in particular, was a result of her wishing to vote, and to vote in that way. In turn, her wishing to vote that way was causally related to her general disposition to endorse Conservative policies. And, Hume wishes to stress, that is precisely how we would want it to be. Human life is at its best and its most desirable when the actions we perform are appropriately related to the wishes, intentions and dispositions that we have. To say that the one is the cause of the other is neither here nor there. That does not constitute a threat to our freedom. What is worrying is when the causes are external and, as it were, foisted upon us. Physically forcing Margaret Thatcher to the polling booth and directing her pencil to the side of the Labour candidate's name would be a paradigm of such worrying causation. The absence of such causes is what makes our freedom.

Putting Hume's position in this way is to see it in its most favourable light: it fully brings out the value of the kind of freedom to which Hume is drawing our attention. What must now be said is that not everyone would agree that this is all that can be meant by freedom. It has been argued by many that Hume's thesis ignores the all-important question. That question is: for any particular action, no matter how free of constraint it may have been, could I have acted otherwise?[4] In more detail, the question is this: if in fact I did X, could

I have chosen to do Y, even if all the causes leading up to X had been exactly the same? For example, could Margaret Thatcher have voted Labour if all relevant preceding circumstances had remained the same? It is argued that, only if we can give an affirmative answer to that kind of question can one genuinely talk about freedom. It is therefore suggested that Hume has provided us with no more than a necessary condition for the compatibilist thesis.

However, though this criticism seems to focus our attention in the right place and perhaps persuades us that Hume really has missed a crucial consideration, one needs to be cautious. There are at least some grounds for thinking that the question we are being required to ask is a hollow one. In the first place, it is very difficult to see how one would establish that one could have acted differently under the same conditions. Hume himself considers one attempt to demonstrate the possibility (*T.*, p. 408). A person might suppose that he could prove the possession of such absolute freedom by doing the opposite of what had been predicted. This would be illustrated by Margaret Thatcher deciding to vote Labour just to be perverse. Hume's retort is that this kind of action does not exhibit the required kind of freedom. To act in such a way would not be to act in the absence of 'governing' motives. It would be to act out of the desire to express such freedom, usually in the face of some challenge to it. That desire simply falls into precisely the class of mental antecedents that constitute the causes of our actions and thus justify the claim that they are 'necessitated' in Hume's sense.

If, on the other hand, one were to try to envisage a situation in which one is outside the net of governing antecedents, the resulting product would seem to be something less than an 'action'. We should be in the realm of Hume's liberty of indifference. We should be talking not about actions but about uncaused events; people's behaviour would be entirely random and unpredictable. When one really thinks about it, who could ever suppose that ultimate freedom must consist in this? It seems to follow that there is an element of confusion in thinking that being able to act otherwise is the ultimate criterion of freedom. To put the point paradoxically, to be able to act otherwise, on this interpretation, is not to act at all.

Of course Hume does not deny that, had the antecedent conditions been different, one might have acted otherwise, but this is not the great concession to freedom that some have taken it to be. It may initially seem to be so if one stresses certain aspects of Hume's thoughts on causality. Thus, it is one of his central claims that things could always be other than they are. The necessity that we see in events is nothing more than a projection of what lies in our minds. On this basis, it seems quite feasible to say that we could always have acted otherwise.

However, the matter is not quite as simple as this. When Hume tells us that it is only a contingent fact that A causes B and that it could be otherwise, this is, as we have already seen, just a way of saying that B is not logically entailed by A. (It is not like saying that the having of four sides is logically entailed by something's being a square.) Nevertheless, in the world that we know, it is the case that A will be followed by B. That is how the world now is, and it would have to be a very different world if causes were not followed by their usual effects. That being so, we are, in some sense, saddled with the view that when people act as they do they could not have acted otherwise.

If it seems easy to say of any particular set of conditions that they might not have obtained, this is perhaps because we tend to isolate certain segments of our experience such that they appear to be self-contained. Thus, had the postman not delivered a certain letter, I would not have gone to the hospital to visit a sick friend. The postal delivery and the hospital visit are picked out as a self-contained pair abstracted from the surrounding context. In fact, however, they are simply part of a longer series of events, all of which have been caused. On Hume's thesis, one is dealing with a whole complex network of causes, stretching backwards. For that reason, it is not easy to select one condition or set of conditions as though it or they existed in a vacuum. And for that reason also it is not easy to say that, had certain conditions not obtained, I would have acted otherwise. Those specific conditions were themselves embedded in everything that had occurred before I acted. Of course it is true that, on Hume's thesis, *everything* might have been different, but that would be a flimsy basis on which to found a viable concept of freedom.

All of this conspires to suggest that the freedom of spontaneity is, after all, the kind of freedom to which we must attach value and that perhaps Hume has focused attention in the right place. Nevertheless, the concept needs a little more scrutiny than he gave it. What must be said in particular is that this kind of freedom is not as prevalent in human experience as Hume depicts it to be. According to Hume, it is a freedom that belongs to everyone 'who is not a prisoner in chains'

(*E.*, p. 95). It is true that, in the *Enquiry*, Hume describes it as a 'hypothetical' liberty, perhaps suggesting that, in order for it to exist, certain other conditions must obtain. But neither in the *Enquiry* nor in the *Treatise* does Hume show any real awareness of the ways in which this so-called spontaneous freedom can be circumscribed. As one commentator puts it: 'The quest for liberty is more than an effort to stay out of prison or out of chains'.[5]

To examine this comment more closely, it is worth developing the following thought. If we attach any value to the freedom of spontaneity, it is because it is the result of motives that we are happy to characterise in two important ways. Firstly, we regard these motives as springing from within ourselves; secondly, we regard them as peculiarly our own. If we were to put the point technically, it would be to say that we regard these two conditions as being jointly necessary to allow us to talk meaningfully about freedom. The point about Hume's position is that, while he certainly emphasises the importance of the first condition, he does not seem to recognise the importance of the second.[6] An exaggerated example will make this point clearer. Under the influence of hypnosis, it is possible to instruct a person to perform a particular action in the post-hypnotic state and even to provide the person with a motive for doing it. When the person finally comes to perform the action, in the appropriate circumstances, he will think of it as his own action, and it will be at least nominally true to say that it emanated from him and, moreover, that it emanated from a motive within him. On the only criterion Hume provides us with, it will then be true to say that he acted freely, having the freedom of spontaneity. However, it is highly unlikely that we should regard it as a free action, and this is surely because we feel that it does not meet the second of the two conditions above. We feel that it would be inappropriate to describe it as free because it was not truly that person's action. There is an important sense in which it did not 'belong' to him.

The example is an extreme one, but there are other classes of action which many would see as approximating to it. Phobias and obsessional neuroses would seem to be one such class. They differ from the hypnosis case since they are not impulses that are imposed from without. Nevertheless, the actions resulting from them fall short of being candidates for freedom for the same reason. The reason is that, in a peculiar sense, they do not properly belong to the agents performing them.

Indeed, the matter does not end there. If we are, in general, wondering about how responsible we are for the motives we possess, other queries naturally arise. Increasingly, there is a tendency to think that human motivation, the incentives for human action, is shaped by forces outside ourselves – economic, social, political pressures, as well as hereditary factors. Now it may well be that there are good grounds for distinguishing such factors from the phobias, obsessions and hypnotic influences mentioned above. For example, one might argue that economic, social and political pressures are to be construed not as forces acting upon us, but, rather, as materials or tools placed at our disposal. They may be seen as the medium in which and through which we make our decisions. Such a view finds expression in the thought that characteristically human life is intimately involved in the activity of coping with such factors. To suppose otherwise is rather like supposing that one could fly more easily if only one could escape the inhibiting pressure of the atmosphere. In this sense, then, it may be possible to preserve a viable notion of the freedom of spontaneity and thus to do justice to the spirit of Hume's position. But all of this must only reinforce the initial criticism of him, namely, that the freedom of spontaneity is a concept that needed a great deal more scrutiny than he actually gave it.

A final comment must now be made concerning the complexion of the deterministic aspect of Hume's position. In one sense, the plausibility of Hume's claim that human behaviour is determined rests squarely upon his particular view of what it is to have a motive, and this view has been frequently contested in present-day philosophy. This therefore casts some shadow over the route by which Hume arrives at determinism. The point requires some elaboration.

It will be remembered that Hume begins his discussion of the general topic by reminding us that we already accept the existence of determinism in the sphere of physical objects, and he spelt out for us precisely what that determinism amounted to. He then argued, quite reasonably, that, if human behaviour could be shown to be on the same footing, it too should be described as determined or 'necessary'. The next move was to establish that human behaviour is in fact on the same footing just by virtue of the fact that the same type of regular conjunctions occur between A's and B's, allowing us to make predictions in exactly the same way as we do with physical objects. It is at this point that we need to look more closely at what is being assumed. In the case of physical objects, or events, we are, by and large, talking abut discrete, isolable entities in such a way that Hume's causal formula is easily intelligible to us. That is, given the occurrence of A (granted its frequently observed conjunction with B), we shall automatically come to expect B. When one transfers this formula to the human scene, the events or entities between which such regular conjunctions are meant to occur are, firstly, actions and, secondly, people's 'motives, tempers, and circumstances'(*T.*, p. 401). In general, Hume concentrates upon the conjunction between actions and motives. The *Enquiry* version of things makes this point clearer and even provides a list of the motives that form the basis of all human action (*E.*, p. 83). The problem is that, at least in many cases, when we speak about a person's motive, we are not speaking about a discrete and isolable event, standing behind the action that it motivates. Yet that is the sense that seems to be required by Hume's analysis. Admittedly, some motives may be of this kind, at least in the sense that one can psychologically pin-point a something going on inside oneself that might constitute a sort of impetus to action. But there are so many other cases where one wants to say that the motive is, as it were, written upon the face of the performance. The point becomes more emphatic if one considers the kind of things Hume lists as examples of motives for his purpose. In the *Enquiry*, he cites ambition, avarice, self-love, vanity, friendship, generosity and public spirit. But could one introspectively pin-point something called self-love, for example, or friendship as items which might intelligibly figure in Hume's causal formula? To put the point rhetorically, where *is* this psychological entity called friendship or self-love that is, on Hume's analysis, supposed to be conjoined with some particular action of X's?

We might indeed conclude that, since Hume's conception of causality seems to rest so clearly on the view that the items which are causally related are *objects* or *events*, and since psychological states such as friendship and self-love are neither, it is not at all clear by Hume's lights how he can claim that human behaviour is determined by our motives. However, we must note that the criticism we have been concerned with is not aimed at the idea that our actions are determined, but specifically at the claim that our actions are determined *by our motives*. And it is, of course, quite possible to reject this idea while still holding that our actions are indeed determined by other factors. Indeed, Hume's own account of the determinants of human behaviour includes not only 'motives and tempers', but also the 'circumstances' in which people find themselves. And, however questionable we may find the idea that motives and character-traits are causes of behaviour, we would surely be much more ready to accept that our behaviour is indeed determined by all sorts of 'circumstances'. It would, therefore, clearly be wrong to assume that Hume's view of human action as determined absolutely stands or falls with the rightness or wrongness of his conception of motives.

At the beginning of the present chapter, we noted Hume's claim that the controversy over liberty and determinism is essentially a verbal dispute. He held that, if only people could be brought to recognise precisely what is meant by these two terms, they would in turn recognise that we are indeed both free and determined, though from two different points of view. They would also come to see that there is nothing unacceptable about such a position. We must now ask ourselves the question whether this claim that we are dealing with a dispute that is merely verbal is well-founded.

The short answer to that question must surely be in the negative. If the operative test is whether we feel that all the important problems have been resolved once we have understood the key-terms as Hume defines them, it must be that Hume's account fails that test. The progression of thought in the present chapter should have made it evident that there are a number of issues that need further exploration and discussion before one can accept Hume's judgement. Firstly, to pick up on the last of our comments, it is simply not clear that motives can constitute the determining factors in the way Hume suggests, and this is certainly not a dispute about words. Secondly, whatever we do put forward as the relevant determining forces upon human conduct, one instinctively feels that Hume's particular account of causality somehow nullifies the deterministic claim itself. To clarify this statement, one has to stress that, for Hume, causality is predominantly a psychological concept. The whole message of his account is that there is no objective necessity in events in themselves: the necessity lies in our minds, and gets expressed in our firm expectations of B's upon the occurrence of their preceding A's. As far as the objective order of things is concerned, things could always be other than they are: the present and the future need not conform to the past. It is just this fact, that causality is a psychological concept, that things could always be different, which seems to remove the sting from Hume's deterministic picture. It is not that one wants to question his analysis of causality. The essentials of this analysis have remained extremely influential ever since Hume's day. It is rather, that, on the basis of this analysis, one wonders quite how determinism could get a foothold. Again, therefore, it seems as though the whole dispute is not just about words, for we find ourselves wondering whether we really are determined even after understanding the precise meaning given to this key-term by Hume.

Next, as we saw above, the freedom of spontaneity needs a great deal more scrutiny before we can accept that that is the freedom we enjoy, if we enjoy it at all. On Hume's account of the matter, it is the freedom that belongs to every man who is not a prisoner and in chains. As we have seen, this certainly casts the net too wide. There are many non-prisoners who do not enjoy freedom, and for a variety of reasons. To say, then, as Hume does, that the traditional dispute between liberty and necessity, or freedom and determinism, is merely verbal is not something we can readily accept.

Finally, we have to ask whether there isn't something more profoundly amiss with Hume's treatment of the topic of freedom and responsibility. Hume very effectively pours scorn on the idea that free action is action which is free from causal determination, arguing that if we suppose that action is not determined by the agent's nature we are left with a mere random event, something for which it would make no sense to hold the agent responsible – something, indeed, which we could not even ascribe to any agent. It thus seemed to him that the idea of responsibility actually requires it to be the case that all our actions are determined. But this cannot be the final word. In the last few paragraphs of Section VIII of the *Enquiry* we find Hume asking whether it can really make any sense to blame someone for his actions if those actions are the ineluctable outcome of a sequence of cause and effect, a sequence which could not have been other than it was. Hume sees that the doctrine of determinism implies that all my actions and choices were determined by the state of the world *before I was born*, and that indeed the ultimate responsibility for my wrong-doing must be traced back to the first cause, or to the Deity himself (*E.*, p. 99ff). Hume candidly admits that the difficulties that have thus emerged are too profound for a ready solution.

With this admission we have the most important reason for rejecting Hume's claim that the dispute about freedom and responsibility is merely about words. Up to this point, Hume has argued that everyone will see on reflection that, not only is our freedom compatible with determinism, but that the very idea of action requires the truth of determinism. The notion of the liberty of indifference can give us only random events, not actions at all. Hence, any dispute about freedom must be simply a matter of words, and that dispute is settled once we see that it is true that we are both determined and free. But in the final few paragraphs of this section, this position appears to collapse. Hume here in effect admits that the claim that everything I do was already determined before I was born really does threaten the idea that I am responsible for my actions. We find Hume at last recognising that we do have a powerful intuition that freedom is incompatible with determinism, and that this cannot be dismissed as a mere verbal confusion.

The truth is that the dispute about freedom and responsibility, far from being a merely verbal dispute, reveals that we have deep and powerful intuitions on both sides of the issue. On the one hand we do feel, as Hume came at last to acknowledge, that the claim that all our actions are determined does indeed pose a profound threat to our conception of ourselves as responsible agents. But on the other hand, we seem incapable of making sense of the idea of an action that is not the outcome of and is not determined by one's nature. The attempt to do so yields nothing but a random event, something which isn't an action at all. It is to Hume's credit that he saw this and argued for it with such clarity and force. But it is a major criticism of him that he failed to recognise the power of the opposing intuition, and that when he finally did, he did not see that the claim that the dispute about freedom was a purely verbal one could not stand. Far from being a mere dispute about words, the problem of free will is one of the most difficult in philosophy.[7]

Having thus surveyed Hume's treatment of freedom and determinism, we must now turn our attention to a question that may naturally have occurred to us. We want to know what it is, exactly, that is either free or determined, or both. Of course it is what we call the person, but what account must we give of that all-important concept? This is a question Hume answers in *Treatise*, Book 1, Part IV, Section VI. His answer will form the basis of the next chapter.

Notes

1. This is how Hume himself describes his thesis: '... this reconciling project with regard to the question of liberty and necessity' (*E.*, p. 95).
2. T. Hobbes, *Leviathan* (1651), edited by Richard Tuck (Cambridge, Cambridge University Press, 1991), ch. XXI.

3. J. Locke, *An Essay Concerning Human Understanding*, Book II, ch. XXI. G. W. Leibniz, 'On freedom' (1689) and 'A letter on freedom' (1689), reprinted in G. H. R. Parkinson (ed.), *Leibniz: Philosophical Writings* (London, J. M. Dent and Sons, 1973).

4. See C.A. Campbell, *In Defence of Free Will* (London, Allen & Unwin, 1967) for an account of freedom which emphasises this question. A discussion of an earlier statement of Campbell's views can be found in P.H. Nowell-Smith, *Ethics*, (Harmondsworth, Penguin Books, 1965), ch. 19.

5. B. Stroud, *Hume* (London, Routledge and Kegan Paul, 1977), p. 146.

6. The final pages of the *Treatise* discussion of liberty and necessity do, however, contains some indication that Hume is prepared to acknowledge the moral significance of actions proceeding from a person's own permanent motives and dispositions. See the *Treatise*, pp. 411–12. Hume's concern with the relations of moral responsibility and character is discussed in Chapter 12, above, pp. 239–40.

7. For a useful anthology of contemporary discussions of free will, see Gary Watson (ed.), *Free Will* (Oxford, Oxford University Press, 1982). Other recent studies of free will are G. Strawson, *Freedom and Belief* (Oxford, Clarendon Press, 1986), D. Dennett, *Elbow Room* (Oxford, Oxford University Press, 1985), T. Honderich, *A Theory of Determinism* (Oxford, Clarendon Press, 1988), P. van Inwagen, *An Essay on Free Will* (Oxford, Clarendon Press, 1985), Anthony Kenny, *Freewill and Responsibility* (London, Routledge, 1978), Anthony Kenny, *Will, Freedom and Power* (Oxford, Basil Blackwell, 1975), and J.R. Lucas, *The Freedom of the Will* (Oxford, Clarendon Press, 1970).

9. *What constitutes the identity of a person?*

▬▬▬

(*Treatise* Book 1, Part IV, Section VI; Appendix, pp. 633–6)

This topic is distinctive for being one of the few topics that has a place only in the *Treatise* and not in the *Enquiry*. In common with his treatment of the concept of belief, discussed in Chapter 7 above, it is a topic about which Hume had reservations. These are expressed, as in the case of belief, in the Appendix to the *Treatise*. In the case of personal identity, however, the reservations are stronger and amount almost to a confession of failure. The particular problem that besets him and to which he returns in the Appendix, is described as 'too hard for my understanding' and is thence abandoned (*T.*, p. 636). We shall spell out Hume's particular worry during the course of the present chapter. Suffice to say at this point that his worry may have been strong enough to explain the exclusion of the topic from the later work.

Like the discussion of belief in the external world, the topic arises as yet one more question about which the philosopher should retain some scepticism. As we saw in Chapter 7 above, although we have a natural and irresistible belief in the existence of external objects, Hume maintains that there can be no philosophical foundation for it. He takes the same general attitude towards the question of personal identity. We have an equally natural and irresistible belief in the abiding existence of persons over a period of time. We believe that some person, X, is the same person now as he was ten years ago, and we believe of ourselves that we have existed, continuously the same person, over any specified period of time. Hume ignores the possibility that this belief may be due to the relatively unchanging physical appearance that we all retain. Instead, he holds that personhood, and the identity of persons, must somehow relate to the life of the mind. Many philosophers would have us hold that there exists an abiding 'soul' or inner spiritual substance that is the subject of all our mental states. Part of Hume's purpose in the section as a whole is to point out that, although philosophers have claimed that we are at all times intimately conscious of this soul or self, there is in fact no empirical evidence for its existence. Nevertheless, he acknowledges that there is something that we *call* the idea of the self, and that we have an idea of abiding selves. The remaining part of his purpose is to show how this can be possible, granted his own philosophical principles.

In more detail, the problem arises in this way. According to the doctrine of impressions and ideas, I can only come to have a coherent idea of something that has been preceded by an impression. This dictates that if I am to have a coherent idea of the self, there must also be an impression of it. But, as Hume is eager to show, there seems to be no such impression. If we perform the piece of introspection required in order to find it, we simply stumble upon various particular mental experiences, but not on the self or soul that is said to stand behind them (*T.*, p. 252). I might recognise, by this method, for example, that I have just been remembering something, or imagining something, or again that I have just been watching something or listening to something. But I have no comparable impression of the self that is supposed to have been doing these things.

The idea of the self is not only empirically excluded by reference to the impressions and ideas doctrine. It is also excluded by reference to another of Hume's philosophical corner-stones. It is one of Hume's basic tenets, as we saw when discussing his account of causality in Chapter 4, that no one object or event ever intrinsically implies another. The existence of any one thing is entirely self-contained: there is nothing contained in its nature that necessarily implies the existence of any other thing. Of course the mind automatically associates one thing with another. Life itself could not proceed if this were not the case. But there is nothing intrinsic to an object or event considered in itself that implies a necessary connection between it and something else. The principle had already been used by Hume in order to show that the physical properties of an object do not demand that they inhere in a subject or substance. Hume wishes to reiterate the same claim here. Nothing about the nature of the perceptions or experiences that 'pass before the mind' can in itself dictate that there must be a soul or self standing behind them.

This all conspires to suggest that the idea of a self that unites all particular perceptions and makes them mine is some sort of 'fiction', to use Hume's own word (*T.*, p. 259). As far as the character of our experience goes, all we are entitled to talk about is a 'bundle' or collection of perceptions. We are, each one of us, a bundle or collection of this kind. Hume's theory of personal identity has been nicknamed the 'bundle theory' ever since. A recent book refers to the theory as 'Hume'n Bundles'.[1] However, Hume's task does not end there. We have seen how he regards the identity we ascribe to persons as being a 'fiction'. The individual perceptions themselves are not intrinsically connected and are, in any case, interrupted by sleep or periods of unconsciousness; and there is no evidence for the existence of a unifying substance lying behind them. His problem, then, is to explain how it is that we come to create such a 'fiction'.

Creating the Fiction

Hume warns the reader that, in order to give an explanation of how we ascribe identity to people where, strictly, there is none, he will have to 'take the matter pretty deep' (*T*., p. 253). In fact, his approach is quite simple. He claims that we create a similar fiction in dealing with objects in the physical world. Therefore, what we must do is to examine the psychological factors involved there in order to see more clearly what is going on in the case of persons and their perceptions. Essentially what Hume wants to say about our perception of many of the objects in the physical world is that, by means of various 'devices', the imagination is able to construe diversity as identity. One might put it by saying that our imagination is able to disguise or conceal from us the recognisable fact that, in many cases, our experience actually consists of a number of isolated and unconnected perceptions. Because of this, we may come to see a certain series of events as being continuous when in fact it is not.

The next move must be to identify some of the means by which the imagination is able to perform the 'trick' in the case of physical objects. In some cases, Hume tells us, the matter is quite simple. The actual change that has taken place may be so small and insignificant that we fail to notice it. Even if we recognise that some small change has in fact taken place, the predominant character of our experience may remain so intact that we continue to regard it as the same entity. As Hume puts it, there is an easy and smooth 'passage of the thought' in such cases, from the perception of the object as it was before the change to the perception of it after the change (*T*., p. 256).

Sometimes, it is the gradualness of a change that causes us to go on calling something the same when in fact it is different. This may be even in those cases in which the change is quite considerable. A heavily used desk, for example, may, over a period of years, have its top replaced, its drawers replaced, and its legs replaced. So long as we ourselves witness these changes, we shall generally be quite happy about calling it the same desk. If we were suddenly confronted with the complete series of changes all at once, the case would be quite different – we would, on the contrary, feel that it was a completely new desk.

Hume also refers to a phenomenon that is something akin to what John Locke called the identity of organisation.[2] Here, what is important to our continuing to call something the same thing is its general configuration of parts, relating to one another in various ways and/or serving some common purpose. One of Hume's examples is that of a ship, most of the parts of which may be replaced during the course of its life, yet we all the while regard it as the same ship, because the various parts remain organised in the same way (*T.*, p. 257). In the case of animals and vegetables also, we may ascribe a continuing identity even though every constituent part has been replaced.

Occasionally, we take an example of qualitative identity to be a case of numerical identity, as when a sound that is regularly interrupted is nevertheless regarded as the same sound. Hume points out that, strictly speaking, when a sound is interrupted we have two or more separate sounds, but that we often regard them as constituting a single continuing sound; we do this, for example, if the distinct sounds are generated by the same cause (*T.*, p. 258).

These, then, are some of the means by which the imagination makes identity out of diversity. Hume describes such identity as a fiction because, in each case, we are not presented with one continuously existing thing, the same thing both at time t1 and at time t2. We are, therefore, not strictly entitled to talk about one and the same thing existing through a period of time. His next move must be to see how a similar fiction is generated in the case of the identity of persons. How does diversity get converted into identity in this sphere? In particular, what is it that allows us to see a series of disparate perceptions as one continuous series, constituting one person?

Hume's immediate response is to refer us to the principles of association we first encountered in Chapter 3. These are causality, contiguity in time and place, and resemblance. These were, it will be remembered, the principles that explained how ideas associate in the mind. Two of these principles are singled out as being relevant in the present context. These are causality and resemblance. To take resemblance to begin with, it is often by virtue of the fact that one perception or mental content is similar to another that one invokes the other. Upon the occurrence of some mental content, X, the mind is automatically transported to Y, to which X bears a resemblance. In a more general form the phenomenon regularly occurs. Thinking about my Aunt Matilda tends to make me think about Margaret Thatcher, because of their similar appearance. On a psychological level, then, this is one thing that helps to produce a smooth transition in the mind from one perception to another.

But it is also a part of Hume's thesis, not readily grasped, that the amount of resemblance between perceptions in the general bundle is actually increased by the activity of remembering the perceptions. His claim is that memory not only observes or discovers the resemblances that are already there; it also *produces* the relation of resemblance between perceptions (*T*., p. 261). To remember something, for Hume, is to have an image or a series of images. Since the image is, in this case, a copy of something that has already been present to the mind, the relation of resemblance between two or more perceptions necessarily obtains on every occasion that one remembers something. One might say, then, that similarity between perceptions is rendered more widespread by the faculty of memory. Memory thus helps, substantially, to facilitate the easy transition of the mind along a line of perceptions.

The other principle of association, causality, is given a rather more specific role in Hume's explanation. In addition to explaining how one perception arises causally from another, owing to the number of occasions on which they have been conjoined in the past, it also helps to 'plug the gaps'. As Hume points out (*T*., p. 262), it is obvious that there are many things from our past that we simply do not remember. We are all happy to concede that there are gaps in our memory. Yet we regard ourselves as having continued as the same individuals through these gaps. The present claim is that it is the causal principle that helps us to bridge the gaps. Suppose, for example, that I have a distinct recollection of composing a paper well in advance of a conference at which I was due to deliver it; but that I have no recollection at all of my activities during the intervening period. What Hume is telling us is that the mind is enabled to make the jump from one episode to the other by virtue of the causal link that obtains between them. There is therefore a smooth transition from the one perception to the other such that there is nothing to inhibit my tendency to regard myself as the one continuing person.

The key features, then, in Hume's account of the 'fictitious' idea of personal identity are memory, resemblance and causality. Memory is, of course, required as the means by which there can be any awareness at all of a series of perceptions over time. But it is enabled to make its journey along a smooth and continuous line by means of the relations of resemblance and causality. In addition, it actually contributes to the idea of identity by creating resemblance between perceptions. It must be stressed, once more, that Hume's reason for regarding the identity involved as 'fictitious' is that there are no necessary connections between the perceptions in themselves. The continuity is something that is attributed to them by the mind. We saw Hume making a comparable point when discussing the nature of the causal connection. We tend to think that necessary connections exist between the things we call causes and the things we call effects. Strictly speaking, however, this is not the case. The connections are psychological and exist in the mind only. In one sense, Hume is saying that the identity we ascribe to the sequence of our perceptions also exists only in the mind. That is to say, the identity is not intrinsic to the sequence of our perceptions, but arises from our reflection on these perceptions.

The Criticisms
There have been a number of criticisms of Hume's account of personal identity, some of the more prominent of which we must now try to collect together. Perhaps the most fundamental charge against his analysis is that, in the end, he seems to presuppose the very entity whose existence he had originally denied. He has told us, very forcibly, that introspection will not yield for us the impression of a soul or self lying behind our various perceptions. Therefore, it makes no sense to say that it exists and that our perceptions are the perceptions of one person by virtue of their relation to this one abiding entity.

He seems, however, to have presupposed what he has denied because his explanation of how we come to think our successive perceptions constitute a single entity in the absence of a soul or self depends heavily upon the idea of a *subject of experience*. To see the force of this charge, one must emphasise, once more, that, according to Hume, in attributing identity we are creating a fiction. That in turn means that we are making a mistake. We are taking something to be what it is not. But that seems to require that the series of perceptions concerning which a mistake is being made are 'presented' to a somebody or a something. To put the point rhetorically, who is it that is making the mistake? Who is it who is imposing identity on a series of perceptions when, strictly, there is no identity there? It is held, then, that some sort of subject is required in order to make Hume's explanation intelligible and that, whether Hume fully recognised it or not, his reasoning actually presupposes it.

The charge against Hume is slightly Cartesian in character, since Descartes had argued that if one can doubt one is thereby committed to the existence of a 'doubter'. However, while the criticism is certainly Cartesian in character, one must be careful not to exaggerate the implications for Hume's position. It is not the case that Hume is straight off necessarily committed to the existence of some inner soul or self. However, the onus would be upon him to respond to the more general charge that his explanation seems to require the concept of a subject. He would need to provide an explanation of how it is that there can be a 'presentation' of perceptions, mistakenly conceived, in a context where it is claimed that only perceptions themselves exist: for to whom or to what are these perceptions presented? Whether or not such an explanation is possible, Hume certainly does not attempt it.

Others have attempted it for him. The most natural move on his behalf, for example, is to say that the act of construing one's perceptions as having identity in the required sense is itself one more perception in the series. It constitutes one more addition to the 'bundle'. F. H. Bradley put the following question to a philosopher called Bain, who held a 'bundle' view of the self: 'Mr Bain thinks the mind is a collection. Has Mr Bain reflected: who collects Mr Bain?'[3] Anthony Quinton has replied: 'The answer is that the later Mr Bain collects the earlier Mr Bain by recollecting him.'[4]

Unfortunately, this move cannot, in the last resort, be of assistance to Hume. It looks like a solution to the problem only if one thinks of such a perception, or 'recollection', as a little self-contained unit added to the general bundle and if one simply ignores the function it has to perform. Once one examines its function, it is immediately evident that the same problem emerges. A perception of the required kind would still have to take the form of a 'presentation' of perceptions to *someone*; and that 'someone' would still have to judge them to constitute an identity when in fact they are not. It remains a puzzle as to how Hume can eliminate the notion of a subject of experience that seems to be so strongly implied here.

In the light of this problem, one is irresistibly led to think that it is generated by the restricted psychology with which Hume is working. As we have seen, the impressions/ideas doctrine dictated that we can only have an intelligible idea of something of which we have already had an impression. We have no impression of a self or soul lying behind and uniting our perceptions. Therefore, it does not make sense to talk about such a thing. A little reflection, however suggests otherwise. A torch-beam will shine upon everything but the torch that lies behind it. Moreover, it is not at all surprising that the torch itself is not caught within the compass of the beam. Was it, perhaps, the straitjacket of impressions and ideas that prevented Hume from thinking this thought?[5]

Quite apart from the fact that Hume seems to be lumbered with the notion of a subject whether he likes it or not, there are other difficulties surrounding the psychological story that he tells. As we have seen, resemblance is one of the factors that helps us to create a fictitious identity linking our perceptions. It enables the mind to glide smoothly from one perception to another, failing to recognise that all perceptions are, in reality, perfectly distinct and separate. But it is left unclear as to exactly how resemblance performs that trick. The puzzle can be highlighted by taking a slightly closer look at the situation as Hume presents it to us. It is as though I must see myself as being confronted by a collection of perceptions and am then required to decide whether, collectively, they constitute a single bundle. Do they belong to *this* particular bundle, as opposed to some other? Now, according to Hume, the relation of resemblance holding between perceptions is partly what enables me to answer that question. But the mere fact that a number of items resemble each other will not in itself persuade us that they belong together in the same group or category, let alone that they constitute a single entity. The pianist Rubinstein was said to resemble Bertrand Russell, but no one would be tempted to suggest that they are parts of one single entity. My Oxford edition of Hume's *Treatise* resembles, from a distance, my copy of the *Concise Oxford Dictionary*, but this does not lead me to suppose that the two books are facets of one identical super-book. How, then, does resemblance play a part in the creating of a fictitious entity?

Of course it is possible to say that the respect in virtue of which all my perceptions resemble each other is just this: they are all perceptions had by *me*. But there is an important reason why this move cannot be made. Essentially, on this view, we should be saying that the collection of perceptions constitutes one bundle because each of the perceptions is mine. But that was not the thesis that Hume was putting forward. Hume's view was that, in ascribing any set of perceptions over time to myself I am engaged in a *fiction*. His aim is to isolate those factors which explain how we come to create this fiction. It would be wildly inconsistent to argue that what explains the fact that I associate a bundle of perceptions together and thus create the fiction that they are all mine is just the fact that they are all mine.

It is tempting to suppose that causality will do the trick that resemblance fails to do. Causality, it will be remembered, was the other factor to which Hume pointed in his explanation of how we come to attribute a fictitious identity to the series of our perceptions. Unfortunately, there are worries about this also. Certainly, if one thinks of a whole series of perceptions, A, B, C, D ... as being causally connected, that seems to bind them together in a bundle. The trouble however is that, for this purpose, it would have to be true of most, if not all, my experiences, that they were causally connected to each other; but a glance at human experience suggests that this is not the case. Some of our experiences are undoubtedly caused by those that have preceded them. My thought about the scar on my little finger will, for example, cause me to think about the accident which led to the scar. If I think about the bloody nose I once suffered at the age of eight, I shall be very likely to think of the boy who inflicted it. But, over a large area of human experience, such causal connections seem to be absent. A typical segment of human mental activity might proceed in the following way. I enter my office to find the sun shining through the window. This is followed by my hearing a knock at my colleague's door. Next, I notice a letter lying on the desk, but, before I can open it, I suddenly remember that the bicycle upon which I have just travelled to work needs to be locked, and so on. It is obvious that, if I later reflect upon this set of experiences, wondering whether they all belong to the same bundle, there are no relevant causal connections which will help me to put them together. Thus, the general picture of human experience is of a whole sea of perceptions, causally generated by all sorts of extraneous factors, but not systematically connected by any intrinsic causal relations. What intrinsic causal connections there are seem to be too sporadic to bear the weight Hume puts on them.

Even if there were to be the universal connections that are required for Hume's explanation, our very use of them would throw up a certain puzzle, granted Hume's previous analysis of causality. As we saw when discussing the topic of causality, above, we come to call something a cause only after experience of repeated cases of A being followed by B. If we now apply that main feature of Hume's account to the case of perceptions, it points to a consequence that may vitiate the very reason for referring to causal connections in the first place. The purpose of referring to causal connections was to show how the mind can construe diversity as identity. It was designed to show, at least partly, how it is that the mind can glide smoothly from one perception to another (quite different) perception, by virtue of the causal connection between them. A whole multitude of perceptions are thus brought together as one identifiable unit. But if Hume's account of causality requires us to observe regular connections between perceptions in order to talk of causes, then, by the very nature of the activity in which we would be engaged, a set of perceptions seems already to have been identified. If I am requested to trace the causal linkages that do or do not exist between the trucks of a railway train, I must already know which group of trucks I am expected to consider. Otherwise, the request could not make any sense. That point seems to be equally appropriate to Hume's perceptions. I can only trace out the causal connections there in so far as I can observe the regular conjunctions that are the basis for them. This seems to imply awareness of a cohesive set of perceptions before the whole process begins. One might put the point by saying that the causal connections in this case already presuppose the very identity they were intended to support. This is not to deny that the causal connections, once they are acknowledged, may strengthen the cohesiveness of the general bundle; but it is difficult to see how Hume can regard them as the *basis* (in conjunction with resemblance) upon which the bundle is construed as a single whole. Causal linkages may strengthen the unity of a group of railway trucks but, even in their absence, we still have an identifiable group of trucks.

It should now be clear that there are two questions at issue in this context which are quite separate and which Hume himself does not distinguish. The first question is: how is it possible for a bundle of experiences to be connected in such a way that we are led to suppose that the experiences belong to a single mind? The second question, however, is quite different. It is: what is it for some particular bundle to be *mine*, or *me*? It is one thing to conduct an enquiry into the way in which the mind organises a series of perceptions into a single bundle. This would be a psychological enquiry that might or might not make a reference to the kind of unifying factors mentioned by Hume, viz., resemblance and causality. It is another question altogether to ask whether that bundle, however united, constitutes *me* or some other person. It is clear that the answer to the first question is not in itself an answer to the second. No description of any particular bundle of experiences and of the connections between them will *entail* that the bundle thus described is *mine*, or *me*. It is a logical possibility that there exists someone else, having experiences which are qualitatively exactly similar to my own, and in consequence standing in exactly the same relations of causality and resemblance to each other. Perhaps he exists in a world which is just like this one, a place we can call Twin Earth.[6] He is my *Doppelgänger* on Twin Earth. He is not me, though he is exactly like me.

It is often seen as an additional criticism of Hume on identity that he makes no mention of physical characteristics as being possible criteria for deciding whether a person is the same person or not over a period of time. This is said to be unfortunate for two reasons. Firstly, his position is counter-intuitive: we do, as a matter of fact, identify people and identify them as being the same people over a period of time by reference to their physical features. Secondly, had he brought the body squarely into the picture, it could have provided the much-needed anchor-point for perceptions. After all, Hume claims that we cannot intelligibly talk about a non-physical subject, capable of uniting perceptions into one bundle. In that case, the body, with its relatively constant features would seem to be the next best thing for this purpose. We should then be saying that a group of perceptions belongs in bundle X by virtue of being experienced by body X. We must now try to assess the weight of this criticism and the way in which it is developed.

To begin with, it is certainly true that Hume does ignore the part played by the body in our judgements of identity. He takes it for granted that what we call a person is essentially composed of what we might call mental predicates. The person, as such, is the mind and the various experiences that it has; the body is to be construed as the shell that houses it. In its emphasis upon mental characteristics as making the person, the view is broadly Cartesian. Descartes had argued for the existence of a spiritual substance or ego:[7] Hume, as we have seen, explicitly denies the existence of such an entity. It is nevertheless true that he sees the person as being encased within the body.

Turning now to the claim that his position is counter-intuitive for the reasons mentioned above, it needs to be said that the claim is not obviously correct. As we saw, it is true that physical characteristics play a predominant role in our everyday judgements of identity. We tend to recognise people on the basis of their physical appearance. But then, this is probably because physical features are immediately apparent and accessible to us, in a way in which mental features are not. The continuity of the mental set-up – that is to say, abiding motives, intentions, interests, long-term goals, and sustained rememberings of things past – is something for which we need evidence. This evidence is normally gleaned from what a person reveals to us in conversation and is therefore more indirect than the palpable evidence of the physical appearance. On these grounds, many would hold that judgements based upon physical criteria are judgements of convenience and therefore provisional in character. Moreover, this view is thought to be confirmed by our standard reactions in situations of conflict. If we feel unsure about the identity of a person when confronted only by his physical appearance, we often regard a reference to mental criteria as clinching the matter. We take it that if the person concerned continues to have an intimate acquaintance with certain things from the past that are particularly associated with somebody called X, then he is that person X. What is more, the reverse is not the case. That is, we do not, in general, appeal to physical features in order to correct or confirm what we have discovered on the basis of mental features. This is, indeed, the thought that had been so well expressed by Locke in the famous Prince and Cobbler example.[8] If we take the soul of a prince and instal it in the soul-less body of a cobbler, Locke takes it for granted that we shall regard the finished product as the Prince; and that is despite the fact that we shall continue to be confronted by the physical appearance of the cobbler. If Locke's insight is correct, then it is indeed the case that judgements of identity based upon the continuity of the body are to be regarded as interim judgements of convenience. They remain open to correction by reference to mental criteria. Of course there is not likely to be universal agreement about Locke's conclusion concerning the Prince and the Cobbler, nor with the more general view of the self which it represents. Nevertheless, the view is sufficiently widespread to inhibit the charge against Hume that his position is counter-intuitive.

As for the development of the charge against Hume that, by omitting a reference to bodily characteristics, he missed an opportunity to 'anchor' a collection of perceptions in one bundle, this too may turn out to be abortive. It surely suffers the same fate as the comparable attempt to unite perceptions in an inner spiritual substance. In order to see why this is so, one must bear in mind once more the two distinct questions we separated above. It is one thing to enquire whether a collection of perceptions constitutes one single whole: it is another thing to enquire whether that whole is me as opposed to some other person. It is the latter question that is central to discussions of personal identity. Now if our concern is merely to know whether a whole cluster of disparate experiences belongs in one bundle, then their being associated with one specific body is at least one very good reason for regarding them as such. This would give us a unified bundle. But if the claim is that some particular bundle is mine because all the individual members of it are experienced by *my* body then the answer to the question of personal identity seems to have been presupposed rather than provided by this move. The fact that the cluster of perceptions belongs to this body will only show them to be mine if I already *know that this body is mine*. I would thereby be operating with an identity claim in the very process of trying to establish identity. What is more, if I can know that this body is mine, by whatever means, presumably by the same token I can immediately know that any particular perception is mine: I would not need to relate it to my body in order to resolve the issue. Indeed, this latter thought is more in keeping with the way in which we normally think about these matters. In a collapsed rugby scrum, I might conceivably establish that some particular leg sticking out from the pile of bodies is mine by confirming that when I pinch it I feel the pinch. But it would be utterly bizarre to suggest that I might seek to establish that the pinching sensation was mine by confirming that it was indeed located in a part of my body. Yet that is what the suggestion under examination would seem to imply. I would be expected to *infer* that a perception was mine from the fact that it was experienced by my body.

We must now sum up our thoughts on this particular criticism of Hume. The original criticism stated that Hume had ignored physical criteria in his discussion of personal identity. The result of this is (a) that his position becomes counter-intuitive and (b) that he is robbed of an opportunity to use the body as the unifying subject of experiences. In response, we agreed that Hume does indeed inherit the broadly Cartesian picture of the self as being something other than the physical. However, we then argued that this view is not necessarily counter-intuitive and that, on the contrary, it actually harmonises with many of our more reflective thoughts on personal identity. Finally, we argued that, even if Hume had brought physical criteria more centrally into the picture, such a move could not have performed the function required of it without actually presupposing the very sense of identity it was intended to establish.

Finally, we must record a certain puzzle that is thrown up by Hume's general treatment of personal identity. It is a puzzle which some commentators have seen as a possible source of Hume's own reservations about the topic in the Appendix to the *Treatise* (pp. 633–6). We can articulate the puzzlement if we reflect back upon the way in which Hume construes the main problem as he sees it. That problem is that, once we have disposed of an inner self to function as a unifying thread, we seem to be left with a succession of discrete perceptions, constantly changing. According to Hume, this is the very opposite of what we mean by identity or sameness. Indeed, 'to an accurate view', he says, this presents us with a 'perfect ... notion of diversity' (*T.*, p. 253). Thus the problem is as we portrayed it earlier, essentially a psychological one. We do, as a matter of fact, regard ourselves as, in some sense, unchanging – that is, retaining an identity over time. How is this possible, granted we are in fact confronted by diversity? In short, Hume takes the view that we somehow manage to disguise the diversity from ourselves and that we deceive ourselves into thinking that we do, after all, have identity. We construe diversity as identity. The puzzle is this: why does Hume suppose that a succession of perceptions constitutes an example of diversity? The question is important, because it is only by virtue of making this assumption that Hume finds himself faced with the psychological task we have just outlined. If we can in fact show that the assumption is unwarranted, this will be a major criticism of the way in which Hume proceeds in his discussion of identity in the *Treatise*.

The key assumption here, then, is that a succession of perceptions is an example of diversity. We must now try to say, more positively, why the assumption may be ungrounded. It is mainly because he seems to be operating with a concept of sameness that strictly excludes change. Some things do remain the same in precisely that respect. The book that now lies before me on my desk would be the same as the one that lay there yesterday if it retained all the same qualities it had yesterday. But what is important is that we also have a concept of sameness that allows for or accommodates quite radical differences. The collection of books that constitutes a library is a case in point. The books may be constantly changing, and the collection itself may expand or contract, but, for most general purposes, we regard it as being essentially the same library over a period of time. What is more, when we describe it as being the same over a specified period, and thus ascribe identity to it, we do not regard ourselves as creating a fiction or as being deceived about anything. We explicitly acknowledge that the books are constantly changing and that, in that sense, we have diversity. Far from diversity being incompatible with the identity claim, such that it requires a kind of subterfuge on our part, one wants to say just the opposite. A reference to diversity is actually *required* in order to say what we mean, in this context, by the identity claim.

Precisely the same comment would seem to apply to the collection of perceptions that, according to Hume, constitutes a person. At the very least it would seem that unchangedness, in any strict sense, is simply not required in order for the collection to retain its identity. Why, then, did Hume think that it *was* required? In a sense, the difficulty is more acute in the case of perceptions than it is elsewhere. This can be brought out by asking what it would be like for the requirement to be fulfilled. What would it be like for perceptions to remain unchanged? When Hume actually defines identity for us, he says that it is the idea of an object 'that remains invariable and uninterrupted through a supposed variation of time' (*T.*, p. 253). In what sense can a bundle of perceptions satisfy this criterion? Of course any specific perception may remain unchanged in some sense, in that I see no intrinsic difference in it on the various occasions on which I remember it; but that is a different matter. The series of perceptions as a whole can hardly be regarded as some single thing, remaining invariable and uninterrupted. One perception gives way to another in the normal run of mental events and, almost always, the one perception is different from the other. Even a sustained sensory experience of a single object may change so radically that we cease to regard it as a single perception. To repeat the basic question, then, what sense can we possibly give to the view that a bundle of perceptions might have the kind of identity about which Hume talks?

These considerations surely support the view that we quite openly recognise diversity for what it is. It is not the case that we try to disguise it from ourselves and construe it as a case of identity when it is not. Rather, the diversity is incorporated into the concept of identity with which we are operating in this context. As a consequence of this, Hume should have seen the two 'devices' – resemblance and causality – not as contributing to a subterfuge but as reinforcing a genuine identity claim. It is not the kind of identity he had in mind but it is identity just the same. Of course, resemblance and causality may not be the effective linking factors Hume took them to be, as we suggested above, but in so far as they are such factors, they would be at least some of the grounds for our sense of identity.

It is evident, then, that there are considerable difficulties associated with Hume's account of personal identity, and it is not surprising that he himself should come to express misgivings about it in the Appendix. The precise nature of his reservations is not known and one can only speculate about them. One plausible view is that he regretted the standpoint to which his impressions/ideas doctrine committed him. No impression of the self as an underlying substance was forthcoming and, therefore, he was obliged to say that there existed no such entity. This, in conjunction with his deliberate omission of a reference to bodily criteria for identity, was bound to leave him in a very peculiar position, at least at an intuitive level. Indeed, the peculiarity of his position was, as we saw, accentuated by his subsequent attempt to make his view acceptable in the absence of an inner self. It resulted in his presupposing the very notion of a subject of experiences he had been so concerned to deny.

Nevertheless, having said this, there is also something to be said for Hume on the credit side. This can be brought out by means of the following considerations.

1. There is still, among contemporary philosophers, no universally accepted theory of personal identity.[9] Theorists vacillate between views that emphasise mental features and views that emphasise bodily features. More crucially, where Hume is concerned, they vacillate between views that posit an inner spiritual substance and those that do not. Granted that state of affairs, the fact that Hume did not produce an acceptable account does not, at least, stand out like a sore thumb.

2. He faced up squarely to the task of explaining how, in the absence of an inner, unifying self, we can come to see a continuity of mental events as constituting one single mental history. In the process, he delineated certain principles at work on the mental landscape: ideas associate by means of resemblance and causality. In the event, we saw that this was not sufficient to explain the general cohesiveness of the bundle of perceptions, but this should not detract from the very commendable character of Hume's scrutiny of what goes on in the mind.

3. There are many who would wish to commend Hume's faithful commitment to the original empiricist dictum, that is, to the impressions/ideas doctrine. The final outcome of such a commitment may well be judged unsatisfactory, as indeed we have suggested, but it did

mean that he felt obliged to ask an all-important question. Essentially, that question asks us whether we can ultimately make intelligible to ourselves the notion of an abiding spiritual entity that can function as the subject of experiences. The question is not alien, even to contemporary philosophers.

With the above review of the topic of personal identity, we have reached a minor turning point in the elucidation and discussion of Hume's thought. It is a turning point because we have been considering some of the more prominent topics in Hume's epistemological writings. Roughly, these have been the topics concerned centrally with the question of *how* we can come to know or believe certain things and *what* it is that we can legitimately know or believe. The freedom/determinism issue, as presented in Chapter 7 above, may seem to be anomalous in that respect since it seems to be more concerned with our status as human beings than with what we can know. Nevertheless, it *was* a natural follow-on from Hume's remarks on causality; and that latter topic is indeed intimately involved in questions about what we can know and how we can do so.

It is now time to turn to another dimension of human nature, as conceived by Hume, namely, the feeling part of us. This will occupy the following chapter.

Notes

1. See Peter Carruthers, *Introducing Persons*, p. 46 *ff.*
2. J. Locke, *Essay Concerning Human Understanding*, II, XXVII, 4.
3. F. H. Bradley, *Ethical Studies*, (Oxford, Clarendon Press, second edition, 1927), p. 39, fn. 1.
4. See Anthony Quinton, *The Nature of Things* (London, Routledge and Kegan Paul, 1973), p. 99.
5. For a further consideration of this issue, see N. Pike, 'Hume's bundle theory of the self: a limited defence', *American Philosophical Quarterly*, vol. 4, 1967. See also T. Penelhum, 'Hume on personal identity', *Philosophical Review*, vol. 64, 1955, reprinted in Chappell, *Hume*.
6. I am here adopting a suggestion first made by Hilary Putnam, in his paper 'The meaning of "meaning"'. See his *Mind, Language and Reality* (Cambridge, Cambridge University Press, 1975), p. 223.
7. 'Accordingly this "I" – that is, the soul by which I am what I am – is entirely distinct from the body ... and would not fail to be whatever it is even if the body did not exist.' R. Descartes, *Discourse on Method* (1638), Part Four, in *The Philosophical Writings of Descartes*, translated by J. Cottingham, R. Stoothoff and D. Murdoch (Cambridge, Cambridge University Press, 1985), vol. 1, p. 127.

8. J. Locke, *Essay*, II, XXVII, 15.
9. For a recent account of personal identity along Humean lines, see D. Parfit, *Reasons and Persons* (Oxford, Clarendon Press, 1984), Part Three. An anti-Humean view of personal identity can be found in G. Madell, *The Identity of the Self* (Edinburgh, Edinburgh University Press, 1981). Further contemporary discussions of personal identity are included in A. O. Rorty (ed.), *The Identities of Persons* (Berkeley, University of California Press, 1976), and S. Shoemaker and R. Swinburne, *Personal Identity* (Oxford, Basil Blackwell, 1984).

10. *How do emotions work?*

(*Treatise* Book 2, 'Of The Passions')

The character of human emotions is an intriguing topic in its own right, but it has a natural place in Hume's thought because it is one more aspect of what we call human nature, and that is what the *Treatise* is all about. Not only are we creatures that think: we also *feel* and this deserves some attention. Indeed, from one point of view, Hume would certainly hold that, in any attempt to understand how human nature functions, we need to begin by recognising the very fundamental role played by feelings. That is a thought to which we shall return when we come to discuss Hume's moral philosophy below.

Most of what Hume had to say about emotion is to be found in the second book of the *Treatise*. The same material, in a slightly modified form, was reproduced in a later work, entitled *A Dissertation of the Passions*. It is quite impossible to do justice to all aspects of Hume's thought in this area. We must content ourselves, in this chapter, with a consideration of some of his more prominent themes, together with an attempt to locate the more important insights he was able to contribute. We shall be concentrating, first, on some of the more general features of Hume's treatment of the passions, and then with four passions in particular to which he attaches a great deal of importance. These are love and hatred, pride and humility.

General Features of Hume's Account

1. Within Hume's psychological scheme, passions are to be regarded as impressions (*T*., p. 276). Broadly, the feeling part of us consists in the having of impressions and the thinking part of us consists in the having of ideas. However, it has to be remembered that the kind of impressions to which he is referring are not sense-impressions but, rather, impressions of reflection, by which he means secondary impressions (*T*., p. 275). The term 'secondary' is intended to convey that they are not primitive; they are dependent upon other impressions or ideas. An example will help us to see what is meant. Let us suppose that I witness one person physically striking another person. This will, according to Hume's scheme, constitute an original impression of sensation: I see it with my own eyes. But let us also suppose that it makes me annoyed or indignant to see it happening. It is this reaction

on my part, this secondary occurrence, that constitutes the particular kind of impression that Hume calls a passion. It is, in that sense, then, parasitic upon a previous idea; for I have to *think of* the situation if it is to produce the emotional reaction.

2. Hume divides the passions into two broad categories which he terms the calm and the violent (*T.*, p. 276). The latter class of emotions are, strangely enough, those for which, nowadays, we tend to reserve the term 'passion'. Hume is referring typically to the more powerfully-felt emotions such as love and hatred, grief and joy. The calm passions, so-called, are rather more difficult to delineate. The first reference to them, in Book II, gives as an example 'the sense of beauty and deformity in action, composition, and external objects' (*T.*, p. 276). A later reference, in Part III, Section III of Book II, tells us that they are 'either certain instincts originally implanted in our natures, such as benevolence and resentment, the love of life, and kindness to children; or the general appetite to good, and aversion to evil, considered merely as such' (T., p. 417). What Hume seems to have in mind is a definite but quietly felt emotion such as that which an antique-dealer experiences when confronted by a superb example of a Chippendale chair. One would describe the dealer as experiencing an informed appreciation of the object. He does not get worked up about it, but we would think it false to assert that he feels nothing. What he feels, then, would appear to comply with Hume's requirements for a 'calm passion'. We shall see, at a later point, how the distinction between the calm and the violent passions assumes a certain significance in his account of moral judgements. For the moment it is sufficient to record it.

3. Hume has the view that every emotion is a mental item that is both simple and unique (*T.*, p. 276, p. 329). This claim is important for two reasons. In the first place, it makes clear that Hume is not a reductionist in his treatment of the passions. That is to say, he does not think, as many contemporary philosophers would, that human emotions can be reduced to, or analysed out in terms of, physical states of the body or characteristic patterns of behaviour. Instead, he takes them to be specific internal sensations that are introspectively identifiable, though not analysable. In that respect, Hume's position conforms to the motto deployed by G. E. Moore in his book *Principia Ethica* – 'Everything is what it is, and not another thing' taken from Bishop Butler.[1]

Secondly the claim is important because it means that Hume's account of the passions necessarily has to be what we might call a causal one. If emotions are to be described as perfectly simple, this entails that they have no parts or aspects in terms of which they can be analysed. It therefore follows that any account Hume gives of them must be in terms of causal conditions or attendant circumstances. In the case of pride and humility, for example, Hume's procedure will be to point to the circumstances, both psychological and external, in which one can expect those passions to arise. Hume's position is thus precisely the same as that of G. E. Moore concerning the indefinability of certain simple qualities. Yellowness, for example, cannot be defined because it has no intrinsic qualities or characteristics in terms of which the defining can be done. On the other hand, a horse *can* be defined because it does have parts in the required sense.[2]

4. Finally, Hume's associationism has an important bearing upon his account of emotions. We saw, in Chapter 3 above that a great deal of human mental activity is to be explained on the basis of three principles of association. Ideas come to associate with one another as a result of the relations of resemblance, contiguity and causality. If one thing resembles another in our experience, for example, then the idea of the one, whenever it crops up in thought, tends to invoke the idea of the other. Hume wants to point out that emotions, that is to say, impressions, behave in a similar manner. The only difference is that, whereas ideas tend to associate by means of the three principles mentioned above, impressions associate only by way of resemblance. The claim being made, then, is that any given emotion can be brought into existence by virtue of its resemblance to another. We shall have cause to comment on this in more detail in due course.

Problems Arising from Hume's Account

It will be obvious from what has been said above that there are a number of quite distinctive claims involved in Hume's position: they give rise to some important questions. The reference to resemblance as a principle of association between impressions (emotions) immediately presents us with one query. If we put it alongside the earlier claim that every impression is perfectly simple, we shall be led to ask whether they are mutually compatible. It is plausible to claim that, if one thing resembles another, it can only do so by virtue of possessing a quality or qualities in common with the other. But if we say that something is perfectly simple, we seem to be saying that it has no qualities by virtue of which it can resemble something else. In the present case, then, how can Hume claim that emotions are perfectly simple and also claim that they can resemble one another? He surely cannot hold both of these propositions. Either passions resemble one another, or they are perfectly simple; but not both. A succinct way of putting the criticism is to say that resemblance requires complexity and is therefore incompatible with the perfect simplicity that is supposed to characterise Hume's passions.

Let us examine this criticism in more detail and try to determine how far it is justified. Whether or not Hume's two claims really are incompatible must partly depend upon what is entailed by a resemblance or similarity statement. As we have just seen, one view, the strong view, is that in order to make an intelligible resemblance claim, one has to be able to identify a quality or qualities that two or more things have in common. You cannot say that X resembles Y and then assert that there is nothing by virtue of which they resemble each other. John Passmore, for example, takes this view in his commentary on Hume.[3] He concedes that we sometimes *say* that one apparently simple thing resembles another apparently simple thing, but he holds that if we properly examine what is involved we shall find that they are not genuine cases of simplicity. Thus, a person might say, for example, that blue and green resemble each other more than, say, blue and scarlet. According to Passmore, such a person would be covertly treating these colours as complex. He is, ultimately, comparing the colours in respect of certain more particular qualities possessed by those colours. For example, he may be referring to such features as dullness or intensity, lightness or vividness, etc. Passmore therefore wishes to preserve the strong line that all resemblance statements entail complexity and are incompatible with simplicity.

A more accommodating line is taken by another of Hume's commentators, P. S. Ardal.[4] His position is that, while most resemblance statements make a reference to a common quality, it is not necessary that they do so. Ardal holds that it is perfectly intelligible to say 'They have nothing in common: they are just similar'. We are often inclined to say that, for example, green resembles blue but, he argues, it would surely be puzzling to be asked to name the quality that both colours have in common. Therefore, on this view, Hume is entitled to speak about passions resembling one another without presupposing complexity, and without running the risk of contradicting himself.

Ardal supports his case by referring us to the following thought. We sometimes pick out similarities between experiences that emanate from different sensory fields. For example, we can talk about a cold drink as well as a cold painting. The use of the word 'cold' to describe both of them surely indicates our perception of a resemblance between them; yet, according to Ardal, we would be hard-pressed to specify a feature that they both share. Indeed, it is his view that there *is* no feature that is identically present in each.

Passmore and Ardal, then, represent the two possible views of this issue. Either resemblance requires complexity, in which case one of Hume's two claims must be surrendered; or it does not require complexity, in which case both Humean claims may stand. Intuitively, one may feel that Passmore's position is the correct one. If the question 'In what respect do A and B resemble each other?' cannot be answered in principle, there does seem to be something suspect about the resemblance that is said to obtain between them. What is more, the example Ardal gives us in support of his view may not be conclusive. It is true that when we describe the painting as being cold, we do not mean that it is literally so. In particular, it does not actually possess the property of feeling or tasting cold in the way in which cold water does. In that precise respect, there are no actually shared properties. But of course this is only to show that the use of the word 'cold' to describe the painting is metaphorical, and all metaphorical uses of words depend, in order to be metaphorical, upon an imagined carry-over of properties. When we say that a person has sharp eyes, we do not mean that they cut like a sharp knife; but we do mean that, just as the sharp knife does not fail to cut whatever it is applied to, so the sharp eyes do not miss whatever appears before them. In that sense, there is a property, vaguely defined though it is, that both the knife and the eyes share. In the case under discussion, we would say something comparable. The painting is not cold to the feel or taste but, for example, what it depicts or the colours in which it is depicted may produce in us the kind of sensations we associate with cold water. Indeed, a painting can sometimes cause us to shiver!

Obviously, a great deal more could be said about the use of metaphor, and what has been said is necessarily sketchy. However, one might hope for agreement upon the general claim that any use of metaphor must depend on *some* continuity of meaning as between the metaphorical and the literal uses of a word. This does not mean that a property that is metaphorically ascribed to something may be an imagined, as opposed to an actual, one. Nevertheless, this does not show that the resemblance statement is not in some sense founded on common qualities. It may simply lead us to modify the position slightly. Thus, we might want to say that any resemblance claim requires that the person making it should in principle be able to specify a shared quality or qualities, even though what he specifies may not be objectively observable.

Enough has been said to show that there is an important issue at stake in this area and, as we have seen, it must raise a question about whether Hume can intelligibly hold both of the propositions mentioned above. Are the passions always perfectly simple in character and, if so, can they be said to associate by means of resemblance? Had Hume been compelled to surrender one of these claims, it is unlikely to have been the second. The relation of resemblance was just one example of the general phenomenon of association in the mental world, and it was a phenomenon that Hume prided himself on having discovered and identified. The significance Hume attached to it is highlighted by his being prepared to liken its influence to that of gravity in the physical world.

If compelled, it is more likely that he would have surrendered the first of the two claims, that is, that each passion is perfectly simple in character. Indeed, on independent grounds, there are very good reasons why he should have given it up. Doing so would have had no significant repercussions for the rest of his philosophy of mind. Besides, the claim is counter-intuitive. To put the point rhetorically, is there really anything simple about emotions like love and hatred, pride, humility, malice, resentment? What is more, Hume himself seems to have had reservations about the simplicity claim as his thought progressed in Book II. That is something we shall have cause to note in more detail at a later point.

We must now turn to some further reactions to Hume's account of the passions. One overall feature of that account is that Hume regards every emotion as being an internal, self-contained occurrence. This is evident, for example, when he begins to speak about pride and humility at Book II, Part I, Section II. The clear message is that pride and humility, like all other emotions, are internal sensations and that, where they are not present, a person cannot be said to be proud, humble, jealous, etc. The response we should now record is that this suggests a very limited account of emotions as we know them. There are two ways in which it is limited. Firstly, we often use the language of emotions when there is nothing that could constitute a mental item involved. This may be brought out by considering that, sometimes, a person has to be *told* that he is in love, or that he is jealous, or that he is proud. If these emotions necessarily consisted in the having of internal sensations, we would expect the agent to be the first to know about them and hardly in need of being told. As observers, our ascriptions of these states will be based upon the external behaviour displayed by the agent. Moreover, if the agent acknowledges the description as being appropriate, this is not necessarily because he looks into his mind and discovers the relevant sensation (like looking into the box and finding the beetle that is said to be there).[5] It is, often, because he too is able to discern the same pattern in his behaviour. The evidence that is cited by the spectator is often the very same evidence that is used by the agent himself to confirm the correctness of the description (c.f. 'Look here, old chap, can't you see – you're in love with her!').

Pride – one of the emotions that figures so extensively in Book II – is a case in point. We often wish to say of a person that he is proud of something even though he has no internal feelings that would constitute his pride. Consider the man who is said to be proud of his wife. The grounds for this description may be, for example, that he is always keen to be at his wife's side at all social gatherings, cocktail parties, etc.; that he is anxious that people should meet her; that he spends much time publicising her achievements or her beauty, and so on. And once again, this may also be the evidence upon which the man himself comes to acknowledge that he is indeed proud of her – despite the fact that he records no feelings that could constitute his pride.

One way of putting the general point against Hume is to say that, in one main respect, he still labours under the Cartesian model of mind. What this means is that, for Hume as well as for Descartes, passions are the kind of things we experience within ourselves.[6] They have their place entirely within a kind of mental abode. The limitation of this model can be brought out in the following way. Consider what we mean when we say that, for example, an aspirin is soluble, that a brick is hard, or again that music is sad or lettuce soporific. In the case of aspirin, for example, we do not mean to imply that solubility is something that is *contained* in the aspirin. Even if we were to take the aspirin apart and examine it under a microscope, the solubility would not thereby be revealed to us. To say that it is soluble is to refer to the way in which it can be expected to behave in certain specified circumstances, in this case when placed in water. Many contemporary philosophers would argue that we should treat emotions in just the same way. The microscope will not reveal some distinctive thing called solubility to us, and introspection will not reveal some distinctive thing called pride, or love, or jealousy. To ascribe such emotions to people is, like ascribing solubility, to talk of certain characteristic forms of behaviour.[7] We are not obliged to accept this analysis of emotions as against Hume's. In all probability, it goes too far in the opposite direction.[8] Nevertheless, it helps us to see that, at least in the case of some feelings, it seems inadequate to characterise them as events that are entirely internal or mental.

There is a second respect in which Hume's account is limited when he stresses that emotions are internal occurrences. It is not just that they are internal in the way in which we have just discussed; Hume also wishes to say that, as internal events, they are single, introspectable items. This is in fact the spelling out of the simplicity claim we considered earlier. His position is made very clear, for example, in Book II, Part II, Section I (*T.*, p. 329). He says "Tis impossible to give any definitions of the passions of love and hatred; and that because they produce merely a simple impression, without any mixture or composition'. All passions are 'simple impressions' in this sense. It may seem as though Hume is actually contradicting this claim in Part II, Section VI, when he speaks of passions as being 'susceptible of an entire union' (*T.*, p. 366), but in fact this is not the case. The kind of union he is talking about is likened to the blending of colours. Colours can blend or mix, but the end-result is still one colour. In that sense we would still have simplicity and not complexity. There would be no separately identifiable elements in the whole.

Now the question we have to ask ourselves is whether it can make sense to suppose that an emotion can be a simple, introspectible item in this way. Consider what might typically be involved on a psychological level in being jealous of somebody – say the husband who is jealous of his wife's lover. It seem very unlikely that one could tell any simple story about his mental state. Could the husband really be expected to point to one, single, discrete sensation and say 'That's my jealousy'? It seems hardly plausible to suppose that he could. Characteristically, the husband's jealousy will consist in his thinking of or picturing the object of his jealousy in certain ways. He constantly pictures his wife's lover in his mind; he imagines situations in which his rival is made to suffer; he thinks about the qualities in his rival to which his wife is obviously attracted and fondly wishes that he himself possessed such qualities, and so on. We would expect to tell a similar

kind of story about most emotions and, if this is the case, to repeat the
point, one really must consider in what sense Hume's claim can be
made intelligible.

It is possible that, in making this claim, Hume is influenced by the
way in which we traditionally think of pains and pleasures. Thus,
when a physical pain is registered in consciousness, there is at least a
sense in which it is one simple thing, without parts or aspects, and
quite indefinable. But the onus would then be on Hume to show that
emotions are like this. On the face of it, they are not.

There is a further difficulty that stems from Hume's general claim
that emotions are internal self-contained items of experience. We have
already made the point that, on many occasions, there is no such
mental item to be found and that the emotion would consist in certain
specified forms of behaviour. It was remarked that the agent himself
may come to be persuaded about his state from such a reference to his
behaviour and indeed deny that he had felt any inner feelings. What
we must now add to this comment is that, even on those occasions
when it is agreed that a person did have certain inner feelings, it is not
clear that the activity of identifying them can be done entirely on an
internal level. Hume would have us believe that we simply have to look
into ourselves in order to identify the feelings we experience. What he
fails to see is that many of our emotions bear an intimate relation to
the circumstances in which they occur.[9] That they sometimes bear
such intimate relation to the circumstances suggests, in its turn, that
there will be occasions on which the circumstances actually dictate the
identity of the emotion. The act of looking into one's own mind might
turn out to be a futile gesture.

The point comes out most clearly if one dwells on those emotions
that are qualitatively very similar. Love and admiration would be a
case in point, as well as anger and indignation, jealousy and malice, and
pride and joy. In these cases, it is not easy to discern a qualitative
introspectible difference. How does pride differ from joy? If one has
to answer this question purely on the intrinsic character of the feeling,
this could present a problem. A reference to the circumstances, on the
other hand, could clinch this issue. Whether what I am feeling is anger
as opposed to indignation, for example, will depend crucially upon
whether there is some aspect of my situation which can be seen as a
challenge or an affront to my dignity. I can be angry with many things
and for many sorts of reasons, but I can only feel indignation under
those more special circumstances. Therefore, to repeat the general

point being made, external circumstances may often dictate the precise character of an emotion. The introspectible qualitative difference that Hume's thesis requires may simply not be there. There is some evidence that Hume himself began to recognise this fact, and we shall come to this in due course.

It was mentioned earlier that many of Hume's assumptions about the passions are Cartesian, but there is one significant respect in which Hume departs from the Cartesian picture. He begins to see that it is part of the logic of passions that they are necessarily *about* something. The modern way to express this point is to say that passions are 'intentional' in character. That is to say, they represent something; they point beyond themselves in a way in which pains, for example, do not. A pain is simply a pain; it has a source and it can be causally explained, but it is not intrinsically *about* anything. Emotions have a source and can be causally explained, but they are also *about* something. Hume, then, did recognise this fact more clearly than Descartes.[10] This is particularly evident when he begins to discuss two of the prominent passions with which he is concerned, namely, pride and humility. In that passage, he says: 'We must, therefore, make a distinction betwixt the cause and the object of these passions; betwixt that idea, which excites them, and that to which they direct their view, when excited' (*T.*, p. 278). What is important about this quotation is its recognition of there being something 'to which they direct their view'. It would seem as though Hume is capturing the notion of 'intentionality' and bringing it into the open.

However, having noticed this promising departure from the Cartesian model, one also has to record a peculiar characteristic of the picture as Hume gives it to us. Hume sees the relation between an emotion and the object of that emotion as being purely contingent.[11] This statement needs careful explaining. There is one sense in which the relation between an emotion and its object is certainly contingent. Thus, for example, it is a contingent fact that I am jealous of X rather than Y, or X's qualities rather than Y's qualities. Again, it is a contingent fact that I feel shame about the dilapidated state of my house rather than about the fact that my car is an 'old banger'. However, what is not contingent is that I can only feel jealous of a person who seems to me to have the kind of qualities or possessions I should like to have myself, or regret not having myself. And it is not a contingent fact, but a necessity that I can feel shame only about something for which I feel responsible. One way of putting the general point is to say that emotions are internally related to the objects at which they are directed. It can also be expressed by saying that every emotion is governed by a certain kind of logic, such that not just anything can be its object.

Hume's treatment of pride illustrates the point being made. In Part I, Section III of Book 2, for example, Hume clearly acknowledges that pride is a passion that turns its attention to the self. The self is its ultimate object. But, though he thinks that this is regularly and psychologically the case, he clearly does not think that it is *logically* the case. His own words on the matter are significant: "'Tis evident ... that these passions are determined to have self for their *object*, not only by a natural but also by an original property. No one can doubt but this property is *natural* from the constancy and steadiness of its operations'(*T*., p. 280). In other words, Hume is maintaining that the association between pride and its object is established inductively. It is something we discover from regular experience, just as we discover that, if we cut our hand, the blood will stream out. What we must surely urge against Hume's position is that the reference to the self in the analysis of pride is something that is established deductively. It is part of what is involved in the very concept of pride. Essentially the same point is made by Philippa Foot in recent literature.[12] The view is that one cannot be proud of just anything. What one is proud of has to bear some relation to the self; otherwise, the claim cannot make sense. A man cannot say that he is proud of the sea, for example, unless, in his insanity, he thinks that *he* made it, or was in some other way responsible for it. To repeat our general point, then, while Hume certainly saw, more clearly than Descartes, that emotions are intentional in character, his account was nevertheless limited in another respect: he failed to grasp the internal, logical relation between an emotion and an object.

Pride and humility – the psychological details

Having listed and assessed some of the general features of Hume's account of the passions, we must now briefly turn our attention to four passions with which Hume was especially concerned. As we saw above, these are pride and humility, love and hatred. Hume never makes it absolutely clear why it is that he singles out these four in particular, but one may speculate. Firstly, he obviously thought that they occupy a very central position in any attempt to understand how human nature ticks. There is, indeed, no doubt that much of what we do is motivated by these emotions. Secondly, as Ardal points out in his commentary on Hume, there is strong evidence for supposing that Hume saw them as essential to our moral judgements.[13] The view is that the making of a moral judgement is essentially the expression of one or other of these four emotions. We shall discuss this in more detail in the chapter on morality, below.

What we have from Hume in the sections devoted to these emotions is an elaborate analysis of what happens, on a psychological level, in the generation of them. There is a tendency, these days, to dismiss the details of Hume's analysis on the ground that it has only curiosity value, its psychology being outdated. It must be agreed that this is partly true. We shall provide a brief sketch of it here for two reasons. Despite the fact that it is couched in the terminology of impressions and ideas, and sounds rather arid and mechanical, it nevertheless reveals just how much painstaking attention Hume gave to the subject. And there are insights involved, once they are properly translated into our terminology. In addition, the explanation gives us a very clear picture of the way in which Hume deploys the famous principles of association to which we referred earlier. It becomes abundantly clear why Hume should be led to describe the influence of these principles as being akin to gravity in the physical world (*T.*, pp. 12–13).

Hume deals with the first of the two pairs of passions listed, namely, pride and humility, in Book 2, Part I, Section II–V (T., pp. 279–90). In order for pride to be generated in me, there has to be an object (in the broad sense of 'object') at which the emotion can be directed. That object has to possess qualities that are a source of pleasure not just to me but to others also. Further, the object and/or its qualities must bear some relation to me. In relation to a specific example, let us suppose that the object at which my pride is directed is a house. In that case, the house must possess qualities that are a source of pleasure to me and to others. For example, it might be beautiful, or architecturally special, or spacious. It may fulfil the requirement of being closely related to me by virtue of being mine, or, again, by virtue of having been designed by me, etc. Once all these factors are in place, one might say that the scene has been set up. We must now see what ensues on the psychological level.

1. I notice that something I own, or is in some other way closely related to me, is a source of pleasure. That it is a source of pleasure may be reinforced for me by my hearing other people remark upon it.

Hence, thinking about my beautiful house, shall we say, gives me pleasure.

2. The thought of this cause of pleasure – my house – quite naturally associates with the thought of myself. That is to say, I cannot think of my house without also thinking of myself, simply because it is *my* house. This constitutes one of the associations at work in Hume's scheme; in this case it is an association between two ideas, as opposed to impressions. The associative principle at work is causality: the thought of the house *causes* the thought of myself.

3. In addition, the impression of pleasure, originally derived from the cause (that is, the house) when I see it as a thing of value, becomes associated with the passion of pride itself, simply because the two passions are similar. Pride, after all, is a pleasant sensation. Here, the second association is in evidence, this time between the two impressions. There is thus, according to Hume's scheme, a double association, one between ideas and the other between impressions. Together, they give rise to pride.

The analysis sounds a little mechanical, but there is every reason to suppose that Hume intended it to be so, bearing in mind his analogy with gravity in the physical world. Indeed, what plausibility the scheme has is best expressed in mechanical terms. Thus, we might say that the idea of the house is constantly 'pushing' towards the self (which is a natural accompaniment of pride on all occasions for Hume). Correspondingly, the pleasurable sensation derived from thinking about the house is constantly 'pushing' towards the pleasurable sensation of pride itself. Two forces combine, as it were, to generate pride.

In the light of this analysis, there are two main responses worth recording. To begin with, of course, it must be acknowledged that Hume is operating with an antiquated psychological apparatus, and it might seem unfair to criticise him from the point of view of modern psychology. Nevertheless, even within the terms of his own psychology, there is a particular query. To put the question very succinctly, if it is merely resemblance that accounts for how the original sensation of pleasure gives rise to the pleasurable sensation of pride, then why should it give rise to pride in particular? Presumably, pleasure also resembles other kinds of pleasurable sensation, for example, gratitude, contentment, relief, love, and many others. Now it is possible that Hume's answer to this question would be that, nevertheless, in these particular circumstances, where the valuable house, for example, belongs to *me*, it is pride that will emerge. But to say this would have strange implications, granted Hume's own assumptions. It would suggest that pride is aided and abetted by the idea of the self (which is provoked by the thought of the house); that the act of turning attention to the self in some way assists in the emergence of pride. Yet he ought, on his own premises, to be precluded from saying this. As we saw above, he had already clearly implied that pride is a perfectly simple, unique, unanalysable sensation which can be located or identified introspectively. The idea of the self is only contingently related to this, and it is something that follows only when pride, as a sensation, is already there. This being the case, Hume seems to be putting the cart before the horse in terms of his own thesis. How can the idea of the self (provoked by the thought of the house) help to generate pride if the idea of the self normally only comes about once pride is already in existence? All of this suggests that the model lacks the explanatory force it was intended to have.

The other response in criticism of Hume's explanatory model concerns the role played in it by the idea of the self. Hume has frequently been taken to task for uncritically employing this idea when, according to the official line adopted in Book 1 of the *Treatise*, we cannot intelligibly talk about such an idea.[14] As we saw in Chapter 9 above, Hume claimed in Book I, Part IV, Section VI, that there could be no impression of the self. It therefore follows from the impression/ideas doctrine that there can be no idea either. How, then, can he be permitted to talk so freely about the idea of the self in the present context? The criticism seems to be all the more acute since the idea of the self plays a key role in the analysis.

Having articulated this criticism, we must now ask ourselves whether it is justified. In one respect, it is not. What Hume was strictly denying in Book 1 was not that there could be no impression of the self. Rather, he was denying that there could be an impression of the self as an underlying substratum or ego substance. As he says in Section VI, 'I never can catch *myself* at any time without a perception' (*T.*, p. 252). He means that there is no introspective consciousness of a subject of experience, over and above the particular perception that we have. Far from denying, he is actually asserting that one can give an account of the self *in terms of* these perceptions. That is precisely why he was said to hold a 'bundle' theory of the self.

It needs to be said on Hume's behalf, then, that the idea of the self, as this is employed in the analysis of pride we have just been considering, is not necessarily inconsistent with Hume's thoughts on personal identity. What is more, Hume is quite explicit about the definition of the self with which he is working in the present context. His words are that the self is 'that succession of related ideas and impressions, of which we have an intimate memory and consciousness' (*T.*, p. 277). Formally, Hume is perfectly consistent and has a perfect right to speak of the self as so defined.

However, that is not the end of the story, if only because it leaves us with a fundamental puzzle about the content of the idea of the self, even when defined as specified. We have seen that the idea of the self is an integral part of his explanation of the generation of pride. The thought of that emotion associates with the idea of the self. The question that has to be posed is; what *is* the self? The bundle theory of the self maintains that the self is the sum-total of all the perceptions that have occurred for a conscious being. But, surely, one cannot pack all of these into one discrete experience, one item of consciousness as this occurs as a component of psychological analysis. To put the matter naively, one cannot have one's whole life-history before one as a regular component in the psychological analysis of pride or humility.

That being the case, one can only suppose that Hume saw the idea of the self as referring to a representative sample of perceptions every time it crops up. But what could possibly constitute such a sample? After all, the term 'perception' was one Hume used in order to refer to all the contents of the mind. One is therefore talking about such varied experiences as memory images, images of imagination, emotions, thoughts, sensory experiences, awareness of pains and pleasures, and so on. How does one obtain a representative sample of perceptions from a list of this kind? Even if that were not a difficulty, one would still seem to be talking about something far more complex than Hume could have had in mind when he introduced the idea of the self into his analysis.

'Limitations'

Before considering the other pair of indirect passions with which Hume is so concerned in Book II we must take notice of an important little section immediately following the account of pride and humility (2, 1, VI). It is entitled 'Limitations of this System' (*T.*, pp. 290–4). Philosophically speaking, Hume is not at his best in this section, but a very 'promising' development in Hume's thought is revealed. What he actually says, by way of a preface to the section is that 'twill be proper to make some limitations to the general system' (*T*., p. 290). The 'general system' refers to the psychological analysis he has offered us in the previous section, and 'limitations' is a slight euphemism for 'qualifications'. It is as though Hume is saying 'Here are my second thoughts on the subject'. What appears to be happening is that, without being properly aware of it, he is groping towards the truth that external factors can often determine the identity of an emotion – a point we raised in criticism of Hume's method above (p. 134). Officially, Hume's story has not altered. That story is that, in order to identify an emotion, all I have to do is to look into my consciousness and see it for what it is. Emotions are, on this view, subjective, self-contained sensations. Here, however, under the misleading title 'limitations', Hume is effectively conceding that there is a kind of logic that determines the character of an emotion, even though he does not consistently hold to this insight. Nevertheless, the fact that he should feel a need to insert such a section is, as we have said, a promising development.

To see this development more closely, we shall briefly glance at the limitations listed by Hume. There are five of them in all, and they are intended to be additional factors that have a bearing upon the origin of pride and humility. The first is a kind of refinement on something Hume had already said. It is the claim that, when a person is proud or ashamed of something, there must be not just a relation but a close relation between the agent and what he or she is proud or ashamed of. The reference to the emotion of joy in this passage perhaps indicates what has happened in Hume's thought at this juncture. After having given us an analysis of pride, it occurs to him that joy is a very similar sensation, subjectively speaking. This presents something of a difficulty for him, since it is not easy to distinguish between them by pure introspective scrutiny. We have already had cause to refer to precisely this difficulty, above (p. 134 *ff.*). Introspective examination may have sounded sufficient so long as Hume confined himself to emotions that seem to stand at opposite ends of a spectrum: pride and humility, love and hatred would fill the bill satisfactorily. But pride and joy are emotions that are qualitatively very close, as Hume has now come to recognise. His response is to refer us back to the circumstances in which pride occurs, and to tell us that, in order for pride to emerge, as opposed to mere joy, there has to be a very close relation between the agent and the object of his pride.

In fact, Hume has still not got it quite right. It is, presumably, not a necessary condition of my being proud that there should actually be a relation of any kind between me and the object of my pride. What *is* necessary is that I should *think* there exists such a relation. Furthermore, the close relation Hume specifies, whether actually existing or merely a fiction of my imagination, is not a sufficient condition for the origin of pride either. That is to say, it is possible for there to be such a relation without my feeling proud.

Hume's second limitation represents a further step in the mapping out of the logic of pride and humility. He argues that I can only feel proud or ashamed of something that is peculiar to me or to just a few people. Thus, to use his own example, when our health is regained after a long illness, we do not feel proud; and this is because good health is something that is shared by vast numbers (*T*., p. 292).

Again, Hume does not have the situation quite in focus. In the first place, considered as a necessary condition, it is not the *actual* peculiarity or uniqueness that matters but, rather, my belief, true or false, that the object of my passion is unique. Secondly, in so far as Hume regards this particular condition as being causally operative in the generation of pride and humility, one wants to say that he has the cart before the horse. In many cases, the tendency to believe that the object is peculiar to me (perhaps by virtue of various imaginative constructions and tricks) will itself be an *expression* of what pride is, rather than its cause. The point is more prominent in the case of shame. In some cases, for example, it is precisely because a person is, to begin with, obsessively sensitive and therefore prone to feeling ashamed that he sees things as being peculiar to him. To this extent, the second limitation is not obviously a causally explanatory factor. And to emphasise this brings out, once more, that emotions are intrinsically more complex than Hume allows.

Much the same kind of reaction must be recorded to Hume's third limitation, though there is also another problem involved here. The condition specified is that the object of pride or humility must be 'very discernible and obvious'(*T*., p. 292) both to ourselves as well as to others. One thing can be conceded to Hume. If some valuable object, related to me, is very discernible and obvious, then it may sometimes be causally operative in generating pride. But, again, this feature may also work in reverse, such that, like the previous limitation, it becomes not causal but consequential. That is to say, there are clearly some cases where it is a consequence of my feeling proud or ashamed that the object of the emotion *becomes*, at least from my point of view, very discernible and obvious. Sometimes, I may strive to make it so. It may not have been so prior to the existence of my pride, as Hume would have us believe.

The additional difficulty is that, whether considered as cause or consequence, being very discernible and obvious is not a necessary feature of situations in which pride and humility exist. There is no logical impropriety in talking about a *secret* pride or a *secret* shame, where we mean that the object of the passion is not known to anybody except the person who feels it. A person can feel shame, just as he can feel remorse, for things in his life that nobody ever knew about, or ever will know about. One can only say, on Hume's behalf, that he has accurately pin-pointed, but rather badly characterised, a feature of pride and humility that is perhaps typically but not necessarily present.

The fourth condition laid down by Hume is that the object of pride or humility must be relatively constant or durable, and it is far from clear why he should want to say this. Many of the things of which we are proud enjoy only a fleeting existence. To adapt an example used by P. S. Ardal,[15] let us suppose that we have a man standing among other spectators on an occasion when the Queen is doing a walk-about. Let us further suppose that he is not an anti-Royalist. By chance, the Queen has a few brief words with him. It would be quite natural for him to feel proud in these circumstances, but what it is that he is proud *of* would be entirely momentary or transitory, probably never to be repeated. The truth of the matter seems, once again, to be the very reverse of what Hume tells us. If the Queen's chat with this person *were* a constant and regular occurrence, then there is every reason to suppose that his pride would simply dissolve.

The fifth limitation, so-called, is something of a misnomer. Indeed, Hume himself asserts that it is more like an enlargement of his system (*T.*, p. 293). However, it represents a further interesting development in Hume's thought. We can approach this development in the following way. Partly as a result of the work of Wittgenstein,[16] we now see many of our emotions as being shaped by language and the concepts that language expresses. To put the position perhaps too briefly, it is the view that an isolated individual in a desert-island situation and without language could not feel shame or pride or resentment, and perhaps many other emotions. To feel shame, for example is necessarily a product of the recognition that *others* can criticise or ridicule or dislike. But that recognition cannot occur except in the context of a common language and, in turn, the community that makes that possible.

Now if one is charitable to Hume, one might say that what he claims under the fifth limitation reflects at least a hint of this insight. For it is here that he introduces the concept of 'general rules'. His words are: 'I may add as a fifth limitation, or rather enlargement of the system, that *general rules* have a great influence upon pride and humility, as well as on other passions'(*T.*, p. 293). The point he then goes on to make is that it is at least partly because society places a certain value upon something that it becomes possible for it to be an object of pride for the person appropriately related to it. Again, it is because society places value on a certain group of personal qualities that a person can become the object of our love, etc. Some further words of Hume are significant in illustrating the development to which we have referred:

> For it is evident, that if a person full-grown, and of the same
> nature with ourselves, were on a sudden transported into our
> world, he would be very much embarrassed by every object,
> and would not readily find what degree of love or hatred, ·
> pride or humility, or any other passion he ought to attribute
> to it. (*T.*, p. 293)

It can be seen from these words that Hume does not go as far as to assert, with Wittgenstein, that such emotions only come into being with the concepts we bring to bear. Nevertheless, the fifth limitation does reveal Hume as recognising that the emotions have an important social dimension.

Love and hatred

It is now time to look at the other pair of indirect passions which Hume singles out for special attention. The psychological story that Hume tells about love and hatred has many of the features already listed in connection with pride and humility. However, there are certain new features which it will be worth our while to notice.

From an official point of view, Hume still holds that love and hatred, like pride and humility, are subjective, self-contained emotions, perfectly simple and unique. But what we may be witnessing in his treatment of the case of love and hatred is the recognition that emotions are really a bit more complex than this. At the beginning of Book II, Part II, Hume reiterates the claim that love and hatred, like all other emotions, are simply impressions 'without mixture or composition' (*T*., p. 329). By the time he reaches Section VI of Part II, he is already beginning to qualify his claim. What he actually says in this passage is that, when a person experiences the emotion of love, it is accompanied by a desire for the happiness of the person loved. Again, when a person feels hatred for another, this is accompanied by a desire for the misery of the person hated. More significantly, he goes on to assert that, in the absence of such accompanying desires, these two emotions are 'not completed within themselves' (*T*., p. 367). In this respect, he concedes, love and hatred are different from pride and humility. On the face of it, even though he would not officially admit it, Hume is abandoning the simplicity claim so prominently asserted earlier.

What is more, it may not be just the simplicity thesis that is now being sacrificed. Hume makes it very clear that the accompanying desires to which he refers are actually impulses to action. He thus makes a connection with behaviour. This seems to mark a departure from the view that passions are entirely internal and subjective. In two respects, then, Hume's view of the emotions is being modified. The modification is in the right direction, in the light of the remarks we made earlier, but the criticism of him must surely be that he cannot have things both ways. Either the passions are simple, or they are complex, but not both.

Despite this difference between the two pairs of emotions, Hume wishes to hold that, in other respects, there is a very close connection between all four of them. This is because he sees them as relating to a set of common qualities. What Hume has in mind is the following, rather strange, thought. If I wish to get other people to love me, I must expect to cultivate and display those qualities of which I am proud, or would be proud under the appropriate circumstances. Thus the qualities of which I am proud are precisely those for which, if I am successful, other people love me. In the case of hatred, people are likely to hate me for possessing those very qualities of which I am, or would be, ashamed.

Hume has undoubtedly captured a truth about some cases of love and hate, but he cannot pretend that it will fit the facts for all cases. It will sometimes be patently false to hold that the qualities of which a person is proud are precisely the same as the qualities for which some other person loves or admires him. Some married men are proud of their conquests with women: it is, to say the least, unlikely that their wives love them for it! However, the charitable view of the point that Hume is making is to say that he is, again, groping towards a more general truth. Let us remind ourselves again of Hume's claim. He wishes to say that pride and love, shame and hatred, make a reference to common qualities. The more general truth to which this approximates is that pride is fed or fuelled by the value that other people put upon the object of a man's pride; and, similarly, shame is fed or fuelled by the disvalue that other people put upon the object of shame. That same general truth is perhaps captured in another way. It is, at the very least, difficult to be proud of something that nobody else values. Again, it is difficult to feel shame about something of which nobody disapproves. We might like to think that this was the more acceptable truth at which Hume was driving.

One thing is evident both from what we have just seen as well as from Hume's use of the principles of association to explain the origin of pride and humility. It is that, when we love a person, it is always *in* virtue of qualities which that person possesses, and correspondingly with hatred. This may seem to be perfectly correct in the case of pride and humility. If I am proud of something, I must surely be able to specify *what* it is about that thing that makes me proud. However, it is not immediately obvious that love and hatred are comparable in this respect. Hume is actually excluding the possibility that I can just love a person, full stop, or hate a person, full stop. Many would regard this exclusion as counter-intuitive. Certainly it deserves some consideration.

D. W. Hamlyn, for example, in a recent article argues that, among emotions generally, love and hatred are distinctive.[17] It is not a logical requirement upon the concept of love that there be some quality or qualities that we love other people *for*; and correspondingly with hatred – we just love or hate them. This is to say that, in one sense, love and hatred are not epistemic emotions in the way in which pride and shame are; they do not necesssarily entail any *belief* about the existence of certain specifiable qualities in the respective objects of the emotions.

However, although Hamlyn's position is one that merits our attention and raises a legitimate query, it is not clear that its truth can be *established* in such a way as to show that Hume is mistaken. We can concede that many a person who finds himself in love with another will be utterly unable to specify the quality or qualities in virtue of which he or she loves the other person. But what needs to be resolved is whether the inability is simply contingent or not. After all, it is often the case that we do actually love people in respect of certain qualities they possess, and recognise that this is the case, without being able to specify those qualities. The position is that we simply cannot get them into focus. After the emotion subsides a little, we may well be able to identify quite precisely what it is about them that has attracted us. Outsiders may often have been able to do this from the start. On the whole, therefore, we must reserve our judgement on this particular aspect of Hume's position.

We shall conclude the present chapter by reiterating a point that was made earlier. We must remind ourselves that, if Hume seems obsessively concerned with the group of four passions we have been discussing, this is not only because he sees them as being so strategic in the understanding of human nature.[18] It is also because he sees them as being at the heart of any explanation of what we are doing when we make moral judgements. In short, he sees them as being species of moral sentiments. One of Hume's problems in his treatment of morality was to say something about the peculiar kind of pleasure and pain that, according to his thesis, constitutes our moral approval and disapproval. He recognised that it could not be just any old pleasure or pain. What he maintains, therefore, is that the pleasure of moral approval is a kind of loving when the approval is directed towards another person, and a kind of pride when it is directed towards oneself. We shall have a little more to say about this connection with moral judgements in the chapter devoted to Hume's moral thought (Chapter 12). Before turning to that topic, we must pause to examine what Hume regards as a very remarkable quality of human nature – our capacity for sympathy. It is an additional, important factor in explaining the generation of the passions. Because the moral sentiments are also passions on Hume's view of the matter, sympathy is as significant to Book III of the *Treatise* (on Morals) as to Book II (The Passions). It therefore constitutes an appropriate bridging section at this stage.

Notes

1. G. E. Moore, *Principia Ethica* (Cambridge, Cambridge University Press, 1903).
2. *Principia Ethica*, Chapter 1, paras. 7 and 8.
3. J. Passmore, *Hume's Intentions* (London, Duckworth, 1968) pp. 108–9
4. P. S. Ardal, *Passion and Value in Hume's Treatise* (Edinburgh,

Edinburgh University Press, 1966), pp. 13–15.

5. This is Wittgenstein's image. See L. Wittgenstein, *Philosophical Investigations* (Oxford, Basil Blackwell, 1973), para. 293.

6. R. Descartes, *Passions of the Soul*, in *The Philosophical Writings of Descartes*, translated by J. Cottingham, R. Stoothoff, and D. Murdoch, vol. 1.

7. See G. Ryle, *The Concept of Mind*, ch. 4.

8. For a recent discussion of philosophical theories of emotion, see W. Lyons, *Emotion* (Cambridge, Cambridge University Press, 1980). For a recent account of emotion sympathetic to, but not uncritical of Ryle's account, see A. Kenny, *The Metaphysics of Mind* (Oxford, Clarendon Press, 1989), ch. 4.

9. For an interpretation of Hume's theory of emotions which gives greater weight to the conditions in which emotions can occur see D. Davidson, 'Hume's cognitive theory of pride', in D. Davidson, *Actions and Events* (Oxford, Clarendon Press, 1980). Davidson's interpretation is discussed by Annette Baier in 'Hume's Analysis of Pride', *Journal of Philosophy*, vol. 75, 1978, pp. 27–40. See also Annette Baier, *Postures of the Mind* (London, Methuen & Co., 1985), ch. 7.

10. For a comparison of Descartes and Hume on emotion see Anthony Kenny, *Action, Emotion and Will* (London, Routledge and Kegan Paul, 1963) ch. 1.

11. On the relation between emotion and object, see Kenny, ch. 3. Kenny's influential analysis is discussed by J. R. S. Wilson, *Emotion and Object* (Cambridge, Cambridge University Press, 1972).

12. See Philippa Foot, 'Moral beliefs', reprinted in Philippa Foot (ed.), *Theories of Ethics* (Oxford, Oxford University Press, 1967), pp. 82–100; also reprinted in P. Foot, *Virtues and Vices* (Oxford, Basil Blackwell, 1978).

13. Ardal, ch. 2.

14. Norman Kemp Smith, *The Philosophy of David Hume* (London, Macmillan, 1941), pp. 178–83.

15. Ardal, p. 23.

16. L. Wittgenstein, *Philosophical Investigations* (1953).

17. D.W. Hamlyn, 'The phenomena of love and hate', *Philosophy*, vol. 53, 1978.

18. Further discussion of the topics of this chapter can be found in A. O. Rorty, *Explaining Emotions* (Berkeley, University of California Press, 1985) and R. Scruton, *Sexual Desire* (London, Weidenfeld & Nicolson, 1986).

11. *The mechanism of sympathy*[1]

(*Treatise*, Bk. II, Part 1, Section XI; Part 2, Section VII)

Our capacity for sympathy is first mentioned in Book II, Part I, Section XI of the *Treatise*, a few short sections after the main discussion of pride and humility, considered in the previous chapter. This first mention of the subject makes it obvious that Hume regards it as being of considerable importance. His words are worth quoting: 'No quality of human nature is more remarkable, both in itself and in its consequences, than that propensity we have to sympathise with others, and to receive by communication their inclinations and sentiments, however different from, or even contrary to our own' (*T.*, p. 316).

Sympathy functions in two ways. It can create sentiments in us where there were none before. Thus a person who is joyful can make me similarly joyful by means of sympathetic communication of what he feels. It can also accentuate or intensify a sentiment that is already present. In the case of pride, for example, the pleasure that others derive from what is possessed by me is communicated by sympathy to me, thus augmenting my own pleasure and, in conjunction with other factors, generating pride.

Sympathy is not itself the name of a sentiment or emotion. It is the name given to a psychological process by means of which somebody else's sentiment is communicated to me. It is thus best regarded as a psychological device or mechanism. There is a strong temptation to think of it as a sentiment because we now associate it with pity or compassion. However, Hume makes it clear that it is not either pity or compassion because he regards it as a *means* by which pity and compassion are themselves communicated. (See *Treatise*, Book II, Part II, Section VII).

We must now set out the psychological details in order to see how, according to Hume, sympathy works. It will simplify matters to set it out in three stages.

1. External behaviour on the part of X produces an *idea* of the sentiment, of which the behaviour is an expression, on the part of Y. This is due to the fact that Y has had experience of a correlation between that kind of behaviour and that kind of sentiment in his own

case. He proceeds as we all do. We cannot see what goes on in other people's minds, but we make inferences on the basis of their behaviour.

2. The idea thus generated is then converted into an *impression* whose force and vivacity is such as to render it equal to the sentiment itself. That is, Y's *idea* of X's anger, for example, becomes Y's own anger. Hume is quite emphatic about the character of this conversion. He does not mean that the anger in Y is in some sense bogus or pretended anger: it is, in Hume's own words, an 'original affection'(*T.*, p. 317).

3. The conversion of the idea into the impression is brought about by means of the impression of the self imparting some of its vivacity to the idea of X's sentiment. The analogy that most helps us here is the way in which something that is potentially luminous is brought into a beam of light and suddenly becomes very vivid.

We must now draw attention to some of the difficulties inherent in Hume's analysis. There is, to begin with, a question about the role played by the impression of the self. According to the thought of Book I of the *Treatise*, there can be no such impression. However, we must be charitable to Hume here and make the point that was made, in the previous chapter, in dealing with Hume's use of the idea of the self in his account of pride. There it was made clear that, when Hume originally denied the intelligibility of an impression of the self, he was referring to the self as an underlying substance or ego, or substance of experiences. He did not deny – in fact, he wished to assert – that there could be an impression of the self as a collection of perceptions. That was, indeed, the essence of the so-called 'bundle' theory of the self. Hume is mindful of that theory in Book II. In the analysis of pride, for example, the self is actually defined as a 'connected succession of perceptions' (*T.*, p. 277). Despite the fact, then, that Hume has been criticised for his use of an impression of the self in his analysis of sympathy, the charge is not well-founded.

However, the particular role that the impression of the self is required to perform does give rise to a more substantial query. It is one of Hume's claims, in his psychological explanation of how sympathy works, that the impression of the self is 'always intimately present with us' (*T.*, p. 317). In fact it is important for him to stress this, given the psychological scheme with which he is operating. It is only by virtue of the impression of the self being constantly present to the mind, and thus a constant source of vivacity, that Hume is able to explain how it can infect an associated idea. It has to be constantly and readily available in order to impart colour and vivacity to the idea of someone else's emotion. The question we must ask is whether the impression of the self, even when defined in the qualified way specified above, is in the centre of the picture in the sense required.

Of course it is true that we are constantly engaged in doing and undergoing things and, as reflective human beings, we are inevitably aware of our interaction with the world. But clearly that does not amount to an assertion of the centrality of the self that is required by Hume's doctrine. What Hume requires is a sort of highlighted consciousness of self, something one might achieve, for example, in moments of meditation or introspection, self-examination or acute embarrassment. There is a well-known illustration in Jean-Paul Sartre's *Being and Nothingness* which brings out clearly the sort of concept Hume actually needs but does not have. 'Let us imagine', says Sartre, 'that, moved by jealousy, curiosity, or vice, I have just glued my ear to the door and looked through the key-hole. I am alone ... But all of a sudden I hear footsteps in the hall. Someone is looking at me. What does this mean? ... It is [the] eruption of the self'[2]. What Sartre thus describes is not altogether uncommon, but it is a very special state of consciousness that one might describe as being 'heightened'. The important thing about it is that no one would suppose that such a state could be a sustained or permanent one. Yet the features of Hume's psychological scheme seem to require that it be so in order for his account of sympathy to be a viable one. In short, the heightened state of self-awareness that Hume's thesis requires occurs only in special circumstances and certainly cannot be described as being 'always present to us'.

There is a feature of Hume's account of sympathy that has not so far been mentioned, and it poses a possible problem. While Hume is normally thought to be talking about the communication of *emotions* by means of sympathy, it is also the case that he sees *beliefs* and *opinions* as being communicated in the same way (*T.*, pp. 320–1). The potential problem here is that the latter are often thought of as being quite different from sentiments or emotions. It is a common view that beliefs and opinions are mental states resulting from reflection and consideration of pros and cons, and this alone may put them beyond reach of sympathy. In considering this possibility, one has to stress, once more, that, on Hume's view of the way in which sympathy works, a belief that was sympathetically induced would be one that was *directly* communicated. That would be to say that there would be no intervening consideration of the object of belief. The thought of some other person's belief would be straightforwardly converted into my belief. The question must be whether this is psychologically possible, granted our usual view of the way in which beliefs are formed.

Before commenting upon this, it will be as well to remind ourselves that Hume had given specific attention to the concept of belief both in Book I of the *Treatise* and in the *Enquiry*. We discussed his position in Chapter 7 above. What we must note here is that the essential ingredient of that original position is retained in the present context. On that earlier position, a belief is brought about when a mere idea of something is rendered more vivid and forceful – rather like seeing a film in colour after having seen it only in black and white. In addition, the means by which the conversion took place is similar to what is involved in the case of sympathy. The earlier view told us that an idea gets transformed into a belief by coming into relation with a 'present impression'. The present impression of sombre cloud formation, for example, leads me to believe that rain is approaching. The impression imparts its natural vivacity to a pre-existing idea. The very same process – that is, the infusion of vivacity from a neighbouring impression – takes place in the sympathising mechanism. The difference is only that the relevant impression is always that of the self.

It is obvious, then, that, as between Books I and II of the *Treatise*, Hume tells us a consistent story about the nature and psychological origin of belief. But what we now have, in the analysis of sympathy, is a claim that the process may be occasioned in an additional way. In the previous context, Hume was mainly concerned with the way in which we arrive at a believing state as a result of conditioning from experience. In the case of sympathy, we are shown how we may acquire a belief simply through perceiving its existence in some other person. It is precisely this that we are now questioning.

Some writers on Hume are happy to accept that beliefs may be sympathetically communicated in the way in which we have depicted it. Ardal is a case in point.[3] He holds that, though the enlivening of an idea of a belief into the belief itself may initially *seem* strange, a closer look at what happens in day-to-day experience will reveal that it does actually happen. Thus, suppose we have a person who mixes in company where it is generally held that the Conservative Party is evil, malicious, and corrupt. He is constantly subjected to this opinion: he hears it being uttered all the time. And eventually he comes to believe it for himself, even though he has given no independent thought to the proposition involved. Here, according to Ardal, would be a belief that had been sympathetically communicated.

Ardal may be perfectly correct. Undoubtedly, something of the sort goes on in social life, but two questions need to be settled before we can assert that what goes on conforms precisely to the model set out by Hume. First, we need to establish that the resulting state of mind really is a case of belief. Secondly, even if we are satisfied that it is, we need to establish that it was truly the result of sympathetic communication, as described.

In relation to the first of these issues, we must bear in mind that the occurrence has to be such that the *idea* of a belief that *p* is succeeded by a *belief* that *p*. Assuming that the example we have used above is representative, can we be sure that the end-product really is a case of belief? In particular, is it necessarily the case that the person concerned has come to *believe* that the Conservative Party is evil, malicious and corrupt? What is clear is that there are other possibilities. Ardal's description of this sort of situation gives the impression of its being one in which the person does not actually believe this proposition. Rather, by virtue of the social pressure put upon him, he finds himself inhibited in various appropriate circumstances. For example, he cannot bring himself to consider Conservative policies objectively; he finds himself unable to socialise with those whom he knows to have Conservative leanings; he cannot seriously consider the possibility of voting Conservative, and so on. It is sometimes this way with non-vegetarians who regularly move in vegetarian circles. It is not that they believe in the rightness of vegetarianism as a policy but, owing to the discreet pressure placed upon them, they find themselves inhibited from eating meat.

Of course it must be conceded that there are those who hold that to behave or react in these ways just *is* what it is to believe something. On this view, Ardal's claim on Hume's behalf would be, correct. But one must be at least wary of going too far in this direction. To assume that a person is in a believing state on *these* grounds, independently of the agent's avowals and denials, is to adopt a radical form of behaviourism, and one which, on the face of it, is strongly counter-intuitive.

What make matters more difficult for the line adopted by Ardal is that there *is* a respectable philosophical position which runs counter to it. It holds that believing something is to be distinguished from certain other mental states that *resemble* it but do not amount to full-blooded belief. Believing has been distinguished, for example, from such states as 'acting as if', 'being under the impression that' and 'taking for granted'.[4] How can we be sure that the example we have considered above does not fall into one of these categories? Until we can be sure of this, it may be premature to assume that we are confronted with a case of belief. Beliefs or opinions are 'formed'. Do we really wish to say that our man has 'formed' the opinion that the Conservative Party is evil, malicious and corrupt?

We said that two questions need to be settled before we can confidently assert that the kind of examples we have considered conforms to the model as set out by Hume. We have now seen that the end-product is not necessarily a case of belief. The second consideration must be whether, even if we are faced with a case of belief, it is truly a situation in which the belief has been sympathetically communicated in the specified sense. After all, there are other, perfectly standard, means by which beliefs are generated before we can be happy about talking of sympathetic communication. For example, a person can be so impressed with the mere force and enthusiasm with which another person holds a certain belief that he proceeds to make independent investigation or gives the matter some thought himself. He may do so without fully recognising what he is doing. This would not constitute sympathetic communication of belief in the Humean sense. Again, a person may be infuenced by the *kind* of people who hold a certain belief. He may regard them as the sort of people who can be relied upon to hold sensible beliefs, and he thus allows himself to hold the same belief himself. Finally, the sheer weight of numbers might lead a person to endorse a certain belief. The thought would be that, if so many people believe it, it *must* be right.

What all three alternatives have in common is that, in each case, the belief is 'grounded' in some consideration or other. There is a minimum sense in which it rests on independent judgement. It is in that sense that the end-product may not be the result of sympathy.

However, we would not be fair to Hume if we did not mention a further consideration bearing upon the general issue. At a later point in Section XI, Hume refers us to something we would now recognise to be a form of psychosomatic illness. It would seem as though he is using it as evidence in support of his view that sentiments and opinions can be transferred by means of sympathy. Thus, he says 'tis certain we may feel sickness and pain from the mere force of imagination, and make a malady real by often thinking of it' (*T.*, p. 319). His argument can be spelled out in the following way. We are all ready to accept that psychomatic illlness occurs, and we have a rough idea of how it occurs. What we must recognise is that sympathetic communication of sentiments and beliefs operates upon the very same principle. In both instances, what we are confronted with, psychologically, is the conversion of a lively idea into an impression.

Many things can be said about this move on Hume's part, but one thing in particular should be noted. The reference to psychosomatic illness may, conceivably, provide some support for the view that sentiments or emotions can be sympathetically communicated. It is by no means clear that this provides an explanation of the transference of opinions and beliefs. On the face of it, there is a crucial difference between the state of being ill, on the one hand, and the state of believing a certain proposition on the other. That is a difference that Hume should not be allowed to ignore. It is best expressed by saying that believing something is essentially a propositional state. It is to say that the mind stands in a cognitive relation to a certain proposition which, in principle, could be specified. But there is nothing 'propositional' about being ill. Of course it is true that, if Freddie is ill, his illness will usually be accompanied by his believing that he is ill. In addition, his believing this may be causally operative in *making* him ill. But this is not to say that the illness is intrinsically propositional. One wants to say that, on Hume's view, the illness should be classed as a matter of having sensations of a certain sort. Consequently, in talking about beliefs and in talking about illness we are talking about two different types of phenomenon. Therefore, Hume cannot simply help himself to the assumption that, because the mechanism of sympathy works for the case of illness, it must also work for opinions and beliefs. It is not that it is necessarily to be ruled out for the latter, but the view that it does so work does need further support.

There are two further worries about Hume's account of sympathy that we must now consider. The first of them concerns the 'object' at which a sympathetically induced emotion is directed. According to Hume's analysis, if I witness a person outwardly expressing grief, then, providing all other conditions are equal, that idea of grief will get converted into *my* grief also, just as anger or fear or sadness might. But that story seems to be incomplete for at least some emotions, and perhaps for all. Some emotions are much more specifically directed at an object than others, and this gives rise to an implication that Hume may not have grasped. If I do not know what it is that X is grieving about, is it possible for his grief to become mine? It would seem to be a precondition of the sympathetic mechanism that I must, at least in most cases, know or be able to identify the object of another's emotion. Yet it is precisely this that I might *not* know merely by observing the external symptoms of a person's emotion. It is rather as though Hume has assumed that, in perceiving the external symptoms of a person's grief, for example, I simultaneously perceive the object at which the grief is directed. It is obvious that this is not necessarily the case. When it is not so, it would look as though sympathy simply cannot function.

Of course the charitable interpretation of Hume here is to construe him as holding that sympathy will only function in those cases where an observer is in fact acquainted with the relevant object of emotion. But, quite apart from the fact that this would render the phenomenon of sympathy much less widespread than Hume claimed, it is unlikely that Hume actually held this view. To see why it is unlikely, we need to refer back to an earlier remark. It was mentioned in Chapter 10 that Hume was beginning to be aware of what we now call the intentionality of emotions – briefly, the fact that they are always *about* something. Nevertheless, his official view was that emotions are perfectly self-contained, subjective sensations, having no necessary reference beyond themselves. Granted *that* view, it was quite natural for him to assume that *any* emotion could be communicated by sympathy. An observer would not have to be acquainted with the object at which the emotion was directed since, on the official view, such an object would be only contingently related to the emotion. This would therefore explain how Hume could come to neglect this particular characteristic of emotions. The effect of stressing it would be to play down the influence and the extent of the sympathetic mechanism.

The second of our two worries is well-expressed by John Passmore in his commentary on Hume.[5] We elaborate it a little. If I witness X displaying anger, the idea I receive is that of X being angry: it is not an idea of anger as such. This being so, and granted that there is merely a difference in degree between impressions and ideas, it follows that, if this particular idea is enlivened, it will not lead to my anger, as Hume's analysis requires. It will simply give rise to an impression, or more vivid experience, of being angry. It could only lead to actual anger in me if there were to be a change of content as between the idea and the impression and that is evidently a view that Hume cannot accept: the doctrine of impressions and ideas itself prevents him from doing so. The criticism is potentially quite devastating since it would seem to apply to all communication of sentiments (and opinions) that is supposed to be generated by sympathy. It therefore undermines the very principle by which Hume laid so much store.

What has to be said about this criticism is that, technically speaking, it is very well-founded. As we saw, when discussing the doctrine of impressions and ideas, Hume adheres very stricty to the claim that there is no difference in content between an impression and its corresponding idea. An impression just is the more vivid of the two experiences. It therefore has to follow that any particular idea whose content is specified as 'X with a certain emotion' will, if converted into an impression, only become a more vivid experience of 'X with a certain emotion'. It will not be the impression (i.e. passion) that constitutes having the emotion itself. On these grounds, Passmore's criticism appears to be sound.

However, there is a little room for manoeuvre in the attempt to defend Hume. It is no doubt correct to state that, if I witness X displaying angry behaviour, this will often lead to my thinking of the feeling of anger that lies behind it. It is then quite natural to state that I have an idea of X's anger which, formally, gives rise to the implications we have mapped out. But, independently of what Hume might actually have thought, this does not necessarily mean that I have the idea of an anger that is peculiarly X's anger. One might put the point by saying that the anger which is the object of my thought is only contingently associated with X. Strictly, what I have been provoked to think about is anger itself. If this is once admitted, there is surely no difficulty in the view that this *idea* of anger becomes an *impression* of anger – that is to say, *my* anger. Importantly, there will have been no change in content.

We must conclude with the judgement that, although Hume undoubtedly attached a great deal of importance to the mechanism of sympathy, his psychological account of it did generate a number of problems. This is not to deny that sympathy, in one form or another, does actually occur. It seems to be an undeniable truth that the 'infectiousness' of certain passions or emotions is a palpable social phenomenon.[6] This is possibly the insight Hume himself was expressing at a later point in Book II: 'In general we may remark that the minds of men are mirrors to one another, not only because they reflect each other's emotions, but also because those rays of passions, sentiments and opinions may be often reverberated ...'(*T.*, p. 365). The problem seems to have been that the terminology of impressions and ideas, in conjunction with the troublesome impression of the self, was simply ill-equipped to capture this insight. It is perhaps for this reason that, although he speaks about sympathy in the *Enquiry Concerning the Principles of Morals* (see, for example, Section V, Part 2), the psychological analysis of it is omitted.

Notes

1. This chapter makes use of material first published in J. Jenkins, 'Hume's account of sympathy – some difficulties', in V. Hope (ed.), *Philosophers of the Scottish Enlightenment* (Edinburgh, Edinburgh University Press, 1984).
2. J-P. Sartre, *Being and Nothingness*, translated by Hazel E. Barnes, (London, Methuen, 1957), p. 259.
3. Ardal, *Passion and Value in Hume's Treatise*, pp. 47–8.
4. See H. H. Price, *Belief* (London, George Allen & Unwin, 1969), pp. 208 ff.
5. Passmore, *Hume's Intentions*, p. 129.
6. For recent discussions see Philip Mercer, *Sympathy and Ethics* (Oxford, Clarendon Press, 1972), I. Dilman, *Love and Human Separateness* (Oxford, Basil Blackwell, 1986), and Jiwei Ci, 'Sympathy and the foundation of morality', *American Philosophical Quarterly*, vol. 28, 1991.

12. *How to make moral judgements*

Hume's account of morality is to be found both in the *Treatise* and in the separate work entitled *An Enquiry Concerning the Principles of Morals*, written some years afterwards. In the earlier work, Hume's moral thinking occupies Book III, though Part III, Section III of Book II is also relevant. The *Enquiry* version of his thought is less complicated and gives us more of a birds-eye view of what is going on. We shall therefore use this latter version as our 'base' and refer to the *Treatise* only where we require some amplification of certain crucial points.

Setting the Scene
Hume's primary concern within the area of morality is firmly stated in Section I of the Second *Enquiry* and the very first section of the *Treatise*, Book III. Granted that there is a class of judgements to which we refer as moral judgements, just what kind of judgements are they? In particular, can they be regarded as rational judgements, in the sense of being founded upon reason? That is to say, can they be construed as necessary truths, arrived at intellectually rather in the way in which we make inferences and deductions in mathematics or logic? If not, is it perhaps possible that they are judgements that simply express, in a sophisticated form, our own feelings and sentiments, rather like judgements about matters of taste? Hume's central question, therefore, is this: is morality a matter of reason, or is it a matter of sentiment?

In the *Treatise*, but not in the Second *Enquiry*, Hume shows us how this central question can be couched in the terminology of impressions and ideas. As we saw when discussing this doctrine, impressions are essentially feelings, while ideas are essentially thoughts. Hence the question must be whether moral judgements are impressions or ideas, or whether they are founded on one or the other.

Hume's general purpose, then, will be to survey the moral scene so as to be in a position, finally, to answer this central question. There will be, as we shall see, other important preoccupations along the way, but his path is clear. He begins, in an unbiased fashion, by telling us that there is a *prima facie* case to be made for both of the claims we have mentioned. Thus, those who support the claim that morality is a rational affair will draw our attention to the fact that we *argue* about moral issues and, they will say, we only argue about things that can be settled by reason or by reference to 'the facts'. As Hume puts it, 'truth is disputable, not taste' (*E.*, p. 171). On the other hand, those who claim that morality is only a matter of how we feel will point out that it is intrinsic to the very nature of virtue that we find it pleasurable and intrinsic to the nature of evil that we find it painful or odious. Surely that must suggest that morality is a matter of taste, feeling, or sentiment. On the face of it, then, there is a case to be made on behalf of both camps. Hume's task will be to decide which of them is correct.

His survey will consist of a broadly scientific enquiry into the way in which morality works in practice. For Hume, this means that we must take a look at those things we call moral judgements and the various contexts in which we use them; and we must also examine the various qualities of character upon which we make such judgements. Now, among such qualities of character, there are two that in their various forms stand out as being more pre-eminently objects of our judgements than others. They are what Hume calls 'benevolence' and 'justice', and he generally refers to them as 'virtues'. The former of the two has a less prominent place in the *Treatise* version, possibly because, in that work, Hume was more preoccupied with the working of sympathy. We shall look at this in more detail in due course.

The term 'benevolence' is a slightly antiquated one these days, but what Hume is actually referring to is something with which we are all perfectly familiar. He means the display of a number of specific qualities, all expressing a kind of fellow-feeling with other people. At the beginning of Section II of the Second *Enquiry*, he spells out the sort of qualities he has in mind; sociableness, good nature, humanity, mercy, gratitude, friendliness, generosity, etc. (*E.*, p. 176). 'Justice', on the other hand, simply designates the virtue of being just. To be just is to conform to the requirements of the system of justice as it exists in one's own society. We shall examine these virtues in more detail below, but two general points concerning them must be made.

It is firstly to be noted that Hume regarded benevolence as a *natural* virtue. This is to claim that it belongs to us by nature – just like the ability to walk or talk. Justice is an artificial virtue for the very opposite reason: it is a quality that we have to acquire through education or upbringing.

Secondly, it is to be noted from Hume's treatment of these virtues that he sees moral judgements as being made not upon actions directly but upon the qualities of character from which they emerge. This position is very emphatically stated in the *Treatise*, where we are told: ''Tis evident, that when we praise any actions, we regard only the motives that produced them, and consider the actions as signs or indications of certain principles in the mind and temper. The external performance has no merit' (*T.*, p. 477). The view is reiterated in Part III, Section I: 'If an *action* be either virtuous or vicious, 'tis only as a sign of some quality or character' (*T.*, p. 575). It is obvious, from these quotations, that Hume is not denying our tendency to describe actions themselves as good or bad, but he holds that our doing so can only be intelligible because of their connection with inner qualities of character. In this respect, Hume falls into the same category as Plato and Aristotle, who also thought that moral judgements are essentially directed at qualities of character. His position is to be contrasted with some forms of utilitarianism, where the emphasis is upon actions and their consequences.[1]

To explain this particular claim of Hume's requires a reference to his more general thesis of morality. Ultimately, what he is going to tell us is that all moral judgements are expressions of how we *feel*. But, in the *Treatise*, we are further told that these feelings will always be forms of love and hatred (when directed at others), and pride and humility (when directed at ourselves). It therefore follows, granted these premises, that we only have such feelings towards *people* and personal qualities. We do not love or hate actions as such: we love or hate the people who perform them.

The plausibility or otherwise of this claim rather depends upon whether we accept Hume's identification of the feelings that moral judgements are supposed to express. It is by no means clear that moral judgements are always expressions of love, hate, pride, or humility. Indeed, in many cases, it seems beyond doubt that they are not. We regularly make judgements on our politicians, for example, and others in public life, but we would hesitate to describe them as expressions of love or hatred. It may be that, if love is reduced to a 'generally benevolent attitude towards' and hatred to 'a mild feeling of dislike or aversion', Hume's case would more naturally go through. But the general point to make is that, unless we endorse some such thesis about the function of moral judgements, we will not necessarily agree with Hume's claim. That is, we shall not necessarily agree that moral judgements are always directed at people and personal qualities, as opposed to the actions they perform.

However, what is more contentious in Hume at this point is the additional claim that the qualities of character in question must be stable and long-lasting. In the *Treatise*, Hume describes them as 'durable principles of the mind, which extend over the whole conduct, and enter into the personal character' (*T.*, p. 575). He supposes that such stability is necessary if our sentiments in reaction to them are to be aroused.[2]

It is to be conceded that Hume has actually captured something of the truth in making such a claim. Thus, if a person, in doing something reprehensible, acts 'out of character', as we say, we have at least some tendency to excuse him. We say, on his behalf, that he acted impulsively, or that he was acting under duress, or that he 'was not quite himself'. In general, we contrive to show that it was 'not really him'. This consideration does rather support the Humean view that we require actions to be the result of stable, abiding qualities of character when we make moral judgements upon them. But it cannot be the whole of the truth. Acting 'out of character' does not completely absolve a person. The man who impulsively murders his wife is still condemned: the fact that his action is impulsive is only a mitigating factor. Indeed, in the case of those actions that we praise, as opposed to condemn, it is clear that we have even fewer inhibitions about making our judgements. It just is a fact that the millionaire who, quite out of the blue, donates an enormous sum of money to famine relief is judged to be morally praiseworthy, despite the fact that it is not part of his character to do this kind of thing. Indeed, to know that such an action is uncharacteristic may increase rather than diminish our moral respect for a person. We sometimes take the view that, if a person performs a benevolent deed in this way, i.e. uncharacteristically, then it must have required an enormous effort on his part to do it. Moral admiration is often appropriate, and sometimes especially appropriate, for the person who has to overcome an obstacle in his personality in order to do what is morally good. The cynical among us might even belittle the person for whom the good action is a natural outcome of his character: for such a person it is easy! In general, then, we should have some reservations about Hume's view that the qualities upon which we make our moral judgements are durable and abiding features of a person's character.

Being benevolent

According to Hume, then, our moral judgements are all about virtues and vices, and these virtues and vices are long-standing qualities of character. It was noted earlier that benevolence and justice are two of the most prominent of these virtues. We must now look at these in turn, beginning with the former.

Section II of the Second *Enquiry* presents us with at least some of the things Hume wishes to say about this virtue. Two main strands can be immediately identified. The first is that the expression of benevolence, in its various forms, is certainly something that pleases us. The second is that at least part of the reason why it pleases us is that it is *useful*. It is useful in this particular respect, that it serves the interests of those at whom it is directed. As Hume says, 'In general, what praise is implied in the simple epithet "useful"! What reproach in the contrary!' (*E.*, p. 179).

However, quite apart from these two empirical claims, which Hume regards as being undeniably true, there are two other propositions he is concerned to establish. They come to the forefront of his thought in Section V of the Second *Enquiry*. First, he is anxious to show that our capacity to be pleased with what is useful to people – itself the expression of benevolence or humanity – is not to be ascribed to education or upbringing. It is not the case that governments, for example, *invented* certain useful practices and then educated and encouraged people to be pleased with them. Hume does not deny that education does have some influence over our judgements of approval and disapproval; but his view is that it can never be the ultimate source or explanation of such judgements. He argues this on the ground that one cannot teach people to have sentiments for which they have no natural capacity. His point is perhaps analogous to the claim that if we had no natural capacity for colour discrimination, it would not be possible to teach us how to have colour sensations.

However, the analogy with colour discrimination does not clinch the issue. If we press the analogy, it will certainly require that we have an original capacity to be pleased with those practices that are useful to other people. But this establishes very little. The capacity or potential to be pleased or to approve is in itself empty of content. It remains a possibility that those things of which we approve are, in fact, dictated by government or education in just the sense that Hume is denying. We can be taught to appreciate – that is, be pleased with – good pictures, good music, good statues, good wine, good food. The sentiments in which our approval consists were not there before the educational process started: only the capacity for them was there. Therefore, why not suppose that we can be similarly educated to appreciate utility, that is, to be pleased with those things that are useful to humanity?

The second proposition that Hume is anxious to establish requires some more detailed attention. He wishes to show that our capacity to be pleased with those things that are useful to humanity is not something that can be given an egoistic twist, and he produces a number of arguments in support of this claim. Essentially, Hume is here arguing against the doctrine of psychological egoism. This is the doctrine which holds that we are, at all times, psychologically predisposed to pursue our own interests. In the present context, this finds expression as the view that we are only disposed to approve of those things that are favourably related to ourselves. Hume resumes the battle against this position in Appendix II of the Second *Enquiry*. We shall consider the material to be found there in conjunction with the material to be found in Section V. Five separate lines of attack may be discerned.

1. Hume draws our attention to the obvious fact that we frequently praise a virtuous action in some distant place or time (*E.*, pp. 215–6). This is significant, he believes, because its being distant in time and place is sufficient to sever any connection with our interest. To put the point rhetorically, what possible benefit could accrue to us from praising such a remote action? This therefore seems to establish the negative claim that at least not all our moral judgements can be egoistically interpreted.

One natural reaction to this is to say that what we do is to *imagine* ourselves to be in those distant places and situations. We thus derive a satisfaction (or, alternatively, a kind of pain) from so doing. This would be to uphold the self-interest theory. However, in fairness to Hume, he anticipates such an objection. He discards it on the ground that imaginative activity of this kind could not produce *genuine* pleasure or pain. In his own words 'it is not conceivable how a *real* sentiment or passion can ever arise from a known *imaginary* interest' (*E.*, p. 217).

There are two comments worth making in response to Hume.

(a) It is clearly part of Hume's case that, even if we can imagine ourselves to be in distant places and situations, any gratification or pain that ensues will be, in some sense, illusory. As we have seen, he holds that it is inconceivable that a *real* pleasure or pain should arise from an *imaginary* interest. (Hume himself italicises these words.) But this is a somewhat strange remark. The fact that a pleasure or a pain is generated in the manner suggested in itself affords no reason for doubting the reality of our sentiments. The manner in which a pleasure is derived has no obvious bearing upon its intrinsic character. We might often have independent grounds for praising or condemning, or otherwise commenting upon, the means by which a sentiment is generated, but this does not impugn the reality of the ensuing sentiment. A person may feel proud of something he thinks he has created when, in fact, he only *imagines* that he created it. This has no tendency to show that he did not genuinely feel pride. Similarly, then, if we, by virtue of our imagination, transport ourselves into Hume's 'distant ages and countries', there is no reason to doubt the reality of any pleasures or pains that follow. The egoist's case may ultimately prove groundless, but it is certainly not felled by this point of Hume's.

(b) Some thinkers would take the view that the judgements we make on historically and geographically remote actions are not significant. It is true that, because the imagined situations are remote, there can be no personal involvement that might suggest a self-interested element. But, just for this reason, the judgements we make about these situations are likely to be what one might call 'rub-off' judgements. That is to say, such judgements are grounded in the perception of a similarity between these situations and those which are the objects of judgements we make about our immediate circumstances. An analogy will help. A person who is proud of the house that he has bought, on account of its distinctive style, furnishings, decoration, etc., will, very naturally, tend to approve of, or look favourably upon, any other house that happens to conform to it in these particular respects. Thus the judgement upon his own house 'rubs off' on any other that is similar to it. The point to make, therefore, is that a similar phenomenon may occur in the case of our judgements upon remote events. In so far as this is true, it will have the implication that such judgements may be neither here nor there. Whether they are to be given an egoistic interpretation or not will depend on what we say about their counterparts in the judgements we make about our immediate circumstances. If the latter are judged to be egoistic, then the former must be similarly described.

2. A slight variation on the same theme occurs immediately after the argument we have just considered. It is to the effect that we have a capacity to give our moral approval to actions performed by enemies (*E.*, p. 216). Even more than this, we can approve of their actions when they are avowedly detrimental to our own interests. This would seem

to support the view that psychological egoism, as a theory of human nature, is false. In so doing, it supports the view that there is a natural sentiment of humanity or benevolence.

Again, one must say that Hume's case remains unproven.

(a) There is the possibility that such appraisals are 'rub-off' judgements in the way described above.

(b) Hume appears to ignore the standard move made by egoists in response to this claim, which is to distinguish between short-term and long-term interest. The egoist need only maintain that the rational person assumes a long-term view of what benefits him. This then commits him to a policy of contributing to and encouraging an orderly society *overall*, on the ground that this is clearly the best way of serving his own interest. He thus takes it for granted that, in some individual situations, he may stand to lose by such a policy, but he holds that the long-term advantages outweigh these. He is prepared to praise his enemy's action, so detrimental to his own immediate interest, because it is the kind of action that contributes to the well-being of a social community ultimately benefiting *him*. Again, such an interpretation may be quite wrong, but Hume has not *shown* it to be so.

3. What we might regard as a third attempt to steer us away from the theory of psychological egoism is to be found in the Second *Enquiry*, Appendix II. It should be seen as a 'consideration' rather than an argument. It amounts to the view that, in trying to persuade people of the truth of his doctrine, the psychological egoist necessarily has an uphill task before him. This is for two reasons. In the first place, what he claims runs counter to the immediate appearance of things. In the second place, since it denies the truth of the immediate and obvious interpretation in this way, it is obliged, in many cases, to produce abstruse and complicated explanations of human conduct. According to Hume, this should put us 'extremely on our guard' (*E.*, p. 299).

Even as a 'consideration' rather than an argument, this line of reasoning is hardly satisfactory. Consider first Hume's assertion that psychological egoism runs counter to immediate appearances. Developing this point, Hume says that 'to the most careless observer there appear to be such dispositions as benevolence and generosity; such affections as love, friendship, compassion, gratitude' (*E.*, p. 299). The obvious retort is that anyone who takes such appearances at their face value *without further ado* is indeed a 'careless observer'. One is reminded of the story told of the philosopher Thomas Hobbes, who was properly regarded as the arch-exponent of psychological egoism.

It is said that he was once observed to throw a coin to a street beggar and was challenged on the ground that the action seems to contradict the theory he was so famous for expounding. Hobbes's reply was to the effect that the observer had misunderstood the situation. Hobbes had not been moved by any altruistic compassion for the beggar's plight. He had, rather, been moved by the desire to relieve his own distress at seeing him. Whether the story is true or not, it is not an implausible account of what might happen in such situations. Moreover, it is neither abstruse nor unduly complicated, as Hume seems to think the egoistic interpretation would typically be.

Even if it were to be established that the egoistic story has to resort, in every case, to 'some very intricate and refined reflections', as Hume calls them (*E.*, p. 299), it is not obvious why we should be 'extremely on our guard'. Human nature just is a very complicated and complex affair. Of course it is easy to make this point these days, using the hindsight that comprehends Freudian psychology and the concept of the unconscious. But Hume, even in his day, should have been capable of acknowledging the complexity of human nature, and of recognising the danger of too easily accepting things at face value. Indeed, this is one of the features on which his reputation as a philosopher is founded. We *think* that we perceive causes objectively at work in the world, but, in reality, we do not. We *think* that determinism does not apply to human nature, but, in a certain sense, it obviously does. We *think* that people witness miracles, but it is very unlikely that they do. Many people *suppose* that God's existence can be demonstrated, but the supposition is almost certainly unfounded. Surely, in the light of all this, Hume should have scrutinised more closely the claim that genuine altruism abounds among us and that our language testifies to this fact.

4. Before considering what is in effect Hume's strongest attack on the doctrine of psychological egoism, we shall briefly glance at a further weak argument deployed in Appendix II. There we are informed that animals display kindness to one another, as well as to us (*E.*, p. 300). We do not, in their case, try to explain their behaviour in terms of self-love or self-interest. Why, then, should we place such an interpretation on comparable types of behaviour in the case of humans?

The short answer to this question is 'because we think that human beings are significantly different from animals'. The longer answer falls into two parts.

(a) It can be conceded that we do not normally ascribe self-interested motives to animal behaviour. However, this is not because we see motives as being simple, straightforward expressions of genuine benevolence: it is because, in a certain sense, we think they have no motives at all. If an action is to be regarded as self-interested, we take it to be a precondition of its being so that there should have been, on the part of the agent performing it some reflection on what is beneficial to him. Such reflection may occur at various levels of consciousness, but it is precisely what we think is missing in the case of animals. By the same token, of course, we should have some hesitation about saying that animals may exhibit kindness or generosity also. In so far as we do ascribe these latter motives, we are, at least on one view of the matter, guilty of personification.

(b) Even if we were quite happy about the ascription of truly benevolent motives to animals, the onus is on Hume to show that human beings are like animals in the relevant respects. As things stand, there is much to be said for the view that there is a considerable difference between the two kinds. In particular, we are the kind of creatures who can clearly intend things, visualise what we intend, deliberate, calculate, and plan ahead. It is a pretty fair guess that animals do not have such capacities. Hume hardly needed to be told such things. Why, therefore, did he so glibly make the jump from animal behaviour to human behaviour?

5. Now let us move to the one argument that does credit to Hume in this area, clearly set out in Appendix II. The basic insight lying behind the argument can be put in the following way. Self-interested action *requires* or *presupposes* certain other motives in human nature that *cannot* be self-interested. Therefore, it cannot be intelligible to claim that all human action is egoistic (*E.*, pp. 301–2). However, this simple thought is supported by Hume in three separate steps, which we shall now summarise.

(a) It is a straightforward empirical fact that we all have certain bodily desires or appetites. We hunger, for example, we thirst, we yearn for sex, or sleep, or warmth. The thing about such impulses or desires is that we regard them as being there, intrinsic to the organism, as it were, quite independently of any pleasure we may derive from satisfying them. If I am extremely thirsty, there is a sense in which my thirst will carry me straight to the water that will quench it. It would seem to be incorrect to say that I pursue the water because I am attracted to the purely sensual enjoyment of drinking it. The latter enjoyment may well be something that usually attends my drinking, and, indeed, once I have discovered that it is enjoyable, the desire for such enjoyment may emerge as a secondary motive. But Hume is concerned to stress that it is a secondary motive that could not come into existence in the absence of the primary one. If I had never thirsted and been moved to satisfy my thirst, I should never have discovered that it was enjoyable to do so. Importantly, the primary motive is not, in the accepted sense, self-interested.

(b) The same thought is then transferred to what Hume calls 'mental' as opposed to physical appetites. For example, it is characteristic of some of us to seek power and fame because we find it gratifying, and certainly there is an egoistic motive involved in this. But Hume's point is that we could not pursue power for the purpose of pleasure unless some other, more basic motive had driven us towards power in the first place. In a similar way, the infliction of vengeance on someone might well turn out to be a pleasing experience, but there must, surely, be something more basic in human nature to impel us towards such an action in the first place, regardless of self-interest or the desire for pleasure.

(c) Benevolence is also to be found among the mental appetites, and surely the same reasoning must apply here. Of course it must be admitted that some of the benevolent acts we perform are motivated by a desire for the pleasure they yield for us. Nevertheless, there must be, in human nature, a natural sentiment of benevolence capable of carrying us into such acts in the first place. How else could we come to discover that they are in fact pleasurable? If this is the case, psychological egoism cannot be true.

As we have already suggested, this is a much more forceful argument against egoism, and it is right that we should respect it. However, for Hume's purpose, it may be limited in its scope. Technically, the argument may show that it is not intelligible to suppose that all our motives could be self-interested ones and that a strict form of psychological egoism is false. But this is perfectly compatible with the claim that, in every case, once a person *discovers* that the performance of a benevolent act is a pleasurable affair, he will thenceforward pursue it for the sake of pleasure. In other words, in practice, it may well be the case that most of our actions are selfish in that sense. This can only run counter to one of the central strands in Hume's analysis of morality, at least in the form in which it appears in the Second *Enquiry*. To make this point clear, we must reiterate

Hume's position once more. Hume's talk of benevolence has two aspects. The virtue of benevolence, in the various forms in which it gets expressed, is very frequently the object of our moral judgements. But it is also the case that our very capacity to take an interest in what is useful or detrimental to people is itself an expression of benevolence – it is what Hume often refers to as the sentiment of humanity, a sentiment which he regards as genuinely altruistic. But in fact it is doubtful if Hume's last argument against psychological egoism does succeed in showing that our interest in what is useful to others is generally motivated by such a sentiment. Everyday moral judgements may well be, by and large, egoistic.

In view of what has been said above, this is an appropriate place to mention that the *Enquiry* version of Hume's account of morality does more obviously than the *Treatise* version posit a natural and genuine sentiment of benevolence. This is because there is a slight change in Hume's thought in this area by the time he wrote the later work. In the *Treatise*, Hume seems reluctant to hold that there is any general sentiment of benevolence. There is 'no such passion in human minds, as the love of mankind as such', he tells us (*T*. p. 481). Of course, he concedes, on an individual level we are easily moved by the plight of others, but this is due to the operation of sympathy, which represents their predicament to us in lively colours. In essence, therefore, his position is that not only is there no love of humanity as such, but there is no love of individuals either, except by means of the intervention of sympathy. This effectively means that our moral judgements are not direct and immediate expressions of benevolence. In the Second *Enquiry*, on the other hand, the mechanism of sympathy largely drops out of the picture as a specific psychological facility. We are left with the view that there is a fairly extensive and natural sentiment of benevolence. This being the case, it was important for him to be able to show that there really is such a sentiment and that it genuinely is a fellow-feeling for other human beings. Without the specific mechanism of sympathy, benevolence must do all the work. It therefore figured more prominently in the later work.

A little recapitulation is necessary at this stage so that we can keep things in perspective. In Section V of the Second *Enquiry*, Hume is concerned to show why it is that the usefulness of qualities and actions pleases us and why their opposite pains us. His answer is that we have a natural sentiment of benevolence which gives us the capacity to be pleased with those actions that are useful to, or serve the interests of, humanity. This constitutes a sort of love of humanity. In the same way, benevolence allows us to be pained by those actions that cause suffering to others. Hume stresses, and argues for, the thesis that the sentiment of benevolence is both a natural and a genuine one.

Being just

What Hume has to say about justice is to be found in Section III and Appendix III of the Second *Enquiry*, and in the whole of Part II of Book III of the *Treatise*. It would be fair to say that, in the former work, Hume states his conclusions about the nature of justice. These are, essentially, that the system of justice as we know it is an artifically contrived set-up, designed to counteract the lack of any extensive benevolence; and that our motives to acts of justice are ultimately founded on a consideration of the general utility of such a system. Any sense of there being a *problem* concerning the nature of justice is almost entirely lacking from the *Enquiry* version. One has to look back at the *Treatise* in order to see that he did at first identify a certain problem and that there was some degree of agonising about it.

The problem is generated in the following way. Hume begins by reiterating a claim we examined earlier, that when we make moral appraisals upon actions it is only in virtue of the motives from which they have been performed. Actions are merely signs of the motives lying behind them. Now it is a plain empirical fact that we do praise, that is, morally approve of, those actions we describe as just. The problem is this: what, in this case, is the natural motive which is the object of the approbation directed to such actions? In the case of benevolent actions, there is no difficulty. We praise such actions because they issue from the natural motive of benevolence. But what is the motive in the case ofjustice? Hume clearly sees that if what makes any action virtuous is the motive from which it is performed, it can only be reasoning in a circle to suggest that the motive behind the performance of a virtuous action is simply regard for the action's virtue. The action cannot be virtuous independently of the motive behind it, and that means that the motive behind a virtuous action has got to be something other than regard for its virtue. As Hume puts it, 'no action can be virtuous, or morally good, unless there be in human nature some motive to produce it, distinct from the sense of its morality' (*T.*, p. 479). But what can that motive be? It cannot be love of mankind as such, since in the *Treatise* Hume insists that there is no such passion. Our natural affections are much more particular than that. Nor could the motive be a regard for the public interest as such, since people in the ordinary conduct of life aren't generally moved by a motive as 'remote and sublime' as this; moreover we feel that an injustice ought to be rectified even though the public may be ignorant of it and therefore may have no interest in it.

How, then, are we to avoid having to admit that the motive for an honest or just action is simple regard for its virtue? Hume has argued that the motive for any virtuous action must be something other than regard for its virtue, yet so far as just or honest actions are concerned it seems that there is no other appropriate motive, and thus that 'there is here an evident sophistry and reasoning in a circle' (*T.*, p. 483).

If we may allow ourselves a brief and simplified account of what becomes a difficult argument, Hume's basic answer to this problem seems to be this. The way out of the circle is provided by the recognition that justice is an *artificial* virtue, something which is to some extent the product of education.[3] The basic difference between justice and benevolence is that every single act of benevolence is quite clearly judged to be good, whereas a single act of justice, taken in isolation, may often appear contrary to the public good. That means that for single acts of justice, taken on their own, there is often no intelligible motive at all. It is only when one takes the system of justice as a whole that it becomes intelligible, and everyone can see that, no matter how individual acts of justice may be to his detriment, the existence of a system of justice is to his benefit.

But justice cannot be just a matter of this sort of prudential calculation, and what makes this obvious is the fact that our ordinary feelings about justice do not involve such a calculation, or 'balancing the account' (*T.*, p. 497). The essential *artifice* of the artificial virtues consists in the cultivation, through education, of a sentiment in favour of every single act of justice, including those which may not be of benefit to anyone. Some acts of justice may seem grossly unfair, but we will nevertheless, if education has been succesful, have a sentiment in their favour.

Such, at least, seems to be Hume's position in the *Treatise*. In the Second *Enquiry* we do not find this puzzle about the motive underlying just actions. Here we find Hume much more disposed to think that there is indeed a natural regard for the well-being of others, what Hume calls the 'sentiment of humanity', and that this, together with a consideration of the usefulness of the system of justice, provides the basic motivation for acts of justice. We approve of, and are thus pleased by, the utility of the system of justice. But this usefulness is not simply a matter of its being of advantage to ourselves. It is also a matter of its answering to the wider sentiment of humanity.

Justice and Utility
Hume's basic position, then, is that justice, as a system of rules generating obligations and duties, is there and continues to be there only because of its utility. Take away its usefulness, the way in which it benefits society, and it would disappear. In Section III of the Second *Enquiry* Hume offers what he takes to be a proof of this claim. Essentially the proof amounts to showing in some detail that if we take away certain contingent features of life as we find it justice would have no role to perform.

Suppose, for example, that we had a situation of absolute abundance such that we had every conceivable material good; if anything was taken from us we would only have to stretch out a hand to replace it (*E.*, p. 183). Surely, Hume says, there can be no room for a system of justice in such a situation. It could serve no purpose. Justice is there essentially to protect property, but where the material goods that constitute property are there in such complete abundance there would be no point in even talking of property, let alone in devising a system of rules to protect it.

Alternatively, let us suppose that we were always governed by the most perfect benevolence, that, as Hume puts it, 'the mind is so enlarged, and so replete with friendship and generosity, that every man has the utmost tenderness for every man' (*E.*, pp. 184–5). Once again, justice would have no place. The whole human race would be like one big happy family, and there is no difference between thine and mine.

Hume then considers the reverse of these situations. Suppose, first, that the basic necessities of life are so scarce that no system of distribution can prevent most people from dying. Any system of justice would be suspended, and people would be driven by the motives of 'necessity and self-preservation'(*E.*, p. 186). We would ignore or override property rights. Finally, suppose that one falls into the hands of a band of ruffians, governed by a 'desperate rapaciousness'. Here, too, one can only set aside all regard for justice and 'consult the dictates of self-preservation alone'.

The situations Hume has described are all situations in which justice would be useless; and, just because it is useless, it is set aside.

Now it is only because, as Hume puts it 'the common situation of society is a medium amidst all these extremes' (*E.*, p. 188) that a system of justice exists. The fact that our actual situation corresponds to none of the extremes he has outlined means that justice has an essential role, and that is why we value it.

All this, then, demonstrates that justice as a system of rules and laws exists only because it is useful. Moreover, the fact that justice, as Hume sees it, is there primarily to protect property indicates another aspect of the artificiality of the virtue of justice. The virtue of being just is only possible because of what is created by the system of rules and laws we call justice. That is to say, the obligation which justice imposes on us to respect the property of others can only exist if there is such a thing as property, and it is Hume's claim that there can be no such thing as property outside a system of justice. Benevolence, by contrast, does not depend on any such artefact of human society. That is a motive which people have by nature, and whose expression does not depend on a set of rules and regulations.

Criticisms

The first doubt to be raised about Hume's account of justice is that in centring round the notion of property it has left out the more general and fundamental notions of fairness and equality, notions which most of us would suppose to be at the core of any proper conception of justice. For Hume, justice looks to be no more than a system of rules and laws which is set up to protect people's property. But what we want to be free to say of any particular such system is that it is or is not *fair*, or *just*; and it is not clear on Hume's account of justice what sort of judgement this would be and how it would be possible.

Hume's answer to this point appears in essence to run as follows. We do have a disposition to criticise a system of justice which embodies and legalises unfairnesses and injustices. Our inclination to do so rests on two factors. First, the natural benevolence, the 'sentiment of humanity', which motivates many of our actions. But this alone is not enough, since this sentiment is generally more inclined to motivate one's dealings with those who are relatively close to us and to operate more weakly in relation to distant situations and persons. It is essentially the need to communicate with each other which means that we must set aside our own particular standpoint and adopt an impartial stance, one from which the actions of everyone may be considered, whether or not one's own interests and affections are engaged. If we are to compare and discuss our moral judgements with others, we can only do so from a standpoint which we can all share, one which is independent of our own particular position in the world. The obligation to judge matters impartially, to transcend the limited reach of benevolence, is imposed on us by the need to understand and communicate with each other (*E.*, p. 228). We shall return to the question of whether this answer meets the criticism somewhat later.

Another possible criticism of Hume's account of justice centres on Hume's insistence that justice is useful only if it is inflexibly observed. As he puts it himself, take one brick away from the vault and it collapses (*E.*, p. 305). Now Hume does not spell out exactly why such inflexibility is demanded, but it is easy to see what he has in mind. Briefly, his view is that the utility of the system as a whole depends on its rules being inflexibly observed. If we were, for example, to suggest that the laws of inheritance could be waived in a particular case because we know that the son who is due to inherit his father's wealth is a wastrel, the consequences of following this policy would clearly be that the whole institution of justice would be gravely weakened; indeed, it is doubtful that it could survive at all. We may think that in this individual case the consequences of our setting aside the dictates of the system of justice would be desirable, but, as the contemporary philosopher John Rawls has argued, the usefulness of such institutions as that of justice can only be secured if we surrender the right to ask of each and every act of justice whether it has beneficial consequences.[4]

This position is now generally known as that of rule utilitarianism.[5] It is the view that what we should consider is not the usefulness or otherwise of every individual action, but that of the particular rules with which we think we ought to comply. A particular rule is justified if the consequences of complying with it are generally beneficial, even though there may be individual cases in which non-compliance may produce more benefit. One more point about it needs to be made, and that is that, although it requires that the rules of an institution like justice be observed inflexibly, it is perfectly compatible with this to require that the rules themselves be framed to take account of a great variety of different sorts of case. To take a simple example, we require that everyone should pay their taxes without exception, but of course we recognise that what anyone pays must take account of his/her particular circumstances, and that some people cannot be expected to pay anything at all.

Reason or Sentiment?

We began this chapter by pointing out that Hume's central aim was to show that moral judgement is not a matter of reason, but a matter of feeling. We must now look at this claim in more detail. Hume takes it that what he has said about the natural and artificial virtues in itself shows that the basis of morality is indeed feeling, but he has a group of arguments, which he sets out in Appendix 1 of the Second *Enquiry*, and which he thinks show that the idea that morality could be a matter of reason is absurd. He begins this section by reminding us of what he means by reason. Reason, he says, functions in two ways: it discovers matters of fact, and it discerns relations between ideas (*E.*, p. 287).

We may feel that there is something odd about the view that the perception of matters of fact is the work of *reason* rather than perception as such. We would not normally term the perception of a straightforward matter of fact, such as that this table is brown, a matter in which one's reason is employed. This sense of oddness can only be increased by the argument Hume uses to show that morality is not a matter of reason in this way. When we call something a crime, he says, we are not discerning a feature of the act or the world. We can describe all the objective features of the action in question, but its being a crime will not be one of them. Its being a crime is not an objective fact about the world, but a matter of how we react or feel about this act.

It seems clear, first of all, that this argument is aimed not so much against those who think that the basis of morality is a matter of reason, but against those who think that an act's being good or bad, right or wrong, is an objective property of the act, along with all the other objective properties.[6] Now this sort of view is not generally thought of as the view that morality is a matter of reason; rather, it is the view that moral properties are discerned by *intuition*. The fundamental doctrine of ethical intuitionism is that human beings have an immediate awareness of moral values, and this first argument of Hume's looks to be aimed at the variant of that view, which holds that something's being good or bad, right or wrong, is an objective property of what we are judging. It is the view that the awareness of moral value is something akin to sense-perception, and that is a view which was held by Shaftesbury and Hutcheson[7] among Hume's contemporaries and by G. E. Moore in the twentieth century. Now if Hume's argument is indeed aimed at this view, it has to be said that as a criticism of it his argument is entirely worthless. What Hume does is simply to point out that if we list all the objective *non*-moral properties of an action or situation its being good or bad would not be one of them. But this is to leave open just the possibility that Hume takes himself to have ruled out, namely that the act's being bad (a 'crime') is indeed one of its objective properties, albeit a moral one. He has entirely failed to show that our deeming some act a crime is basically a matter of how we feel, rather than a judgement grounded on our perception of an objective state of affairs, that state of affairs being the possession by the act of a certain moral property.

Hume goes on to argue that, if morality cannot be a matter of the perception of properties or matters of fact, neither can it be a matter of the grasping of relations between ideas (*E.*, p. 288). This argument seems to be aimed at that variant of intuitionism which holds that the basic truths of morality are known in much the same way as the fundamental axioms of geometry – by *rational* intuition. This is a view which was held by Samuel Clarke and Richard Price among philosophers of the eighteenth century.[8] But once again Hume's argument is quite unsuccessful. His argument is that inanimate objects may stand to each other in the same relations as those which we observe to hold between moral agents, a fact which would render the former just as much a matter for moral assessment as the latter, if morality consists 'merely in relations' (*E.*, p. 293). A young tree which over-tops and destroys its parent stands in just the same relation to its parent as did Nero when he murdered his mother Agrippina. Yet, he says, we condemn the one but not the other, a fact that would be inexplicable if morality were a matter of reason, or the discerning of relations.

The first thing to be said about this argument is that if the two cases, or two 'relations', *were* the same in all relevant respects, then the fact that we *feel* differently about the two cases would itself be something utterly inexplicable and bizarre. We cannot suppose that two situations can be alike in all relevant non-moral respects and that we are free nevertheless to react morally to these two situations in quite different ways. Of course Hume is right that we do react to these two cases in quite different ways: to the one our reaction is one of abhorrence, whereas we have no moral reaction at all to the other. That means that there must be a crucial difference between them, and it is not difficult to see what that is. The case of matricide involves consciousness, self-awareness, and intention, factors which are entirely absent in the other case. If Hume's argument were valid, moral judgement would be something quite inexplicable and positively *irrational*.

Some people have argued that, for example, when one makes a promise one places oneself under an obligation to keep that promise. A certain relation has been created, and it is a relation such that one ought to keep one's promise, that it would be right to do so and wrong not to do so. Nothing in Hume's argument shows what, if anything, is wrong with this position.

Equally, it cannot be to the point to argue, as Hume does, that, while in geometry we grasp certain facts and from these deduce others, in morality we must have all the facts before us before a moral judgement is made; hence, morality cannot be a matter of reason (*E.*, pp. 289–90). We could argue that geometrical reasoning is not so much the deduction of new facts, but the making clear of what is already in some sense contained in the premisses of one's argument; and so for all deductive reasoning. We may well go on to say that moral reasoning is rather like this, and point to the example about promising to illustrate how this could be so. Alternatively, we might want to accept Hume's characterisation of geometry as involving the deduction of new facts, but insist that Hume has simply stated, rather than shown, that moral reasoning cannot be like this.

Hume also argues that 'the ultimate ends of human actions can never, in any case, be accounted for by reason' (*E.*, p. 293). We may ask someone why he exercises, and he may well say it is to preserve his health. If we ask why he wants to preserve his health he can only say that it is because sickness is painful and being healthy is pleasant. But if we ask why he desires pleasure, he can go no further: there is no further reason he can offer.

Now it may well be that our ultimate ends are like this, something we simply value and pursue without being able to offer any reason why we pursue them. But what this claim does not establish, even if we admit it, is that morality itself is not a matter of reason. We might well think, for example, that the fact that one sees one's own pleasure as ultimately desirable means that one has a rational obligation to recognise that, since there is no crucial objective difference between one's own pleasure and that of other people, it cannot be just one's own pleasure that is worthy of desire but the pleasure and interests of every human being; and that this in turn means that one is rationally obliged to pursue, not only one's own good, but the good of all impartially. This is the position which is argued for Sidgwick.[9] What is missing from Hume's treatment is any real consideration of the claim that taking an impartial viewpoint, and, more particularly, acknowledging the rights of others, *is itself a requirement of reason*. He therefore does not consider whether this basic requirement of impartiality can yield a morality which is truly a matter of reason rather than feeling. It is true, as mentioned above, that he argues that we are obliged to take an impartial view if we are to converse with each other (*E.*, p. 228), but a view can be generally agreed on yet still embody the most fundamental injustice: consider the past universal acceptance of slavery, for example. The need to converse with each other, while requiring that we at least understand each other's viewpoint, cannot support the view that we are rationally obliged to respect the interests of every human being, or even that we share the same fundamental moral outlook. The greatest proponent of the view that morality is indeed a matter of reason is the German philosopher Immanuel Kant,[10] much of whose basic approach to the nature of morality underlies the work of many contemporary moral philosophers.[11] Hume may well be right that the claim that morality is a matter of reason cannot withstand critical scrutiny. But it would be overstating the case to claim that Hume's treatment of morality provides us with an answer to the opposing conception of Kant.[12]

Notes

1. See Plato, *Republic*, translated by Desmond Lee (Harmondsworth, Penguin Books, 1974), Aristotle, *Ethics*, translated by Hugh Tredennick (Harmondsworth, Penguin Books, 1965), and J. S. Mill, *Utilitarianism*, edited by M. Warnock (London, Fontana Press, 1989). For a useful introduction to these ethical theories, see R. Norman, *The Moral Philosophers* (Oxford, Clarendon Press, 1983).

2. Hume's emphasis on character in his discussion of moral judgement can be related to his remarks on 'durable or constant' motives for action in his discussion of liberty and necessity (*T.*, pp. 411–12).

3. In saying that justice is an *artificial* virtue, Hume is not saying that justice is in any sense unreal or illusory. 'Artificial' here means 'created' or 'manufactured' and is to be contrasted with that which exists naturally or prior to human artifice. To use an analogy: a monument in stone is no less real than a molehill, even though it is artificial and the molehill natural. On this point, see *E.*, p. 307, fn. 2.

4. J. Rawls, 'Two concepts of rules', *Philosophical Review*, vol. 64, 1955; reprinted in P. Foot (ed.), *Theories of Ethics* (Oxford, Oxford University Press, 1970). See also J. Rawls, *A Theory of Justice* (London, Oxford University Press, 1973), ch. 1.

5. On rule utilitarianism, see S. Toulmin, *An Examination of the Place of Reason in Ethics* (London, Cambridge University Press, 1950), K.E.M.

Baier, *The Moral Point of View* (Ithaca,N.Y., Cornell University Press, 1958), and the essays by J. O. Urmson, J. D. Mabbott, J. Rawls and J. J. C. Smart in P. Foot (ed.) *Theories of Ethics.* See also J. J. C. Smart and B. Williams, *Utilitarianism: For and Against* (Cambridge, Cambridge University Press, 1973).

6. For recent discussion of the nature of moral judgement influenced by Hume's approach see W. H. Hudson (ed.) *The Is/ Ought Question* (London, Macmillan, 1969), J. L. Mackie, *Ethics: Inventing Right and Wrong* (Harmondsworth, Penguin Books, 1977), and T. Honderich (ed.), *Ethics and Objectivity* (London, Routledge, 1985).

7. Lord Shaftesbury, *Characteristics of Men, Manners, Opinions, Times* (1711), and F. Hutcheson, *An Essay on the Nature and Conduct of the Passions and Affections* (1728). For excerpts from these works see D. H. Munro (ed.), *A Guide to The British Moralists* (London, Fontana Press, 1972) and D .D. Raphael, *British Moralists* (Oxford, Clarendon Press, 1969), vol. 1.

8. S. Clarke, *A Discourse of Natural Religion* (1728), in D. D. Raphael (ed.), *British Moralists*, vol. 1. Richard Price, *A Review of the Principal Questions in Morals*, ed. D. D. Raphael (Oxford, Clarendon Press, 1948).

9. H. Sidgwick, *The Methods of Ethics*, 7th edition, (London, Macmillan, 1907).

10. I. Kant, *Groundwork of the Metaphysic of Morals* (1785), translated by H. J. Paton as *The Moral Law* (London, Hutchinson University Library, 1972). For an introduction to Kant's ethics, see Onora O'Neill, *Contradictions of Reason* (Cambridge, Cambridge University Press, 1990).

11. See, for example, Thomas Nagel, *The Possibility of Altruism* (Oxford, Clarendon Press, 1990).

12. For further discussion see R. M. Kydd, *Reason and Conduct in Hume's Treatise* (Oxford, Clarendon Press, 1946), A. Baier, 'Master passions', in A. O. Rorty, *Explaining Emotions*, M. Ayers, *The Refutation of Determinism* (London, Methuen, 1968), Roy Edgley, *Reason and Theory in Practice* (London, Hutchinson, 1969), and J. McDowell, 'Are moral requirements hypothetical requirements?' *Proceedings of the Aristotelian Society*, Supp. vol., 1978.

13. *Is religious belief rational?*

During his lifetime Hume had the reputation of being an atheist, although he was perhaps closer to being what we would call an agnostic. Whatever his personal convictions, in his writings Hume never asserts that God does not exist or argues that religious belief can be demonstrated to be false. This does not merely reflect Hume's desire to avoid provoking the theologians and ministers of religion who held positions of power in his day. It is also an expression of that moderate or 'mitigated' scepticism which Hume advocates in Section XII of the First *Enquiry* and which is characteristic of so much of his philosophising. This is not to suggest that Hume's discussion of religion is in any way lacking in forcefulness or depth. On the contrary, as one contemporary philosopher of religion has written, 'Hume's reflections on religion have had an enormous influence and have formed for many who have come after him the essential terms of reference within which philosophical reflection about religion is to be carried on'.[1]

In this chapter we shall examine Hume's discussions in the *Enquiry Concerning Human Understanding* of the topics of miracles and the argument from design. The latter topic is explored at length and with great subtlety in the *Dialogues Concerning Natural Religion*, the literary and philosophical masterpiece written when Hume was in his early forties though not published in his lifetime.[2]

Miracles (*Enquiry*, Section X)

'A wise man, therefore, proportions his belief to the evidence' (p. 110). This seemingly innocent remark is at the centre of Hume's discussion of miracles. It links this discussion with Hume's predominant interest in epistemological issues and at the same time indicates the approach Hume takes to the subject of miracles. The continuity with Hume's familiar enquiries into knowledge and belief can be seen from the fact that, in the discussion of miracles, he is very much concerned with the nature of evidence and particularly with that special kind of evidence which we call testimony; though not only with religious testimony but more generally with reports we get from other people about events we ourselves have not witnessed. Hume is concerned to investigate the criteria we employ in assessing this kind of evidence as reasonable or unreasonable grounds for belief. By raising such questions with respect to reports of miracles, Hume addresses one of the most sensitive and significant of religious issues. For belief in a miraculous event constitutes the basis of Christian faith, viz., belief in the Resurrection of Christ from the dead as reported in the Gospels. Although he does not explicitly refer to the Resurrection, Hume does consider the miracle 'that a dead man should come to life' (*E.*, p. 115 and p. 128). And at the end of Section X he refers to the 'prodigies and miracles' recorded in the opening books of the New Testament, thereby underlining, as it were, the relevance of his discussion for religious believers.

We must first ask what Hume means by 'miracle'. In fact, he provides two definitions: 'a miracle is a violation of the laws of nature' (*E.*, p. 114); and 'a miracle may be accurately defined, a transgression of a law of nature by a particular volition of the Deity, or by the interposition of some invisible agent' (*E.*, p. 115, fn. 1). Hume's use of the phrase 'may be accurately defined' in the second definition suggests that he thinks of the first as merely an abbreviated or informal version. The second definition includes a reference to a causal explanation of the miraculous event. But, we saw in examining Hume's analysis of causality, he takes the view that an event need not have a cause, that an event can occur with its usual identifying features even if it lacks a cause. So, it is actually the first definition which specifies what for Hume is essential in the idea of a miracle, though it may well be the case that in thinking of some event as a miracle we would naturally expect that it should have been caused by the volition of the Deity or the interposition of some invisible agent.

Both definitions make use of the notion of a law of nature, by which Hume means a completely regular sequence of natural events. As formulated by scientists, a statement of a law of nature is a descriptive generalisation based upon observation of an absolutely constant conjunction of a cause and its effect or of a thing and its properties. For example, at standard pressure fresh water boils at 100 degrees centigrade; unsupported bodies near the surface of the earth fall to the ground. A miracle, then, on Hume's definition, is an event which 'violates', 'transgresses', or fails to conform to, such a regular natural sequence.

Now it is important to notice that the thrust of Hume's discussion of miracles is not to argue that miracles cannot occur. Instead, what Hume tries to show is that it can never be rational to believe that a miracle has occurred. It can never be rational, Hume argues, because we can never have good evidence for believing that a miracle has occurred. And, the argument goes on, we can never have such evidence because there will always be greater evidence for believing that a law of nature continues to hold. Thus, a wise man, who proportions his belief to the evidence, will never believe in miracles.

In order to bring out the force of this argument, Hume first considers events which, as he puts it, 'partake of the extraordinary and the marvellous' (*E.*, p. 113) rather than the miraculous. He refers to a tale of an Indian prince who refuses to believe 'the first relations concerning the effects of frost' (*E.*, p. 113), that is, refused to believe that water becomes solid in freezing temperatures. The prince 'reasoned justly' (*E.*, p. 113), says Hume. To someone who has spent his life in a hot climate, there has been an absolutely regular conjunction between water and the property of being liquid; so it was reasonable for him to disbelieve reports of water becoming solid, to dismiss them as fantastic.

Even though the prince's judgement was a reasonable one in the circumstances, it was mistaken. The prince's experience, though 'constant and uniform', was limited. The solidifying of water might have seemed miraculous, but it was not; because, as Hume explained in a footnote, 'it is not ... contrary to uniform experience of the course of nature in cases where all the circumstances are the same' (*E.*, p. 114). We, having observed the behaviour of water in very cold conditions, realise that its becoming solid is a regular natural occurrence. However, we might question Hume's claim that the prince 'reasoned justly' in refusing to believe reports about the freezing of water. Given the limited range of the prince's experience, it would surely have been more reasonable of him to have suspended judgement, to have kept an open mind on the matter. Hume appears to concede the point in his footnote:

> The inhabitants of Sumatra have always seen water fluid in their own climate, and the freezing of their rivers ought to be deemed a prodigy: But they never saw water in Muscovy during the winter; and therefore they cannot reasonably be positive what would there be the consequence. (*E.*, p. 114)

A miraculous event is similar to an event which is merely unusual or extraordinary in that it does not conform to our understanding of how things ordinarily behave. The crucial difference is that in the case of the miraculous we are aware that the challenge to our understanding is not a consequence of our ignorance of natural processes. What makes the story of Jesus turning water into wine a report of the miraculous is precisely that we know that this is not a natural occurrence. There are no circumstances in which water turns into wine. That is why His (allegedly) bringing this about is a reason for regarding Jesus as divine: wine turning into water is a violation of the laws of nature and only God can interfere with the laws of nature.

It is at this point that we can appreciate the force of Hume's argument. A report of a miracle will necessarily conflict with the 'constant and uniform experience' of mankind in favour of the operation of the laws of nature. This means that there will always be overwhelmingly strong evidence against believing that a miracle has occurred. Thus, suppose someone tells us that he has seen water being turned into wine. In deciding whether to believe the report, we will have to consider, in Hume's words, 'whether it be more plausible that this person should either deceive or be deceived, or that the fact, which he relates, would really have happened' (*E.*, p. 116). In other words, we have to weigh up the evidence: on the one side, we have the alleged eye-witness report of seeing water being turned into wine; on the other side, we have the agreement of innumerable people from all times and places that water does not turn into wine. It seems more likely that our informant is either trying to hoodwink us or that he himself has been hoodwinked, and so it is reasonable to believe that a miracle has not happened. The pattern of reasoning here will be repeated whenever a report of a miracle is provided, because it is grounded on our understanding that a miracle is a violation of the laws of nature. As Hume succinctly puts it:

> There must, therefore, be a uniform experience against every miraculous event, otherwise the event would not merit that appellation. And as a uniform experience amounts to a proof, there is here a direct and full proof, from the nature of the fact, against the existence of any miracle ... (*E.*, p. 115)

From this, he proceeds to his conclusion, 'That no testimony is sufficient to establish a miracle ... ' (*E.*, pp. 115–16). This is the main thesis of Part One of Hume's discussion of miracles.

We begin our assessment of Hume's argument by noting that it is entirely concerned with what our reactions should be to reports of miracles. While this is a legitimate enquiry, it is nevertheless a distinct issue separate from the question of the interpretation of the events themselves. That is, setting aside questions about how we know it happened, the reliability of the evidence, and so on, we can still go on to ask about the nature of the event, about the criteria for establishing that it is or is not a violation of a law of nature. Apart from laying down his definitions, Hume does not pursue this kind of question.

Take the case of someone suddenly recovering in the final stages of what has been diagnosed as a terminal illness. There is no doubt about what happened. The patient was dying; he is now getting better, and the cancer is receding. The interesting question is whether or not this was a miracle: what features of the event would justify us in saying that a violation of a law of nature had occurred? Doctors and scientists might be unable to find satisfactory explanations of the patient's sudden recovery, but this could be an indication of their failure to understand the relevant natural processes rather than an indication of a miraculous occurrence. Now, since it appears unlikely that we could ever be in a position to say that we have complete understanding of all the laws of nature, it seems to follow that we could never be in a position to say that a miracle had occurred and, therefore, that the title of the miraculous is just another name for ignorance. To be justified in believing that we had reached the limits of our present understanding of natural processes, we would require positive evidence that the event in question had been brought about by the intervention of the Deity; that is, evidence that the event had supernatural rather than natural causes. If, for example, the allegedly miraculous event, such as an inexplicable recovery from terminal illness, always, and only, occurred in response to exhortations of a religious figure or after prayers were said for a patient's recovery, then we might indeed think that this was evidence of divine intervention in the natural world. The absence of such evidence in so many cases of what are now called 'spontaneous remissions' of terminal illness is taken as a reason for believing that these events have natural causes which require further investigation.[3]

Secondly, Hume's concentration on the assessment of testimony leads him to neglect the question of how we should judge our own experience or observation of a possibly miraculous event. This links up with a further point, which is that Hume concentrates on the quantity rather than the quality of evidence. That is, his argument turns on the fact of the uniformity of the evidence against miracles; whereas quality, or kind, of evidence also needs to be taken into account. First-person present tense evidence is likely to be more 'telling' than reading historical reports of events in the distant past. To realise this, imagine yourself as the witness of some extraordinary event. For instance, suppose or imagine yourself to be standing at the edge of a lake watching someone walking on the surface of the water; now consider the way in which that evidence from your own senses compares with evidence from a written report of the same event and how you would react to someone who argued that it is impossible for people to walk on the water. Ordinarily, you would be more reluctant to admit that you were mistaken in what you saw than you would be to allow that the author of the report might be mistaken; indeed, before doubting what you saw with your own eyes you would surely require specific evidence of fraud or optical illusion, etc., in addition to general considerations about the tendency of heavy objects to sink in water. By ignoring factors relevant to first person observation, as opposed to third person testimony, Hume's argument appears more plausible than it otherwise might.[4]

A further consideration relating to the quality of evidence concerns the reliability of the witnesses of the allegedly miraculous event. By contrasting the comparative scarcity of reports in favour of the miracle with the enormous quantity of reports in favour of the regular natural occurrences, Hume implies that the former reports lack genuine inductive corroboration. But inductive support for factual claims can come from two sources: the number of occasions on which human sense-experience has been reliable; or the number of occasions on which this particular person's or these persons' sense-experience has been reliable. We need to remember that the report of a miracle is based upon the sense-experiences of the person or persons allegedly witnessing the event. And the veracity of those experiences is grounded upon a countless number of past occasions on which the people concerned have been reliable witnesses of ordinary natural occurrences. So if the person reporting the miracle is known to be a reliable and accurate observer, then the support for his claim will be proportionately stronger. A wise man will clearly have to take these considerations into account and doing so may well lead to a result less heavily balanced against reports of the miraculous than Hume's argument proposes.

Hume's treatment of miracles, if followed to the letter, has an odd implication for scientific procedure. In a broad sense, science is concerned to record the ways in which the world works. Hence, scientists must always be on the lookout for any revisions needed to be made in their theories of the world, their descriptions of the natural laws. But if they were to follow the method implicit in Hume's argument they would be precluded from recognising a potential revision or alteration of their understanding of the laws of nature. For the weight of evidence in favour of the accepted view would always be greater than that in favour of the purported exception to the law. Hume's methodology seems to rule out the possibility of progress in our understanding of nature. But is this a fair criticism? Surely, it might be said on Hume's behalf, the scientist only has to go on recording the counter-instances until they are numerous enough to warrant a revision of the existing statement of the natural law. But this response misses the real difficulty, which is that Hume's methodology will not entitle the scientist to record the first counter-instance. Since there will be a uniform experience in favour of the existing law, the alleged counter-instance will be dismissed as an illusion – perhaps the instruments were faulty or the observer was careless, etc. And, if the alleged counter-instance cannot count as a counter-instance, then, logically, the procedure of enumerating counter-instances cannot begin. So it will never be rational to revise our accepted theories of how the world works. This is evidently absurd.

A further bizarre consequence can be derived from Hume's argument. It is a feature of Hume's analysis that we can decide in advance, before any claim in favour of a miracle has been put forward, that it will be irrational to believe a miracle has occurred. Put into the first person, this means that I can say, in advance, that if I were to have an experience which I am tempted to call 'witnessing a miracle', then I should regard it as some kind of deception. What is worse, I am committed to telling other people that if I should ever claim to have seen a miracle they had better not believe me. All this is determined in advance because Hume's argument is based on a conceptual analysis, indeed, a definition, of what a miracle is. Hume is in effect informing us that we do not need to examine the features of any experience we might have when we claim to perceive a miracle. But this is surely an unacceptable piece of a priori legislation. Moreover, it runs counter to the open, enquiring spirit that Hume, as an empiricist, has long been advocating.

Our examination of Hume's views on miracles has so far been directed at the argument he employs in Part One of Section X of the *Enquiry*. Whereas that argument is concerned with the concept of a miracle in the abstract, in Part Two of Section X Hume turns to the consideration of more concrete details of the circumstances in which people put forward reports of the occurrence of miracles. In Part One Hume had taken for granted that the report of a miracle was well founded, arguing that even then it would not be rational to believe it; in Part Two he argues that in point of fact no reports of miracles have ever been adequately grounded.

To begin with, Hume lists the conditions which need to be met if reports of miracles are to count as reliable testimony.

1. There must be a sufficient number of witnesses of such 'good sense, education and learning' as to preclude the possibility that they have been deceived.

2. The witnesses must be of such integrity that we could not possibly suspect them of trying to deceive us.

3. Their moral standing in the community must be so high that they would have a great deal to lose if they were detected in a lie.

4. The event that is reported must be so publicly accessible that it would have been quite easy to find out whether the witnesses had been lying. 'There is not to be found in all history', Hume asserts, any testimony reporting the miraculous which meet these conditions (*E.*, p. 116).

Some comments are called for. Firstly, Hume has made the conditions for reliable testimony so stringent that reports of miracles are ruled out from the start. Indeed, if these are to count as the conditions for the reliability of any human testimony, Hume has virtually made most of history impossible: few, if any historical reports will meet all these conditions. As an historian himself, Hume would have relied in writing his *History of England* upon all sorts of reports which by these criteria were unreliable. To evade the charge that he has arbitrarily raised the standards for reliability of testimony pertaining to miracles, Hume would have to claim that these higher standards are demanded by the nature of the subject in question, viz., the miraculous, in the same way in which more rigorous tests would have to be applied before accepting reports of extremely improbable behaviour by familiar historical personages. Secondly, Hume's assertion that no report of a miracle meets the conditions of reliability is a bold, even astonishing, claim. But how could Hume know that as a matter of fact no testimony has ever, 'in all history', been reliable? He has no more privileged access to history than we do, and we, surely, must allow that there may have been some reliable reports. As Antony Flew concedes, 'There is good reason to believe that many of the phenomena he dismisses with such contempt did in fact occur'.[5]

The second reason Hume gives for saying that no testimony has been sufficient to establish the occurrence of a miracle is that, in effect, we are too eager to believe such things and so our judgement is inevitably biased. In Hume's words, 'The passion of *surprise* and *wonder*, arising from miracles, being an agreeable emotion, gives a sensible tendency towards the belief of those events, from which it is derived' (*E.*, p. 117). Hume's claim is that, really, we want to believe in miracles; consequently, we easily accept reports of miracles without giving the evidence proper scrutiny.

Hume's point is not all that persuasive. We can agree with him that we all want to believe in miracles and other extraordinary events but without agreeing with the implication Hume draws from the fact, that we become more gullible. Often, our reaction is just the opposite: the realisation that it would be nice to believe the story, that we want to believe it, puts us on our guard such that we are more than usually concerned to scrutinise the evidence. A contemporary illustration of this tendency can be observed in our reactions to the mysterious phenomenon of corn-circles which appear from time to time in fields in southern England. There is a strong temptation to believe that these circles are made by extra-terrestrial forces or beings, a temptation which some people cannot resist. This is the reaction Hume ascribes universally to human nature. On the other hand, just because there is this temptation, other people are especially scrupulous in their assessment of the evidence.

Hume's third reason for doubting the existence of genuine testimony in favour of miracles is provocatively phrased.

It forms a strong presumption against all supernatural and miraculous relations, that they are observed chiefly to abound among ignorant and barbarous nations; or if a civilized people has ever given admission to any of them, that people will be found to have received them from ignorant and barbarous ancestors ... (*E.*, p. 119)

It is difficult to see how Hume can have the right to generalise in this fashion. There are, even now, plenty of well-attested reports of 'miracles' put forward by civilised and intelligent people, just as there must have been in Hume's time. In any case, even if most miracles were reported by 'ignorant and barbarous' people, the inference that their reporting is unreliable is contestable. It might be said that ignorant people, just by virtue of lacking 'civilised' inhibitions, are more reliable witnesses than educated people. The same point can be made about children: often they are the best witnesses because they are not afraid to say what they see and what they think.

Hume's fourth reason takes the form of an ingenious argument (*E.*, pp. 121–2). Different miracles are claimed in support of many different religions. And that means, Hume argues, that there is a mutual destruction of evidence. That is, a miracle supporting the truth of one religion will automatically be evidence for the falsity of the miracles allegedly supporting the truth of the various other religions, and vice versa. The situation is similar, Hume suggests, to that in a court of law when the evidence of two witnesses against the man in the dock is cancelled out by the contrary evidence of two equally reliable witnesses (*E.*, p. 122). In commenting on this argument we should note, to begin with, that Hume has conflated two distinct issues. There is first, the question of whether a miracle has occurred, that is, whether there has been an infringement of a law of nature. The second question is whether that miracle does or does not support the truth of any particular religion. The former question can be answered independently of any answer to the latter question; in principle, even an atheistic scientist might decide that a violation of a law of nature has taken place; and the evidence in favour of any one miracle occurring does not necessarily undermine the evidence for the occurrence of any other miracle. The pertinent question for religious believers would be that of the identity of the God or gods or other 'invisible agent' who caused the miracle to occur. It is no doubt at this level that the mutual destruction of evidence alleged by Hume would come into play. But, as our earlier consideration of Hume's two definitions of miracles showed (p. 182), the determination of the cause of the miraculous event is separable from the identification of the event as miraculous. It may well be the case that in practice the description of the miracle will be given in terms which indicate that it counts as evidence in favour of one particular religion as opposed to others. Thus, the miracles recorded in the New Testament are specifically Christian miracles, proofs of the divinity of Jesus of Nazareth. And yet we can distinguish on Humean principles between the miraculous event itself – the turning of water into wine, the raising of Lazarus from the dead -- and the religious interpretation of the event as indicative of the truth of the claims of the Christian faith. Religions distinct from Christianity might dispute the Christian interpretation of the miraculous event without denying the occurrence of the event itself. Hume's 'subtle and refined' (*E.*, p. 122) argument fails to distinguish disputes over the religious significance of miracles from disputes about the existence of miracles and it does so in a manner reminiscent of the religious writers he is so anxious to criticise.[6]

In response to the above criticism it might be objected that it is too superficial to think that the occurrence of a miracle can be established independently of its religious significance. For, some have maintained, an event can be identified as a miracle only within the context of a religious tradition.[7] Outside the framework of religious beliefs, the miraculous event would be regarded as something bizarre or bewildering for which the appropriate natural explanation would be forthcoming sooner or later. The effect of this line of reasoning is not, however, to establish the credibility of Hume's point about the mutual destruction of evidence; rather, it leads to a reconsideration of the idea that miracles can count as evidence for religious belief at all. That is to say, if an event is identified as a miracle only from within the system of beliefs of a given religion, then the occurrence of the miracle cannot function as logically neutral evidence in favour of accepting those religious beliefs. Miracles are significant for religious believers in so far as, for example, they see them as God's way of entering into their lives. To disparage the role of miracles as evidence for religious belief is perhaps to misunderstand their nature as religious events.

Surprisingly, this is a point that Hume himself appears to make at the end of Section X when he writes that '[o]ur most holy religion is founded on *Faith*, not reason; and it is a sure method of exposing it to put it such a trial as it is, by no means, fitted to endure' (*E.*, p. 130). Taken literally, this remark seems to place Hume in the position of defending religion against rationalist criticism and so defending himself against the charge of being anti-religious. But since this reading would require us to regard the whole section on miracles as an exercise designed to show up the strength of faith by revealing the weaknesses in rational theology, it surely makes more sense to understand Hume's remark as an ironic comment on the credulity of religious believers. This reading is confirmed by the even greater irony of the final sentence of Section X:

> And whoever is moved by Faith to assent to [the Christian religion], is conscious of a continued miracle in his own person, which subverts all the principles of his understanding, and gives him a determination to believe what is most contrary to custom and experience. (*E.*, p. 131)

Hume employs such literary devices in order to provide a smoke-screen for his assault on the blinkered orthodoxies of his day. In Section XI the elaborateness of the literary disguise conceals a yet more powerful attack on theological dogma.

The 'Argument from Design' (*Enquiry*, Section XI).

Even the title of this section 'Of a particular providence and of a future state', is slightly misleading,[8] for it is really a discussion of the so-called 'Argument from Design', one of the three or four standard philosophical proofs of the existence of God and the proof most commonly employed by eighteenth century apologists for religion.[9] Hume further obscures the real content of the section by couching his analysis of the argument in the guise of a dialogue between himself and a friend who in turn assumes the role of the Greek philosopher Epicurus haranguing the Athenian people (see *E.*, p. 134). This contrived and cautious presentation of his own views indicates Hume's awareness not only of the sensitivity of the subject for eighteenth century readers, but also of the severity of the attack he is launching upon deep-seated convictions.

At its most general the Argument from Design may be said to be an inference from world to God. Its starting point is the world as we observe it to be. This is one reason why the argument is of particular interest to empiricist philosophers. Hume is also interested in the nature of the inference itself. He brings his earlier conclusions about cause and effect and the character of reasonings concerning matters of fact to bear upon his scrutiny of the inference. Hume's aim is to show that, in spite of its special religious significance, the Argument from Design must be assessed in terms of the principles of reasoning which govern our thinking in other areas of human experience. Indeed, Hume tries to demonstrate that religious preconceptions have interfered with the rational assessment of the design argument and that once they are discounted it is then possible to appreciate its limitations.

The argument which philosophers call the Argument from Design consists in a piece of reasoning which is familiar to most people who have ever wondered about the existence of the world as a whole. Surely, it is said, the order and beauty of the universe cannot be the result of 'either chance or the blind and unguided force of matter' (to quote the words of Hume's imaginary friend speaking on behalf of Epicurus, *E.*, p. 135); it is more compelling to believe that the universe was deliberately created to be the way it is by some supernatural, all-powerful, all-knowing being or God. Thus the argument starts from a claim that the world has certain features, say order and beauty; then it is inferred that these features are the product of a maker or designer. In short, the existence of a creator God is postulated as the best explanation of the world being as it is. This is what Hume calls 'the religious hypothesis' (*E.*, p. 139).

It is important to notice that Hume does not initially contest the validity of the inference at the heart of the design argument. 'I shall not examine the justness of this argument. I shall allow it to be as solid as my antagonists and accusers can desire' (*E.* p. 135). That is, Hume does not at first question the inference that there is a maker or designer. Instead, Hume argues that this is not enough to justify the conclusions that religious apologists have based on it; he sets out to show the weakness of the religious hypothesis without disputing the legitimacy of the hypothesis. The apparent caution of this approach appears to imply that Hume is prepared to acknowledge some merit in the Argument from Design. But, as we shall see, there is a sting in the Section's tail. At the end of his discussion Hume challenges the validity of the inference which he has conceded throughout.

Hume's first step is to point out that the Design Argument is 'an argument drawn from effects to causes. From the order of the work, you infer, there must have been project and forethought in the workman' (*E.*, p. 136). The next move is to examine what consequences can and cannot be justifiably derived from an argument of this form. Here we can see that there is a connection between Hume's analysis of the Design Argument and his earlier analysis of the relation between cause and effect. In the latter, Hume had concentrated on the inference from causes to effects: having observed A's followed by B's on many occasions, we call A the cause and B the effect, and when we see A alone we expect to see the effect B. This account also implies that when we see B, the effect, alone, then we will be led to, expect to see the cause A, to infer the cause on observing the effect. The principles Hume had established in his analysis of the cause–effect relation underlie his discussion of the Design Argument, providing the framework within which he is able to assess the claims made about the nature of the divine or supernatural cause postulated to explain the observed effects in the natural world.

Hume states a principle which structures the ensuing analysis of the religious hypothesis. 'When we infer any particular cause from an effect, we must proportion the one to the other, and can never be allowed to ascribe to the cause any qualities, but what are exactly sufficient to produce the effect' (*E.*, p. 136). The best way to appreciate the significance of this statement is to look at the examples Hume employs, the weighing-scales and the picture of Zeuxis (*E.*, pp. 136–7).

Take the second example first. Zeuxis was a famous painter, sculptor and architect in ancient Greece. One of the legends about him is that his painting of a bunch of grapes was so realistic that birds flew down to peck at them. Hume's claim, however, is that just by looking at his paintings we could not be justified in inferring that he was also a sculptor and an architect. (As a matter of fact, none of Zeuxis' paintings has survived.) By examining the paintings, we could decide that the painter, Zeuxis, possessed certain painterly skills which were the causes of the effects we see in the painting. If we went further, and said that Zuexis was a sculptor and an architect, we would be indulging in a speculation beyond what the evidence of the paintings entitles us to infer.

In Hume's first example, he supposes that we can see only one side of the weighing-scales or balance consisting of a beam resting at its mid-point upon a fulcrum and suspending a scale pan at each end. If the scale pan we can see has a ten ounce weight on it, and if this pan is raised up, then we can reasonably infer that there is a weight on the other, hidden, scale pan greater than ten ounces. We infer an unobserved cause – a weight greater than ten ounces – to explain the observed effect – the ten ounce weight being raised. What we cannot justifiably do, according to Hume, is to say by how much the hidden weight exceeds the visible one. We have no reason to justify believing that the hidden weight is twenty ounces or thirty or eighty ounces: the claim that it is one or other of these would be arbitrary speculation or guess-work, or what Hume calls ' the licence of conjecture' (*E.*, p. 136). When we say that Zeuxis possesses skills at painting or when we say that the weight on the hidden side of the balance exceeds ten ounces, we are in Hume's words proportioning the cause to the effect, that is, ascribing to the cause qualities exactly sufficient to explain the known effect. That is all that we are entitled to infer by the 'rules of just reasoning' (*E.*, p. 136).

The nub of Hume's argument in Section XI of the *Enquiry* is that those who employ the Argument from Design to support the tenets of the Christian religion offend against the 'rules of just reasoning' both by ascribing to the inferred cause 'qualities beyond what are precisely required to produce the effect' and by inferring 'other effects from it beyond those by which alone it is known to us' (*E.*, p. 136). Although Hume concedes, temporarily, that we are entitled to infer the existence of a maker or designer of the world, he denies that the evidence entitles us to ascribe to that maker all the qualities attributed to the God of Christianity. Thus, God is traditionally regarded as the sum of all perfections, infinitely powerful, wise and good. And yet the world as we know it contains death and disaster, pain and misery, sufficient to cast doubt on the perfection of the designer. If he were all-powerful, he could intervene to prevent much of the suffering that occurs; the fact that he does not suggests that he is either not all-powerful or not all-good.[10] If we attribute to the maker 'the precise degree of power, intelligence, and benevolence, which appears in the workmanship' (E., 137), then we surely fall far short of perfection: the imperfection of the world is balanced, explained, by the imperfection of its designer. Again, it is traditionally believed that, although in this world the wicked prosper at the expense of the good, God will punish the wicked and reward the good in a future life. Hume points out that this is again to derive effects from the inferred cause in addition to those we are actually aware of – it is to predict the course of future events in line with a conviction about God's goodness and benevolence for which there is inadequate evidence in the world as we observe it to be (*E.*, pp. 140-1).

Hume is not denying the existence of a perfect designer. 'That the divinity may *possibly* be endowed with attributes, which we have never seen exerted; may be governed by principles of action, which we cannot discover to be satisfied: all this will freely be allowed' (*E.*, p. 141). Hume's claim is that the argument from design does not provide rational justification for belief in such a designer. It is imagination rather than reason which is the source of that belief. Having inferred the existence of a maker, we project on to him the qualities we deem it fitting that such a being should possess and we then interpret events by reference to the actions of this imaginary being. Stripped of these make-believe attributions, the religious hypothesis is useless because it cannot extend our understanding of the world beyond telling us that the world is as it is because it was designed to be the way that it is. As Hume puts it:

> The religious hypothesis, therefore must be considered only
> as a particular method of accounting for the visible phenom-
> ena of the universe: but no just reasoner will ever presume to

infer from it any single fact, and alter or add to the phenomena, in any single particular. (*E.*, p. 139)

Before examining some difficulties in Hume's argument, we need
to consider his answer to an important objection which he presents in
his own voice during the fictitious dialogue with his friend. The
objection is that, contrary to the 'friend's' argument, we do, frequently
and legitimately, attribute more to an inferred cause than we can
strictly find in the observed effect. For example, suppose we
encountered 'a half-finished building, surrounded with heaps of brick
and stone and mortar, and all the instruments of masonry' (*E.*, p. 143).
In such a case, we would rightly infer not only that there was a builder
but also that 'the building would soon be finished and receive all the
further improvements, which art could bestow upon it' (*E.*, p. 143).
Similarly, if we saw a footprint on a sandy beach, we would be justified
in concluding that it had been made by a person with two feet and that
the other prints he had made had been 'effaced by the rolling of the
sands or inundation of the waters' (*E.*, p. 143). In both cases we go
beyond the observable evidence and it is reasonable to do so. Why,
then, is it not legitimate to 'admit the same method of reasoning with
regard to the order of nature?'

'The infinite difference of the subjects' (*E.*, p. 143) – that is
Hume's answer to the above question. In the two examples, we can
find abundant independent evidence to support our inferences. We
have seen builders constructing buildings; we have seen builders take
holidays and return from them to complete their work. Similarly, we
know from experience that normal human beings have two feet, that
they leave pairs of prints on soft sand, and that winds and incoming
tides wash some or all of the prints away. Our inferences in these two
cases are justified by reference to the innumerable experiences we have
of similar effects brought about by similar causes:

> The case is not the same with our reasonings from the works
> of nature. The Deity is known to us only by his productions,
> and is a single being in the universe, not comprehended
> under any species or genus, from whose experienced at-
> tributes or qualities, we can, by analogy, infer any attribute
> or quality in him. (*E.*, p. 144)

The crucial difference between the two examples and the
inference from world to God is that we have no experiences of the
inferred cause, God, independent of the observable effect, the world
in which we exist. So, we have no corroborative evidence with which

to justify our inference. Moreover, since God, or the designer of the world, is unique, we cannot reason by analogy in order to support our assertions. That is, there is nothing in our experience which is remotely analogous to the Deity or the designer – he, she or it is 'a single being in the universe' – and so there is nothing from our own experience we can draw on in order to construct a fruitful hypothesis; a hypothesis, that is, which would enable us to make predictions about hitherto unobserved effects.

The argument of the previous paragraph is used by Hume in defence of his criticism that, according to the rules of just reasoning, the conclusion to be drawn from the Design Argument must be significantly weaker than the one traditionally drawn. But this criticism, we should remember, is developed by Hume on the basis of his concession that the initial inference from world to God is a valid one. In the very last paragraph of Section XI Hume withdraws that concession and casts doubt on the inference which is at the heart of the Argument from Design. He does so by emphasising and extending his point that the Deity is a single being not comprehended under any species or genus.

> I doubt whether it is possible for a cause to be known only
> by its effect (as you have all along supposed) or to be of so
> singular and particular a nature as to have no parallel and no
> similarity with any other cause or object, that has ever fallen
> under our observation. It is only when two *species* of objects
> are found to be constantly conjoined, that we can infer the
> one from the other; and were an effect presented, which was
> entirely singular, and could not be comprehended under any
> known *species*, I do not see, that we could form any conjec-
> ture or inference at all concerning its cause. (*E.*, p. 148)

In this passage we can clearly see the connections with Hume's analysis of the cause-effect relation in terms of constant conjunction. The assertion that fire causes smoke implies that fire and smoke are, and will continue to be, constantly conjoined in our experience. In such an assertion the terms 'fire' and 'smoke' refer to kinds of objects or events, that is, kinds of fires, kinds of smoke, rather than any particular fire or smoke. It is on these conditions that the old adage, 'There's no smoke without fire,' makes sense. On observing smoke, even a kind I have not previously observed, I can reasonably infer that the cause is fire, perhaps a kind of fire I have not previously encountered. Hume's argument is that the terms 'Deity' and 'universe' do not refer to kinds of thing; and that we do not and cannot have experience of a constant conjunction between the Deity and the universe which would entitle us to regard them as causally related. For these reasons there is no possibility of inferring the existence of God as a cause for the observable universe.

In examining Hume's treatment of the Argument from Design in Section XI of the First *Enquiry*, we have to remember the distinction between the two stages in Hume's discussion corresponding to his initial acceptance of the inference from world to maker or designer and his final rejection of that inference.

Hume's criticism of the very possibility of inferring a cause of the world appears to be a strong one. It is certainly true that we have not observed the Deity creating the universe; and as created beings (according to the religious hypothesis) it hardly makes sense to suggest that such an experience could occur. What is more the description, 'Deity creating the universe', cannot be understood in the way that we understand, say, 'Beethoven creating the *Eroica* Symphony'. Beethoven was only one man among many, albeit a distinguished man, and the *Eroica* only one symphony among many, albeit a great one. But the Deity as postulated by the design argument and worshipped by Christians is not one deity among many. He is the necessarily unique cause of all created things. Similarly, the universe is not one thing among many possible universes, though this is perhaps obscured by science fiction talk of parallel universes, negative universes, and so on. The term 'universe' stands for everything that is the case, everything that exists; in this sense there cannot be more than one universe – the universe is necessarily unique. Hence, Hume's claim is that the Deity and the universe are of the wrong logical type to be conjoined in a causal relation.

Hume's reliance on the notion of uniqueness is questionable. After all, there is a sense in which everything is unique, a sense in which every particular thing is distinct from every other thing. The point might be expressed by saying that anything can count as unique under some description or from some point of view. Thus, Beethoven is unique in that only he was born at a specific time and place to those specific parents; but being unique in this sense does not exclude him from possessing properties of a general kind such as being human, male, German, etc. Similarly, even if it is true that there is no other God than the God of Christianity, He nonetheless is believed to possess properties of a general kind such as being powerful, wise, and good. And we surely can imagine that the one and only Deity might have had different properties, for example, that he was not all-powerful or perfectly good. Again, it seems conceivable that the Deity could have created a different universe from that which he did create; that is to say, it is possible that the things which might have now existed should have been different from the things which actually do now exist. Although the Deity and the universe are unique, that does not mean that they cannot be described in ways which are appropriate for items in a causal relation.

The next point to notice is that we have no scruples about speaking of the causes of things which are unique in a quite straightforward sense. The human race, so far as we know, is unique. But that does not mean that there cannot be a causal explanation for the existence of the human species.[11] Of course, the causes of human life have to be inferred; the origins of the human race are not observable by its members. But these facts are not insuperable obstacles to rational enquiry. If we can intelligibly seek the causes of humanity in nature, then it is difficult to accept Hume's rejection of an attempt to seek the causes of nature in the Deity. Were we to accept Hume's reasoning, we would inevitably be forced to reject much serious science as well as natural theology.

The above points concern the possibility of inferring a cause of the world. Even if Hume is incorrect in denying the validity of such an inference, that does not affect the soundness of the bulk of his discussion which is devoted to showing the limited character of the conclusions that can be drawn from the design argument when it is employed according to the rules of just reasoning. As we have seen, he argues that the religious hypothesis is only one method of accounting for the order and beauty of the world. In the *Dialogues Concerning Natural Religion* he argues that there are other hypotheses equally capable of explaining the observable features of the world. For example, instead of a single all-powerful God we could postulate 'a numerous society of deities' (*D.*, Part VI, p. 85) in which 'several deities combine in contriving and framing a world' (*D.*, Part V, p. 77). Again, it is surely question-begging to pick on intelligence as the source of order in the world. If we are attentive to experience, we will recognise that intelligence is itself only one of the means by which order comes about. There are in nature other forces capable of organising arrangements of matter, such as the vegetation and generation observable in the life of plants and animals. 'A tree bestows order and organisation on that tree, which springs from it, without knowing the order: An animal, in the same manner, on its offspring: a bird on its nest' (*D.*, Part VII, p. 89). The inference that the world originates in intelligence is itself a further symptom of the anthropomorphising tendency to which Hume has drawn attention. It would be no less reasonable, Hume suggests in the *Dialogues*, to regard the whole world as similar to an animal or a vegetable whose cause, therefore, 'we may infer to be some thing similar or analogous to generation or vegetation' (*loc. cit.*).

But are the social and vegetable hypotheses just as reasonable as the religious hypotheses? One problem with the proposal that the causes of the world as we know it are akin to the generation and vegetation of plants is that these processes themselves stand in need of causal explanation. However, as Hume indicates, a similar problem besets the religious hypothesis. If the order and arrangement of nature are explained by 'an intelligent cause or Author', we can ask, 'what is the cause of this cause?' (*D.*, Part IV, p. 74). If all explanations have to stop somewhere, the only difference between the vegetarian and the religious hypothesis is that they stop at different places (*cf. Dialogues*, Part VII). And yet it might perhaps be argued that the kind of explanation offered by the religious hypothesis is intrinsically more satisfying because it involves the idea of an agent bringing something about.[12] Thus, in ordinary life the discovery that something happened because of somebody's deliberate decision is usually accepted as a satisfactory explanation, even though we may want to go on to ask why he decided to act in the way he did. By suggesting that things were deliberately arranged to be the way they are, the religious hypothesis is more appealing than a hypothesis which tells us that things are the way they are because that's the way they are.

But why should we acknowledge the existence of only one God? The order and arrangement of things could just as well be the outcome of the decisions of many gods. One response to this suggestion would be to maintain that postulating the existence of many Deities is a kind of intellectual extravagance. Hume recognises that 'to multiply causes, without necessity, is indeed contrary to true philosophy' (*D.*, Part V, p. 78), but claims that this principle does not apply because the existence of a single god has not been independently established. However, this is to misunderstand the character of the principle. Where there are competing explanations, we should prefer the simplest, most economical explanation unless we have some reason for not doing so. This is a principle which is employed in everyday as well as scientific reasoning. Consider the situation of scientists trying to discover what causes the disease known as AIDS. The supposition that the disease is caused by a number of distinct viruses is in itself no less reasonable then the supposition that it is caused by a single virus, but as a working hypothesis it is more complicated than it needs to be and should only be adopted if we have some independent reason for supposing that what causes the disease is not unitary. By postulating the existence of a single designer of the world, the religious hypothesis conforms to our customary practice of choosing the more economical explanation.

Whereas in the *Dialogues* Hume is prepared to explore alternatives to the religious hypothesis, in the first *Enquiry* he argues that it is 'useless' (*E.*, p. 142). Because our knowledge of the inferred cause, the maker or designer, is 'derived entirely from the course of nature, we can never, according to the rules of just reasoning, return back from the cause with any new inference, or making additions to the common and experienced course of nature, establish any new principles of conduct and behaviour' (*E.*, p. 142). It might be suggested that Hume's account of these rules is too narrow. The value of a theory is not necessarily a simple function of the predictions it generates. Darwin's theory of the origin of the species through natural selection is valuable not primarily in virtue of any power to make predictions about the future course of experience but because of the way it seems to make sense of the historical development of an immense variety of natural phenomena. In a similar way the religious hypothesis imposes a meaningful pattern on a diversity of things. Even the bare assertion that the world is designed to be the way it is seems to have implications that are far from trivial: it means, for instance, that human life is not a matter of chance or accident, but that it has a definite place in the scheme of things; it means that the evil of human suffering is not merely arbitrary or pointless, but that there are reasons for its existence. However, little comfort can be drawn from these conclusions. For, according to Hume's argument, the alleged designer can be understood only as the utterly vague postulate of *that which* causes or explains why the world is at it is.[13] This carries no implications concerning the nature of the designer or of the reasons for things being as they are. Indeed, were things entirely different from what they are, were the order of the world the reverse of what it is, we could still infer the existence of something which causes or explains why it takes that form. The bare postulate of the designer provides no endorsement, indicates no preference for the world being arranged in one way as opposed to any other way.

But isn't Hume unfairly limiting the scope of the religious hypothesis? After all, if we infer the existence of a hidden weight on the other side of a weighing-scales, we can justifiably assume that it will possess properties of colour and shape, and so on, which bodies normally have. Similarly, if we infer a maker capable of designing the order and beauty of the natural world, we can surely also assume the usual accompaniments of rationality such as motives and desires, aims and purposes, etc. By thus giving greater content to the inferred cause, we enrich the religious hypothesis in a way that enables us to derive interesting implications which may have consequences for ethical conduct.[14] The religious hypothesis would be consonant with much everyday causal reasoning as well as scientific theorising in which imaginative conjectures are justified on pragmatic grounds, by their success in helping us to solve other problems and achieve further goals. Nevertheless, it has to be said that the religious hypothesis cannot be tested in the ways other theories can. Thus, though the theory of evolution, with its images of competition for existence and fitness to survive, provides a compelling picture of the organisation and development of plant and animal life, it also generates detailed factual implications – for example, concerning the fossil records. It is the confirmation or disconfirmation of such implications which enables us to adjudicate its claims in relation to rival theories, and which entitles us to regard it as genuinely explanatory. In the absence of such testable procedures, there is no control on the imagination, and we are left with make-believe rather than insight. It may be pointed out that there is indeed a factual test for the religious hypothesis, viz., whether or not there is a future life in which goodness is rewarded and evil punished. But since this is evidently more a matter of faith than knowledge, it only serves to underline Hume's claim that the religious hypothesis is not rationally demonstrable.

Notes

1. D. Z. Phillips, *Religion Without Explanation*, (Oxford, Basil Blackwell, 1976), p. 10.
2. For further details of Hume's attitude to religion and of the character of his philosophy of religion, together with the text of the *Dialogues*, see Hume's *Dialogues Concerning Natural Religion*, edited by Norman

Kemp Smith (Edinburgh, Thomas Nelson & Sons, 2nd edition 1947). A more recent edition of the *Dialogues* can be found in *David Hume on Religion*, editied by A. W. Colver and J. V. Price (Oxford, Oxford University Press, 1976).

3. For further discussion of this issue, see R. G. Swinburne, The Concept of a Miracle, (London, Macmillan, 1970).

4. It could be argued in response to this point that Hume's concern was exclusively with the question of whether a certain type of historical evidence could authenticate the Christian revelation, and that the question of how one judges one's own experience or observation of a possible miraculous event therefore does not arise. It must be said, however, that if this is indeed Hume's sole concern then his treatment of miracles suffers from a serious limitation. In brief, while it may succeed in casting doubt on the use of certain historical claims to support Christian belief, it has nothing to say on how one is to regard the claim that the Christian revelation may well be authenticated, not just by historical 'miracles', but also by well-attested claims about possibly miraculous events in one's own day, and, in particular, by one's own experience of such events.

5. A. Flew, *Hume's Philosophy of Belief*, (London, Routledge & Kegan Paul, 1961), p. 194.

6. One might attempt to answer the criticism that Hume conflated the two questions of whether a miracle has occurred and whether that miracle does or does not support the truth of any particular religion in the following manner. Hume's question is precisely whether it is possible to prove that a miracle has occurred in such a way as to establish the truth of the Christian revelation. Thus, it is quite proper for Hume to suggest that when miracles are used to confirm some religion, the evidence for such miracles is diminished by whatever evidence can be produced in favour of the miracles which might confirm some contrary religion.

   In so far as Hume's concern is with historical miracles, we may grant that if the sole testimony to the effect that a particular supposedly miraculous event has occurred comes from the supporters of a particular religion, a religion claiming a unique revelation, then it is obviously the case that any trust one may put in such testimony is very much weakened by the fact that similar claims are made by supporters of rival religions. The point remains, however, that in principle it is possible to have evidence that water has changed into wine quite independently of any religious interpretation of this event.

7. R. Holland, 'The miraculous', *American Philosophical Quarterly*, vol. 2, 1965; reprinted in R. Holland, *Against Empiricism* (Oxford, Basil Blackwell, 1980).

8. Hume's original title for Section IX of the *Enquiry* was 'Of the

practical consequences of natural religion', a title which gives a more accurate indication of its contents.

9. The Argument from Design, or the Teleological Argument, should be compared with the Ontological Argument and the Cosmological Argument. The Ontological Argument is an a priori argument which starts from the idea or the concept of God. The Cosmological and Design Arguments are a posteriori arguments; but whereas the Cosmological Argument starts from the fact that something exists, the Argument from Design starts from the fact that what exists possesses certain distinctive features. For a discussion of these, and further arguments for the existence of God, see Brian Davies, *An Introduction to the Philosophy of Religion* (Oxford, Oxford University Press, 1982).

10. This is an abbreviation of the classic statement of the problem of evil attributed to Epicurus (341–270 BC), the Greek philosopher whose identity Hume's 'friend' adopts in the imaginary dialogue. Hume's examination of the problem of evil can be found in Part X of the *Dialogues*. For a thorough examination of the problem and its historical sources, see John Hick, *Evil and the God of Love* (London, Macmillan, 1966).

11. This example is taken from R. G. Swinburne, 'The Argument from Design', *Philosophy*, vol. 43, 1968, an examination of Hume's arguments in the *Dialogues* against the Design Argument. See J. C. A. Gaskin, Hume's *Philosophy of Religion* (London, Macmillan, 1988) pp. 24–27, for a criticism of Swinburne on this point. See also R. G. Swinburne, *The Existence of God* (Oxford, The Clarendon Press, 1979), ch. 8, for an important defence of the Argument from Design.

12. Swinburne, *The Existence of God*, ch. 5.

13. J. L. Mackie, *The Miracle of Theism*, (Oxford, The Clarendon Press, 1982), p. 137; see also p. 149. Mackie provides a sympathetic examination of Hume's discussion of the Design Argument as well as criiticism of Swinburne's arguments.

14. It has been argued, for example, that the purpose of human suffering is to provide the opportunity for the development of such virtues as courage and sympathy: see Swinburne, *The Existence of God*, ch. 11. For a searching examination of Swinburne's views, see D. Z. Phillips, *Belief, Change and Forms of Life* (London, Macmillan, 1986).

Bibliography

Hume's Writings

A Treatise of Human Nature, edited by L. A. Selby-Bigge, revised with notes by P. H. Nidditch (Oxford, Clarendon Pres, 1978).

Enquiries Concerning the Human Understanding and Concerning the Principles of Morals, edited by L. A. Selby-Bigge, revised with notes by P. H. Nidditch (Oxford, Clarendon Press, 1975).

An Abstract of a Treatise of Human Nature, reprinted in the above edition of the *Treatise*.

Dialogues Concerning Natural Religion, edited with commentary by Norman Kemp Smith (Edinburgh, Thomas Nelson, 1947).

The above are now the standard editions of Hume's most important philosophical works. Alternative editions are available, including the following:

A Treatise of Human Nature, edited by E. C. Mossner (Harmondsworth, Penguin Books, 1969).

On Human Nature and The Understanding, edited by A. Flew (London and New York, Collier Books, 1962). This edition contains the whole of the First *Enquiry*, plus selections from the *Treatise*, as well as the *Abstract* and 'My Own Life'.

Hume's Ethical Writings, edited by A. MacIntyre (Notre Dame, University of Notre Dame Press, 1985). This edition contains the whole of the Second *Enquiry* as well as selections from the *Treatise*, the *Dialogues*, and some of the essays.

Dialogues Concerning Natural Religion, edited with an introduction and notes by Martin Bell (Harmondsworth, Penguin Books, 1990). This is the edition to which reference is made in this book.

Dialogues Concerning Natural Religion, edited with accompanying essays by Stanley Tweyman, (London, Routledge, 1990).

'My own life', in *Essays: Moral, Political and Literary*, edited with notes by Eugene F. Miller (Indianapolis, Liberty Classics, 1985).

'A dissertation of the passions', in Hume's *Philosophical Works*, edited by T. H. Green and T. H. Grose (London, Longman Green, 1878), vol. 4.

New Letters of David Hume, edited by R. Klibansky and E. C.

Mossner (Oxford, Clarendon Press, 1969).
A Letter from a Gentleman to his Friend in Edinburgh, edited by E.
C. Mossner and J. V. Price (Edinburgh, Edinburgh University
Press, 1967).

Commentaries on Hume

The following publication is a guide to work which will be useful to
students.
Hall, R. *A Hume Bibliography from 1930* (Edinburgh, Edinburgh
University Press, 1978).

1. Books

General Introductions to Hume's Philosophy
Ayer, A. J., *Hume* (Oxford, Oxford University Press, 1980
Capaldi, N., *David Hume, The Newtonian Philosopher* (Boston,
Twayne, 1975).
Flew, A., *David Hume: Philosopher of Moral Science* (Oxford, Basil
Blackwell, 1986).
McNabb, D. G. C., *David Hume: His Theory of Knowledge and
Morality* (Oxford, Basil Blackwell, 1966).
Passmore, J. A., *Hume's Intentions* (London, Duckworth, 1968).
Penelhum, T., *Hume* (London, Macmillan, 1975).
Priest, S., *The British Empiricists* (Harmondsworth, Penguin Books,
1990).
Stroud, B., *Hume* (London, Routledge and Kegan Paul, 1977).
Woolhouse, R. S., *The Empiricists* (Oxford, Oxford University
Press, 1988).

Studies of one or more aspects of Hume's Philosophy
Ardal, P. S., *Passion and Value in Hume's Treatise* (Edinburgh,
Edinburgh University Press, 1966).
Beauchamp, T. L. and Rosenberg, A., *Hume and the Problem of
Causation* (New York, Oxford University Press, 1981).
Bennett, J., *Locke, Berkeley, Hume: Central Themes* (Oxford,
Clarendon Press, 1971).
Church, R. W., *Hume's Theory of Understanding* (London, Allen &
Unwin, 1968).
Danford, J., *David Hume and the Problem of Reason* (New Haven
and London, Yale University Press, 1990).

Flage, D. E., *David Hume's Theory of Mind* (London, Routledge, 1990).
Fogelin, R. J., *Hume's Scepticism in the Treatise of Human Nature* (London, Routledge and Kegan Paul, 1985).
Gaskin, J. C. A., *Hume's Philosophy of Religion* (London, Macmillan, 1978).
Harrison, J., *Hume's Moral Epistemology* (Oxford, Clarendon Press, 1976).
Hendel, C. W., *Studies in the Philosophy of David Hume* (Indianapolis, Bobbs-Merrill, 1963).
Jones, P., *Hume's Sentiments* (Edinburgh, Edinburgh University Press, 1982).
Livingston, D., *Hume's Philosophy of Common Life* (Chicago, Chicago University Press, 1984).
Mackie, J. L., *Hume's Moral Theory* (London, Routledge and Kegan Paul, 1980).
Norton, D. F., *David Hume: Common-Sense Moralist `and Sceptical Metaphysician* (Princeton, Princeton University Press, 1982).
Noxon, J., *Hume's Philosophical Development* (Oxford, Clarendon Press, 1973).
Pears, D., *Hume's System* (Oxford, Oxford University Press, 1990).
Price, H. H., *Hume's Theory of the External World* (Oxford, Clarendon Press, 1963).
Smith, N. K., *The Philosophy of David Hume* (London, Macmillan, 1941).
Stove, D. C., *Probability and Hume's Inductive Scepticism* (Oxford, Clarendon Press, 1973).
Strawson, G., *The Secret Connexion* (Oxford, Clarendon Press, 1989).
Wright, J. P., *The Sceptical Realism of David Hume* (Manchester, Manchester University Press, 1983).

2. Articles

Collections
Chappell, V. C. (ed.), *Hume: A Collection of Critical Essays* (London, MacMillan, 1966).
Livingston, D. W. and King, J. (eds.), *Hume: A Re-evaluation* (New York, Fordham University Press, 1976).
Merrill, K. R. and Shanan, R. W., *David Hume: Many Sided*

Genius (Oklahoma, University of Oklahoma Press, 1976).

Morice, G. P. (ed.), *David Hume: Bicentenary Papers* (Edinburgh, Edinburgh University Press, 1977).

Pears, D. (ed.), *David Hume: A Symposium* (London, Macmillan, 1963).

Sesonske, A. and Fleming, N. (eds.), *Human Understanding: Studies in the Philosophy of David Hume* (California, Wadsworth, 1965).

Individual Articles (additional to those referred to in the notes to each chapter)

Anscombe, G. E. M., 'Hume and Julius Caesar', *Analysis*, vol. 34, 1973, reprinted in G. E. M. Anscombe, *Collected Philosophical Papers* (Oxford, Basil Blackwell, 1981), vol. 1, *From Parmenides to Wittgenstein*.

Anscombe, G. E. M., '"Whatever has a Beginning of Existence must have a Cause": Hume's Argument Exposed', *Analysis*, vol. 34, 1974, reprinted in Anscombe, as above.

Baier, A., 'Hume on heaps and bundles', *American Philosophical Quarterly*, vol. 16, 1979.

Baier, A., 'Frankena and Hume on points of view', *The Monist*, vol. 64, 1981, reprinted in A. Baier, *Postures of the Mind: Essays on Mind and Morals* (London, Methuen, 1985).

Baier, A., 'Hume on women's complexion', in P. Jones (ed.), *The 'Science of Man' in the Scottish Enlightenment* (Edinburgh, Edinburgh University Press, 1989).

Baron, M., 'Hume's noble lie: an account of his artificial virtues', *Canadian Journal of Philosophy*, vol. 12, 1982.

Beck, L. W., '"Was-must-be" and "Is-ought" in Hume', *Philosophical Studies*, vol. 26, 1974.

Blackburn, S., 'Hume and thick connections', *Philosophy and Phenomenological Research*, vol. L, 1990.

Brett, N., 'Substance and mental identity in Hume's *Treatise*', *Philosophical Quarterly*, vol. 22, 1972.

Bricke, J., 'Hume's volitions', in V. Hope (ed.), *Philosophers of the Scottish Enlightenment* (Edinburgh, Edinburgh University Press, 1984).

Butler, R. J., 'Hume's impressions', in G. Vesey (ed.), *Impressions of Empiricism*, Royal Institute of Philosophy Lectures 1974/5 (London, Macmillan, 1976).

Cohen, M. F., 'Obligation and human nature in Hume's philosophy', *Philosophical Quarterly*, vol. 40, 1990.

Cook, J. W., 'Hume's scepticism with regard to the senses', *American Philosophical Quarterly*, vol. 5, 1968

Craig, E., 'Hume on thought and belief', in G. Vesey (ed.), *Philosophers Ancient and Modern*, Royal Institute of Philosophy Lectures 1985/6 (Cambridge, Cambridge University Press, 1986).

Dilman, I., 'Reason and feeling in moral judgement', in I. Dilham, *Studies in Language and Reason* (London, Macmillan, 1981).

Dilman, I., 'Reason and feeling in moral decision', also in the above.

Dimm, E., 'Hume and the monkish virtues', *Philosophical Investigations*, vol. 10, 1987.

Ferreira, M. J., 'Hume's naturalism – "proof" and practice', *Philosophical Quarterly*, vol. 35, 1985.

Flew, A., 'Inconsistency within a "reconciling project"', *Human Studies*, vol. IV, 1978.

Flew, A., 'Hume's philosphy of religion', in G. Vesey, (ed.), *Philosphers Ancient and Modern* (Cambridge, Cambridge University Press, 1986).

Fogelin, R. J., 'Kant and Hume on the simultaneity of causes and effects', *Kant Studien*, vol. 67, 1976

Garrett, D., 'Hume's self doubts about personal identity', *Philosophical Review*, vol. 90, 1981.

Hacking, I., 'Hume's species of probability', *Philosophical Studies*, vol. 33. 1978.

Hanfling, O., 'Hume and Wittgenstein', in G. Vesey (ed.), *Impressions of Empiricism*, Royal Institute of Philosophy Lectures 1974/5, (London, Macmillan, 1976).

Lindley, F. T., 'David Hume and necessary connections', *Philosophy*, vol. 62, 1987.

Livingston, D., 'Hume on the natural history of philosophical consciousness', in Jones, *The 'Science of Man' in the Scottish Enlightenment*.

McIntyre, J. L., 'Is Hume's self consistent?', *McGill Hume Studies* (San Diego, Austin Hill Press, 1979).

Merrill, K. R., 'Hume's "Of miracles", Peirce and the balancing of likelihoods', *Journal of the History of Philosophy*, vol. 29, 1991.

Morreall, J., 'Hume and the missing shade of blue', *Philosphy and Phenomenlogical Research*, vol. 42, 1981–2.

Mounce, H. O., 'The idea of a necessary connection', *Philosophy*, vol. 60, 1985.

Nelson, J. O., 'The conclusion of Book One, Part Four of Hume's *Treatise*', *Philosophy and Phenomenological Research*, vol. XX, 1964.

Pakaluk, M., 'Philosophical types in Hume's dialogues', in Hope, *Philosophers of the Scottish Enlightenment.*

Passmore, J., 'Enthusiasm, fanaticism in David Hume', in Jones, *The 'Science of Man' in the Scottish Enlightenment.*

Patten, S. C., 'Hume's bundles, self-consciousness, and Kant', *Hume Studies*, vol. 2, 1976.

Platts, M., 'Hume and morality as a matter of fact', *Mind*, vol. 97, 1988.

Pears, D. F., 'Hume's account of personal identity', in D. Pears, *Questions in the Philosophy of Mind* (London, Duckworth, 1975).

Penelhum, T., 'Hume's theory of the self revisited', *Dialogue*, vol. 14, 1975.

Robertson, J., 'Hume on practical reason', *Proceedings of the Aristotelian Society*, vol. 90, 1989–90.

Robinson, W. L., 'Hume on personal identity', *Journal of the History of Philosophy*, vol. 12, 1974.

Root, M., 'Miracles and the uniformity of nature', *American Philosophical Quarterly*, vol. 26, 1989.

Smith, M., 'The Humean theory of motivation', *Mind*, vol. 96, 1987.

Strawson, G., 'Realism and causation', *The Philosphical Quarterly*, vol. 37, 1987.

Vesey, G., 'Hume on liberty and necessity', in G. Vesey (ed.), *Philosophers Ancient and Modern* (Cambridge, Cambridge University Press, 1986).

Wooton, D., 'Hume's "Of Miracles": Probability and irreligion', in M. A. Stewart (ed.), *Studies in the Philosophy of the Scottish Enlightenment* (Oxford, Clarendon Press, 1990).

Index

Hospers, John, 74
humanity, 170–1, 172–3, 174
humility, 128, 131, 135, 137–46
  moral judgements, 161
Hutcheson, F., 176
hypnosis, 101–2

ideas, 16–29
  belief, 79–81, 84, 86
  causality, 43, 49, 55
  emotions, 137, 138, 139–40
  mechanics of thought, 31–8
  moral judgements, 159
  necessary connection, 58, 59, 60
  personal identity, 109, 114–15, 123
  relations of, 41
  sympathy, 149–51, 153, 156–8
identity, personal, 108–24
  emotions, 139–40
identity of organisation, 111
ignorance
  contrary causes, 94–5, 97
  miracles, 185
illness, 154–5
images, 20–1, 26
  mechanics of thought, 31, 33–5
  personal identity, 112
imagination
  belief, 80, 83, 85, 88
  causality, 40, 52
  mechanics of thought, 31–8
  imoral judgements, 164–5
  perceptions, 18, 23
  personal identity, 110–11
  religious belief, 195, 202
impartiality, 178–9
impressions, 14–15, 16–29
  belief, 80–1, 82–4
  causality, 43, 49, 55
  emotions, 126–7, 128, 137, 138, 139
  mechanics of thought, 31
  moral judgements, 159
  necessary connection, 57–8, 59–61
  personal identity, 109, 114–15, 123
  sympathy, 150–1, 152, 155, 156–8
impressions of reflection, 58, 60
impulsive behaviour, 162, 168–9
indifference, liberty of, 96, 99, 105–6
indignation, 134

indirect factual claims, *see* inferences
induction
  belief, 79
  emotions, 136
  problem of, 40, 68–77
inferences
  causality, 42, 44
  free choices, 93
  induction, 68, 69–70, 73
  personal identity, 120
  religious belief, 192–202
innatism, 10, 21, 22
instinct, 72, 87
intelligence, 199–200
intentions, 36
  of emotions, 135–6, 156
interfering causes, 63–5, 94–5
internal experience, *see* psychological
  experience
introspection
  belief, 85
  emotions, 133, 134–5, 139, 141
  personal identity, 109, 113
intuition
  free choices, 106
  moral judgements, 176–7
irrationality, 72

jealousy, 29, 133
joy, 141
just reasoning, rules of, 194–5, 197, 199,
  201
justice, 76, 160, 171–5

Kant, Immanuel, 59–60, 179
Kemp Smith, Norman, 22
knowledge, 17, 27, 32

language, 21
laws of nature, 182–7
Leibnlz, G. W., 92
liberty, *see* free choices
licence of conjecture, 194
Locke, John
  association of ideas, 36
  empiricism, 9–10
  free choices, 92
  identity of organisation, 111
  perceptions, 14, 21